THE OEDIPUS PLAYS OF SOPHOCLES

THE OEDIPUS PLAYS
OF SOPHOCLES

OEDIPUS THE KING

OEDIPUS AT KOLONOS

ANTIGONE

Translated by ROBERT BAGG
Introductions and Notes by Robert Bagg and Mary Bagg

University of Massachusetts Press   Amherst and Boston

Printed in the United States of America

LC 2004005674
ISBN 1-55849-453-7 (library cloth ed.); 454-5 (paper)

Set in Adobe Garamond by Graphic Composition, Inc.
Printed and bound by The Maple-Vail Book Manufacturing Group

Library of Congress Cataloging-in-Publication Data

Sophocles
    The Oedipus plays of Sophocles : Oedipus the king, Oedipus at
Kolonos, and Antigone / translated by Robert Bagg ; introductions
and notes by Robert Bagg and Mary Bagg.
        p. cm.
    Includes bibliographical references.
    ISBN 1-55849-453-7 (library cloth : alk. paper) — ISBN 1-55849-
454-5 (pbk. : alk. paper)
    1.   Sophocles—Translations into English. 2.   Oedipus (Greek
mythology)—Drama. 3.   Antigone (Greek mythology)—Drama.
I. Bagg, Robert. II. Bagg, Mary. III. Title.
    PA4414 .A2B34 2004
    882'.01—dc22

                                          2004005674

British Library Cataloguing in Publication data are available.

I dedicate this translation to the memory of
John Andrew Moore,
Thomas Fauss Gould,
and Charles Segal

ΦΙΛΟΙΚΑΙΔΙΔΑΣΚΟΛΟΙ

Contents

In translating the three plays by Sophokles that deal with Oedipus, Jokasta, and their children, as well as with Kreon and his family, I have tried to preserve as much of the poet's meaning, both primary and ramifying, as possible—and to do so in language clear enough to have dramatic effect. Given our imperfect and often contested knowledge of what Sophokles' Greek means at many points—and the difficulty (even the impossibility) of discovering exact English equivalents for an inflected language that can compact several different meanings within a single phrase or word—total literal accuracy is beyond reach. Nor is it always desirable, especially if it produces the eccentric-sounding locutions that literal translations of Greek sometimes impose on English. Thus my goal has been to achieve maximum playability with the least sacrifice of accuracy.

Some scholars have approached literal accuracy, including the late Thomas Gould, my teacher and friend, in his translation and absorbing commentary on *Oedipus the King* (1970). I have worked with the exacting examples of Gould, Sir Richard Jebb, and Sir Hugh Lloyd-Jones in my mind, but with the actors' and audiences' need for verbal clarity and strong speech rhythms in my ears. Oedipus' thoughts (at the start of the *Kolonos*) on surviving with meager rations suggest a useful mantra for a translator: *Suffering teaches patience. So does time.* And when in doubt, Tom Gould advised, look again and again at the Greek.

No modern production can reproduce the conditions of ancient theatre, especially the irrecoverable cultural elements of the Athenian Festival of Dionysos, a holy occasion attended by priests, protected by gods, and witnessed by an audience that believed the gods were intimately involved in their welfare. The story the play told was itself part of a living religious tradition; in performance it combined music, dancing, and acting in a style (and with an authority) now lost. Because ancient manuscripts lack stage directions I have supplied my own, most often to suggest an appropriate entrance or exit line, but also to propose stage business that seems textually prompted. I should warn, however, that several of my stage directions are driven by a critical interpretation. In the introductions to each play, particularly for *Oedipus the King*, I comment more fully about issues of staging.

Surviving texts not only lack stage directions, more crucially they lack the playwrights' original music and choreography. Modern productions usually suffer when directors make no effort to restore that musical dimension; Greek revivals in which the choral odes are raggedly chanted and the chorus rooted are rarely inspiring. The odes make their best dramatic sense when their words are set to music and sung, and the thought in the words expressed in a dance. I urge any director planning to stage a Greek play to join forces early on with a choral composer and a choreographer; doing so will improve the odds of giving an ancient text a robust modern fulfillment.

Another resource for such productions are the professional Hellenists who attempt to recapture performance implications embedded in specific plays; an early and valuable practitioner of this essential recovery operation is Oliver Taplin; David Wiles and Rush Rehm have recently joined him. Relevant works are listed in the bibliography.

Too often the Oedipus plays are treated less as scores to be sung than as ones to be settled—bitter arenas in which the moral and philosophical forces of the cosmos contend, and where we imagine our own contribution might carry the day. Because so much of our cultural tradition radiates from it, and because the nerves it touches are so sensitive and its issues so large, *Oedipus the King* provokes the most passionate debate. Is Oedipus innocent or guilty? What does the play imply about the nature of divinity? Of the family? Of the human psyche? If this is the ultimate tragedy, how should we define *tragedy?* Though fascinating in themselves, such debates also have a practical theatrical bearing. How we resolve them will affect how we imagine the plays in performance. Accordingly, rather than simply interpret a play, I try to visualize several moments of its action in the light of that interpretation.

The late Professor Gould of Yale (who, as my teacher at Amherst embarked me on a good part of my life's work by suggesting I translate Euripides' *Kyklops* for my roommate, Ralph Lee, to direct as his senior thesis project) greeted each successive draft of the 1982 edition of *Oedipus the King* with wise comments and suggestions. His translation of that play concurrently illuminated many dark passages for me and suggested English renderings of several elusive Greek expressions. During the final weeks of work on this volume I returned to his *summa, The Ancient Quarrel between Poetry and Philosophy,* and was grateful anew for his immense learning and energized by his enthusiasm—not only for formulating in modern terms the issues that have always bedeviled Sophoklean drama, but for honoring them by offering unhedged solutions.

For their reading and comments on the 1982 edition of *Oedipus the King* I remain obliged to both Richard Wilbur and Richard Trousdell, who each offered timely encouragement and asked questions that pointed the way to useful revisions. Richard Trousdell (once again) and Michael Birtwistle provided invaluable feedback from the perspective of theatre professionals on drafts of *Antigone* and *Oedipus at Kolonos.* James Scully, Donald Junkins, Normand Berlin, Robin Magowan, and my sons Jonathan Bagg and Hazzard Bagg, all read at least one draft of *Antigone* and *Oedipus at Kolonos* and weighed in with scores of suggestions, rephrasings of awkward lines, and salutatory warnings. The three Hellenists who were the readers for the University of Massachusetts

Press provided a healthy balance of encouragement and learned criticisms of both the translation's accuracy and its style. Their detailed comments drove my work on the plays through many months and countless drafts. All these writers and scholars have my gratitude.

I am deeply grateful to Bruce Wilcox, director of the University of Massachusetts Press, for his encouragement of this project and his patience during the years it took me to complete it. Many thanks also to Kay Scheuer for her expert and careful attention to the manuscript.

My warm thanks to the Department of Theater at the University of Utah for staging premier productions of *Oedipus the King* in 1980 and *Antigone* in 2001. The John Simon Guggenheim Memorial Foundation supported the 1982 translation of *Oedipus the King* with a fellowship that enabled me to work without interruption until it was complete. Thanks also to the American Academy in Rome and its directors, Sophie Consagra in 1980 and Caroline Bruzelius in 1996, who welcomed me as a Visiting Writer. That remarkable institution provided opportunities for stimulation and productive work more than equal to the distractions of Rome. More recently, the Rockefeller Foundation granted me a residency at its deservedly legendary Villa Serbelloni in Bellagio, Italy, where walks through its own sacred grove daily refreshed my work on *Oedipus at Kolonos*.

My wife, Mary Bagg, who initially brought her unblinking and inventive editorial eye to bear on every aspect of the work, improved its prose sections so dramatically that I began to say of each new draft, *Well, this still sounds like me, only much better.* Mary's contributions to the research and writing of the notes and introductions became so substantial that I gratefully acknowledge her as their coauthor and welcome her to the title page.

A word on my dedication. Professors John Moore and Thomas Gould were my teachers at Amherst College as well as lifelong friends. Professor Charles Segal of Harvard I knew best from his many extraordinary books on Athenian drama—though I spent a vivid year in his company in 1962–63 at the American Academy in Rome and corresponded with him from time to time. Segal's work is uniquely valuable for a translator, especially one whose Greek is limited, because he digs so deeply into every kind of background: textual, linguistic, interpretive, mythic, and cultural. All three men were *didaskoloi* in a very modern sense, as teachers who "produced" the great plays throughout their lives—in conversation, in translations and books, and in the classroom—joining their learning and intelligence to Sophokles' enduring creations as they interpreted them in the last century and beyond.

I remember John Moore leaving the dining room before heading to class one afternoon; he rose from his chair abruptly and said to his companions, "Sorry to leave so unceremoniously, but I must deliver

Thebes from the plague." It falls to the fraternity—the *thiasos*—of translators to deliver, every generation or so, the great ancient plays from the gradual estrangement inflicted by an inexorably evolving modern idiom.

ROBERT BAGG

The text, introduction, and notes of *Oedipus the King* printed in this volume are substantially revised from the form in which they were first published by the University of Massachusetts Press in 1982.

I have generally relied on Sir Richard Jebb's indispensable edition of Sophokles for textual and interpretive guidance. I consulted also throughout my work Sir Hugh Lloyd-Jones' Loeb edition of Sophokles, as well as *Sophocleia,* the volume of incisive solutions to textual confusion and despair he coauthored with N. G. Wilson. Mark Griffith's edition of *Antigone* with its comprehensive introduction and commentary was also invaluable.

I have usually noted particular and significant readings I've adopted for textually uncertain passages (especially where I depart from Jebb) and explained the reasons for my choice. In addition to Thomas Gould's translation of *Oedipus the King* I found Mary Blundell's excellent translations with commentary of *Antigone* and *Oedipus at Kolonos* alternately reassuring and corrective.

My spelling of Greek words in English favors the reproduction of the consonant and vowel structure of the original, rather than their Latin intermediaries, and is most noticeable in the replacement of the letter "c" by the letter "k." I have not been rigorously consistent, however. When consistency would result in an awkward or unfamiliar pronunciation of a word, I've kept the standard spelling, viz., Oedipus rather than Oidipous. I have retained the services of the letter "c," moreover, for one crucial role. On the cover and the title page, and thus in the databases of the world, the author I translate is named Sophocles—this to ensure the book's presence in certain databases that refuse to recognize Sophokles as the great Athenian playwright. For this ingenious solution to a vexing problem I am indebted to Oxford University Press, publishers of Gibbons and Segal's translation of *Antigone,* from which I have borrowed it.

In citing lines from the plays in the introductions I have given first the line numbers of the Greek text and second the lines as they are numbered in my translation. For each play I have included the range of Greek line numbers that correspond to my translation in the running heads at the top of each page.

THE OEDIPUS PLAYS OF SOPHOCLES

Greek Theatre in the Time of Sophokles

For seven or eight days each spring, during the fifth-century heyday of Greek theatre, Athenians flocked to the temple grounds sacred to Dionysos on the southern slope of the Acropolis.[1] After dark on the first day, a parade of young men hefted a giant phallic icon of the god into the nearby theater, having just transported it from a temple on the outskirts of the city where hymns had been sung in its honor. The "introduction" of this icon—a huge wooden shaft festooned with garlands of ivy and a mask of the god's face—initiated a dramatic festival, the City, or Great Dionysia, and proclaimed the festival's origins in Dionysian myth and rural celebrations of the god.[2]

The shaft also recalled an embarrassing (surely mythical) moment in the city's history. When worshippers of Dionysos first attempted to organize his cult in Athens, citizens rejected the upstart god. To punish them—and demonstrate his power—the offended Dionysos imposed permanent erections on all Athenian men. Their condition was relieved with the city's subsequent agreement to worship him, and on the advice of an oracle, the once-afflicted men manufactured large numbers of outsized phalloi to confirm their devotion.[3] As certain aspects of Dionysiac cult worship dovetailed with the city's burgeoning democracy—an emphasis on collective activity; an outlook that valued life's pleasures; rituals that diminished barriers of class, gender, and age; a propensity to punish enemies—Athens began to develop a healthy relationship with the god.[4]

Some ancient Greeks questioned (as modern scholars have, as

---

[1] Unless otherwise noted, all dates will be BCE (Before the Common Era). Spelling note: *theatre* refers to dramatic performance as an art, *theater* to the physical space in which drama is performed.

[2] An icon of the god, called Dionysos Eleuthereus, was first brought to Athens from the temple at Eleutherai, north of the city, possibly as early as the sixth century, and probably by a missionary of the Dionysiac cult. Its permanent home in the fifth century was the temple of Dionysos within the theater precincts. Shortly before the festival, young men of military age moved the icon to a different temple on the road to Eleutherai so that the processional back to Athens would reenact its first arrival in the city. Pickard-Cambridge, 57–62. See also Csapo and Slater, 105–6 for a discussion of the procession and photographs of ancient vases depicting the icon (plates 19A and 19B).

[3] Pickard-Cambridge, 37. Earlier rural ceremonies of the cult typically enacted plots in which Dionysos' divine wrath punished human resistance to him, but they also enticed the god to ensure the fertility of their fields and their women.

[4] The city's gradual adoption of democratic governance began with the liberalizing reforms of Solon in the mid-sixth century and continued in earnest, after the last tyrants were finally deposed, with Kleisthenes' widening of the electorate in the late sixth century. Democracy, Athenian style, was fully achieved in the mid-fifth century when Perikles expanded the assembly and granted citizenship and voting rights to every free male of military age whose parents were both Athenians.

well) why Dionysos presided over Athenian theatre. "Nothing to do with Dionysos!" was (and is) the doubters' cry.[5] But the role-playing, mask-wearing, life-enhancing properties of drama have an undeniable affinity with the god who liberates his devotees from their ordinary lives. And the prevalence of satyr drama is the most powerful evidence of Dionysiac influence on the Athenian festival.[6]

Each of the three playwrights selected in a given year to present three of his tragedies also staged a satyr play.[7] Song and dance were intrinsic to both dramatic forms. But the chorus of satyrs (those mythical followers of Dionysos, "playful, violent, sensual creatures, part-human, part-animal") performed in a wilder key—in "vehement contrast with the tone, style, music and costume of the choruses of tragedy."[8] The potent effect of satyr plays, as one scholar writes, was akin to exploring "human culture through a fun-house mirror."[9] Bestial revelers engaged somberly intelligent heroes within the same play—an incongruous but explosive fusion of the playful and the serious. In Euripides' *Kyklops,* for instance, an exhausted Odysseus and his nearly mutinous crew, sailing home from the Trojan War, come to the rescue of satyrs enslaved on a "dry" island by a "man-gobbling" one-eyed giant. The grim fun ensues when Odysseus devises a wily plan "laced with deceit." Using equipment at hand—wine from his galley and a giant carpenter's auger tipped with fire—he attempts to get the Kyklops drunk and poke out his eye. When the deed is done, the satyrs go back to the "Bakkhic business of life," and Odysseus continues his long journey home.[10]

But satyr plays were not grotesque afterpieces merely intended for comic relief. The raucous carousing of the satyr chorus put the audience in touch with the rural energies of the Dionysiac cult and with their own animal natures. For the chorus members who danced as devotees of the god—almost certainly the same actors who had just performed more soberly in the tragic dramas—the experience allowed

[5] The late John J. Winkler and Froma I. Zeitlin, the editors of *Nothing to Do with Dionysos?,* argue that dramatic festivals had everything to do with the god.

[6] Easterling, 38.

[7] The most important of Athens' nine chief magistrates, the "eponymous archon" for whom the year was named, chose the playwrights; the criteria he used, other than talent, remain obscure. Csapo and Slater, 105.

[8] Easterling, 38. Besides Euripides' *Kyklops* and a large portion of Sophokles' *The Trackers,* no satyr play survives in complete form or with a date.

[9] Easterling, 41, quotes François Lissarague, whose interpretation of satyr drama is based on the study of sixth- and fifth-century vase painting.

[10] The *Kyklops* opens with Silenus, the horse-eared, -tailed, and -hoofed leader of the satyrs, pouring a libation of goat's milk for Dionysos and praying that the god not take offense. Passages in quotes are from my translation of the play in *Liberations* (Spiritus Mundi Press, 1961).

them to embody, literally, a part of the worship itself. The satyr play, a culmination of a playwright's four-part presentation, brought Dionysiac ritual center stage.[11]

If one Dionysian theme erupts into most tragedies (and some comedies as well) it is extreme, often frenzied, and occasionally insane behavior by both men and gods. Medea kills her children, Zeus tortures a fellow immortal, and Ajax commits suicide. Pentheus' mother and her sisters tear him to pieces at a god's command. Agamemnon sacrifices his own daughter. Klytemnestra kills her husband and in turn is killed by her son. Poseidon, disguised as a bull, spooks the horses pulling Hippolytos' chariot and causes it to crash, leaving him a dying wreck. Corrosive poison, in which Herakles' wife soaked the cloak she gave him as a gift, dissolves his skin. What better-credentialed candidate than Dionysos—the god who inspires the release of all inhibitions and whose vengeance is terrifying—to preside over such savagery?

On the morning after the young men installed Dionysos' icon within the theater precincts, a much larger procession arrived, some carrying other phallic images of the god.[12] A cross section of Athenian society brought provisions for a sacrifice and feast: a young virgin of aristocratic family carried a golden basket of fruit; male citizens lugged wineskins and huge loaves of bread; resident aliens, called *metics,* contributed honeycombs and cakes while their daughters hauled in jugs of water. At the huge altar before the temple, priests of Dionysos sacrificed several hundred bulls that had been herded in the pageant by young men of military age; the animals' joints and haunches were then wrapped in fat, seared on the altar, and distributed to the people, who finished roasting the meat on portable braziers.[13] Five days of theatrical competition ensued: one day of dithyrambic contests, in which fifty-member male choruses sang and danced in homage to Dionysos; five comedies the next day; and three days more of tragic drama (with related satyr plays).[14]

Performances began at dawn and must have lasted well into the afternoon. The 14,000 or more Athenians present very likely watched in a state of pleasurable anxiety. Whatever else it did to entertain, move, and awe, Athenian tragedy dramatized human vulnerability to the gods.

[11] The "Pronomos Vase" (Attic, c. 400), now in Naples' archaeological museum, is the best-preserved and single most important representation of Athenian drama. It depicts the backstage excitement of actors and chorus members costumed and masked for a satyr play. Dionysos, thyrsus in one hand and opposite arm embracing a female figure, dominates the scene.

[12] Mock phalloi were also frequent props in the satyr plays and comedies presented during the festival.

[13] For documentation of the details of the procession see Csapo and Slater, 106.

[14] Winkler and Zeitlin (p. 4, n. 3) agree that this was the probable order of events.

Athenian audiences expected this essentially religious experience,[15] and that expectation separates their ability to appreciate the tragedies from our own. Modern audiences are least receptive to a feature of Greek tragedy that was constant and essential to the ancients—mournful keening that lingers on ruined lives and the disasters inflicted by the gods. Athenians wept openly during these scenes, of which Plato thoroughly disapproved. He warned against both the playwrights' wringing of the audience's emotions and the audience's enjoyment of such unwarranted grief.[16] Nightmarish creatures could also cause extreme visceral reactions. The sudden arrival of the glaring, snake-haired Furies in the original staging of Aeschylus' *Eumenides* caused women in the audience to miscarry.[17]

The visual and aural impression tragedy delivered was often spectacular. Aristotle, who witnessed only productions in the fourth century, identified "spectacle" as one of the basic elements of tragic theatre: oboe music; the singing of set-piece odes and dancing; masks that transformed the same male actor into a swarthy-faced young hero, a dignified matron, Argos with a hundred eyes, or the Kyklops with one; painted scenery and large-scale special effects engineered with sliding platforms and towering cranes—all suggest that Greek tragedy had a great deal in common with Italian opera. Indeed, odes were a precious commodity that saved the lives of some who knew them by heart. Athenian soldiers captured in 413 by the Syracusan army received special treatment (and many were set free) if they could teach or sing choral odes from Euripides to their Sicilian captors—who even then were ardent fans of soaring arias.[18]

Athenian politicians deliberately scheduled the Dionsysia after winter storms had abated so that foreign visitors could attend, and they orchestrated festival ceremonies to impress the Mediterranean world with more than their city's flair for music and drama.[19] Indeed, Athens

---

[15] Taplin, 162, disagrees that religious ritual was intrinsic to the festival: "[T]he Great Dionysia was an occasion to stop work, drink a lot of wine, eat some meat" and witness ritual and ceremony "part of such holidays the world over." But Gould (1990, 130–40) and Simon Goldhill (in Winkler and Zeitlin, 96–129) both argue persuasively in favor of the festival's religious nature.

[16] *Republic*, Book X.

[17] Pickard-Cambridge, 264–65. Since it's not certain that women attended the Dionysia, the anecdote may be apocryphal. Jeffrey Henderson sums up the most convincing case for women's attendance in "Women and the Athenian Dramatic Festivals," *TAPA*, 121 (1992): 133–47.

[18] Plutarch, Nicias, 29.

[19] Thuycidides (1.70) records the qualities, as identified by Korinthians, that enabled Athenians' dominance in the ancient world: "[They] are addicted to innovation, and their designs are characterized by swiftness alike in conception and execution. . . . [T]heir bodies they spend ungrudgingly in their country's

exhibited sheer civic and imperial power: by displaying the treasure received during the year from its subjugated cities; by parading in battle armor the sons of soldiers killed in the wars; and by awarding gold crowns to citizens whose achievements it wished to honor. Theater attendance itself was closely linked to citizenship; local town counsels awarded the price of a festival ticket to citizens in good standing.[20] A herald read aloud the names of slaves whose masters had dedicated them to Dionysos, thus setting them free; the ten generals who conducted Athens' military campaigns poured a libation to the god. In the front row (eventually on stone chairs, some of which exist today) sat priests and priestesses of the city's chief religious cults, as well as the gold-crowned, honored citizens. Members of the Boulê (the five hundred–member council) and the *ephebes,* or newly inducted soldiers, filled ranks of wooden seats, while the city's tribal units congregated in their own wedge-shaped sections. The theater's bowl seethed with a heady, sometimes unruly, brew of military, political, and religious energy.[21]

Both drama and democratic politics rely on two or more characters who face off in front of an involved audience. Hillsides, whose slopes were wide and gentle enough to seat a crowd, made perfect settings for such encounters and were the earliest theaters. Ancient roads that widened below the hills, or open ground at the hill's base, provided suitable, flat performance space. In such settings, archaeological find-

---

cause; their intellect they judiciously husband to be employed in her service. . . . [T]o them laborious occupation is less of a misfortune than the peace of a quiet life. To describe their character in a word, one might truly say they were born into the world to take no rest themselves and to give none to others." Throughout the entire range of human accomplishment Athenians exercised the same imagination, skillful organization of resources, and political assertiveness that were evident in their Dionysian Festival. Their concepts, formal models, vocabulary, standards of judgment, even the imperative to innovate itself, are permanently embedded in modern culture and science, from Architecture to Zoology. Athenians asked the right questions: "What is the prime virtue of a good person?" "What is the most powerful and inexhaustible artistic subject?" "Who should rule a nation?" Their answers, "wisdom," "the human form," and "its people," retain their authority.

[20] Winkler and Zeitlin, 4.

[21] Athenian audiences often fortified themselves during the lengthy performances with wine, sweets, and dried fruit, the latter being perfectly suited to pelting actors they didn't like. Spectators raucously applauded and cheered in appreciation—and booed, hissed, or clicked their heels against the seats in disapproval. But physical violence in the theater was against the law and, in extreme circumstances, punishable by death. The sanctity of and laws governing the festival were taken seriously. After the Dionysia ended, the Ekklesia met in the theater to investigate the complaints of misconduct lodged against both officials of the festival and participants in it, and of injuries received. Pickard-Cambridge, 69 and 272–73.

ings and the written record tell us, people gathered to celebrate a rite, perform dithyrambs, meet a crisis, hold a legal proceeding, or join in grief. Such sites (along with every city's marketplace, the *agora*) were the main arenas of community life. Usually a temple dedicated to Dionysos or some other god stood nearby. Inscribed stone markers along roads leading to the theaters commemorated local victors: athletes, actors, playwrights, singers, and the plays' producers, or *choregoi*.[22] Theaters, in every sense, were open to the flow of life.

More formal theaters were hewn from the rugged and already dramatic Greek countryside; archaeologists have excavated hillsides all over the Greek world that were architecturally transformed, most spectacularly those at Delphi and Epidauros (the latter constructed in the fourth century). Besides the Theater of Dionysos, Athens possessed several theater venues for democratic confrontation: the great assembly of all-male citizens (the Ekklesia) met to pass laws at the Pnyx hill; the five hundred Boulê members convened (in the building called the Bouleterion) to set the assembly's agenda. But the rural components of the earliest theaters—and the Greek names that reflect their countryside origins—were incorporated into these urban settings and designs. Two roads that led into the Theater of Dionysos, for instance, connected it to Athens' population center to the northeast and to the sacred city of Eleusis to the northwest. Dancers and actors used these roads (called the east *parodos* and the west *parodos*) as passageways, entering from and exiting toward destinations in which fictive and real topography sometimes coincided. (In *Antigone,* characters going to or from the battlefield would leave via the west *parodos* toward open country, while city-bound characters exited via the east.) *Theatron,* the root of our word theater, translates as "viewing place" and hence designated the curved and banked seating area. *Orchestra* was literally "the place for dancing." The costumed actors emerged from and retired to the *skenê,* a word that originally meant, and literally was in the rural theaters, a tent. As theaters evolved to become more permanent structures, the *skenê* developed as well—into a "stage building" whose painted façade changed, like a mask, with the characters' various habitats. Depending on the drama, the *skenê* could assume the countenance of a

[22] Production costs for the festival—costumes, props, actors' and dancers' salaries—were paid for by *choregoi* (sing. *choregos,* or chorus-person), wealthy citizens appointed as producers by the archon, the city official in charge of the Dionsyia. The "honor" of the appointment was considered part of a citizen's tax base. To assure equal access to acting talent, the state assigned actors according to their abilities to the three competing dramatists. Winkler (in Winkler and Zeitlin, "The Ephebes' Song: *Tragoidia* and *Polis,*" 20–62) makes an interesting argument that young men of military age served as the dancers for the Dionysia productions.

king's grand palace, the Kyklops' cave, a temple to the gods, or (reverting to its original form) an army commander's tent.

Debate, the democratic Athenian art practiced and perfected by politicians, litigators, and thespians—and relished and judged by voters, juries, and audiences—flourished in theatrical venues. Debate permeated daily Athenian life. Thucydides used it as an effective technique to narrate history and explain its participants' motives by reproducing the speeches of politicians, generals, and diplomats who argued the case for a particular policy or a strategy in war. Many of Thucydides' dialogues are indeed highly charged.[23] Plato, recognizing the open-ended, exploratory power of the *agon,* or verbal battle, wrote his philosophy almost entirely in dramatic form. The *agon* was the most readily available version of the Greeks' addiction to all forms of competition, and it remains to this day our most powerful medium for testing and judging issues across the spectrum of civilized life; superior arguments emerge from debate and dialogue, and in them character is laid bare. Sold on the value of conducting their affairs in dramatic mode, the Athenians grasped the potential of artfully composed (and performed) drama—to tell exciting stories, to rouse healthy emotions, and to heighten awareness of the dangerous issues heroes and ordinary folk, past and present, must face.

In official Athenian civic parlance playwrights were called *didaskoloi,* or "teachers," to indicate their practical role in coaching lines, blocking actors, and rehearsing musical numbers with the dancers. But the plays these *didaskoloi* wrote delivered the most powerful lessons. Consider the "Hubris Ode" of *Oedipus the King,* in which the Chorus distinguishes between two kinds of intense ambition. The ode voices disgust for an overreaching tyrant full of hubris, or "the will to violate," who scales the heights and stumbles to his death. But it immediately follows with praise for a healthier exercise of competitive spirit in public life, the kind that sustains and protects cities:

> But there's another fighting spirit
> I ask god never to destroy—
> the kind that makes our city thrive. (879–81/1015–17)

[23] Thucydides chronicles the most chilling and famous political debate on record in his *History.* In that exchange, which took place on the island of Melos, a delegation of Athenians patiently explain to the Melians—who had rebelled and wished to detach themselves from the Athenian empire, or Delian League—the reasons why they must ruthlessly suppress the revolt, the most calculated reason being that any leniency shown to the Melians would encourage other of Athens' subject cities to defect, a most unacceptable prospect. Athens did not extend its own democratic principles of self-determination to cities whose loyalty was exacted by force.

Even a dramatic voice from another era had the power to stop a passerby in his tracks. The poet Simonides wrote the following couplet to be inscribed on the funeral monument for the three hundred Spartan warriors who were killed, in 480, defending the pass at Thermopolae from the Persian invaders:

> Stranger, go tell the Lakedemonians: we lie
> here still, obedient to their commands.[24]

The care Greeks took in siting and building their theaters measures their reverence and respect for dramatic form. Good acoustics were indispensable in projecting dialogue and choral song to audiences of thousands, especially since the intonation of an actor's voice could drastically change the meaning of some ancient Greek words—one slight variation of a vowel might render an entire passage ambiguous. Accordingly, the Greeks constructed technological marvels from earth and stone. The director Peter Sellars sees these theaters as giant ears carved into the sides of mountains, ears capable of receiving intact both whispers of despair and roars of pain—in short, communal listening and transmitting devices of still unsurpassed simplicity and fidelity.[25]

The written dramas and their stone amplifiers survive, but we're still uncertain as to how country dances and dithyrambs enacting incidents from myth evolved into the beautifully structured and remarkably pertinent plays we possess. In the mid-sixth century a Greek actor named Thespis might have made the crucial leap from narrative to dialogue by speaking in the first person as Dionysos, for instance, or as a Homeric hero like Hector or Agamemnon, and then engaging the chorus in a conversation. Some scholars question ancient texts that claim Thespis was the first performer to dramatize a narrative, but the Parian Marble identifies him as the winner of a dramatic competition in Athens c. 534. The prize that year was a goat. Since tragedy translates literally as "goat-dance," it's possible that the modest reward for which actors competed lent the great art form its name.

Could tragic drama as we know it actually have come not from the choral dithyramb but from some surprising unknown source? P. E. Easterling explains why the problem might be insoluble: "The early history of performance at the Dionysia . . . is a notoriously unclear and disputed area, with almost no reliable evidence to work from. One . . . [fact] that is definitely known is that satyrs in Dionysiac cult . . . predate the introduction of plays . . . into the Dionysia, but there is no

---

[24] For the Greek text of the poem I translate here see Moore, 42.
[25] Sellars has directed memorable revivals of Greek drama, notably *The Persians* and, most recently, *The Children of Herakles*. He spoke about the theater as a "giant ear" during a talkback session after a performance of the latter play at the American Repertory Theater in Cambridge, Mass., on January 25, 2003.

record of the process whereby the tragic competition came to be defined as a contest of three tragedies and one satyr play."[26] Jean-Pierre Vernant sums up the situation succinctly: we can and do know tragedy's "antecedents" but not its "origins."[27] Still, tragedy's raw material, its immediate relatives, and its "contributing institutions" are not in dispute; they all derive from and inform Athenian political, cultural, and religious life. Every surviving playwright, including the comedian Aristophanes, confronted aspects of the agonizing and not easily resolvable political and moral problems that beset Athens. The debates and speeches of the assembly and the law courts honed (and sometimes echoed) the plays' verbal infighting. Carved figures of gods and mortals (and painted ones that enlivened pottery) inspired and reflected the masks worn by actors. The frequent public recitations of Homeric poems provided a world-view in which personal honor, compulsory retaliation, and meddling gods were prominent.

Structurally, Athenian tragedy was somewhat formulaic but never static: five to seven dramatic scenes usually separated by four to six choral interludes, or odes, although Sophokles' *Philoctetes* had but one. The odes, performed originally by twelve male members (until Sophokles, always a theatrical innovator, increased the number to fifteen), were most likely accompanied by rhythmic, dance-like movements and by music of an *aulos,* a reed instrument similar to the oboe. The Chorus, in unison or represented by its Leader, participated in the spoken dialogue with the characters. In Aeschylus' earliest tragedies two masked actors were hired to perform all the dramatic roles, so that each exited several times to return in a different guise. Later, when he and other poets employed three actors, the opportunities for complex conversation increased. (Occasional additions to the cast, or "mute" stand-ins, allowed characters to remain on stage for long periods of time to witness, but not verbally participate in, the action.) The dramatic episodes themselves included formal ingredients: several long expository speeches in which characters voiced their opinions on crucial issues; intervals of stichomythia, or rapid-fire one-liners exchanged by two, or sometimes three, characters; at least one speech by a Messenger, almost always the bearer of bad news who vividly described disastrous events that happened offstage; and the *kommos,* an extended polyphonic passage by characters who grieve for what they've lost. In the *threnos,* the concluding portion of the tragedy, the characters discussed and concluded their suffering or, in the case of Euripides' later tragedies, their *escape* from disaster and suffering, the divine source of which was sometimes explicit and at other times only implied.

The radical strangeness of ancient Greek divinities, so different

---

[26] Easterling, 39.
[27] Vernant and Vidal-Naquet, 25.

from their Judeo-Christian counterpart in significant respects, is a potential source of confusion for modern audiences. Though gods from both traditions could denounce, inhibit, and punish forbidden conduct, Greek gods, unlike those from the Hebraic tradition, represented the full range of human engagement with life. A vast, intricate network of myth, poems, and plays showed the gods in action—and enhanced the Greeks' ability to comprehend and deal with virtually anything they might encounter in their own lives from birth until death. The gods provided imaginative writers with an emotional, intellectual, and moral vocabulary: Zeus is the fatherly source of power and authority, Ares the hated god of warriors. Athena is the patroness of the wise and clever, Aphrodite of the wanton and the fecund. Eros provokes desire and encourages its fulfillment; Dionysos intoxicates and deranges via life-transforming fluids (blood, wine, sap, and semen). Artemis is both huntress and midwife; Poseidon gives men power over horses and the sea. Hephaestus inspires the craftsman, Hermes the news-bringer. Apollo is the source of human destiny and its historian, artistic creativity.

The typical tragic plot, judging from the thirty-three surviving plays, dramatizes the gods' destruction of a household or an extended family.[28] The range of issues and human predicaments explored is both exotic and familiar: the consequences of sexual desire and adultery; the futility of resistance to a god; disputes over unburied warriors; the ravages of guilt on an individual conscience; sacrifice of innocent lives; and stark issues of justice and morality, such as the treatment of defeated peoples by their conquerors, a recurring theme of Euripides. Each playwright altered the mythical stories he inherited and reused—sometimes radically, and frequently with both ingenuity and genius. As we will see in the case of Sophokles' Theban plays, these alterations seem inspired by an understanding of human potential and responsibility that deepened during his lifetime.

Tragedy in time became a mode of learning in which there was substantial give and take between the city and its playwrights. The archon, an elected official, chose the playwrights—and most likely listened to influential citizens who lobbied for favorite poets or for popular stories and themes. Though it seems that prior censorship was rarely a factor, playwrights could get into trouble. Aeschylus was tried for revealing sacred Eleusinian mysteries. Phrynichos was heavily fined for depressing the festival audience. His play *The Capture of Miletus* reawakened memories of a massacre perpetrated by the Persians against a valued ally, and the assembly banned any future performance of the tragedy.[29] Euripides was excoriated (by Aristophanes, repeatedly) for

---

[28] Seaford, 334–62.
[29] Csapo and Slater, 11.

presenting women as treacherous, overbold, and oversexed. He rewrote *Hippolytos* in apparent response to such criticism. In the first version Phaidra directly propositions her stepson. In the revised version, the one we possess, Phaidra becomes so desperately lovesick that her nurse begs Hippolytos to "cure" his stepmother by sleeping with her; his refusal proves deadly to both.

Ancient Greek playwrights gravitated to the worst possible violence mortals could suffer and commit, and for the Greeks the most feared and hated crimes were incest and parricide. The story of Oedipus organized these fears in their most powerful, concentrated form. Sophokles first used the Oedipus myth (most likely, but not certainly) in *Antigone*. He returned to Oedipus twice more, each time shifting his attention backward in time from Antigone's death to trace how incest and kin murder worked themselves out through three generations of the Labdakid clan. We see Oedipus, his mother, and his children internalize the deadly grip of Fate, so that the greater interest that links all three plays becomes the psychological distortion that Oedipus' "crimes" impose on himself and his blood kin. The evil mechanism by which Fate or the gods harm families becomes less interesting, particularly to a modern audience, than the characters' experience of living through the havoc the gods wreak—they fear it, suffer it, and wait for it to strike again.

Oedipus, for instance, is compelled to learn new meanings for words that name his closest relationships: son, husband, parent, friend, enemy. His children become his siblings; his wife his mother; his protector his destroyer. He also must cease for a time to trust the justice of the gods. As he discovers his horrific new identities during the final phase of *Oedipus the King*, all he can do is proclaim his disgust at the very source of human life. Oedipus extrapolates from his own and his parents' marriage to all marriages, and he no longer conceives of marriage, at its best a joyful, nurturing, and hopeful partnership, as anything but a destroyer of humankind.[30] Vernant believes that such disorienting discoveries involving language are central to Greek tragedy, and that the dilemma is salutary:

> The tragic message, when understood, is precisely that there are zones of opacity and incommunicability in the words that men exchange. Even as he sees the protagonists clinging exclusively to one meaning, and thus blinded, tearing themselves apart or destroying themselves, the spectator must understand that there really are two or more possible meanings. The language becomes transparent and the tragic message gets across to him only provided he makes the discovery that words, values, men themselves,

[30] See *Oed King,* 1591–96 and *Oed King* introduction, p. 33.

are ambiguous, that the universe is one of conflict, only if he re-
linquishes his earlier convictions, accepts a problematic vision of
the world and, through the dramatic spectacle, himself acquires a
tragic consciousness.[31]

Aristotle provides anecdotal evidence that Sophokles could step
back and view his own personal conduct during a violent political era
with the complex awareness that he builds so consistently into the language of his plays. As Aristotle tells it, Sophokles, one of ten elder states-
men elected to rescue Athens from the aftermath of the catastrophic invasion of Sicily, had just agreed to replace the democratic assembly of
male citizens with an oligarchy of four hundred aristocrats. One of the
new oligarchs asked Sophokles if he had approved abolishing the assembly, the founding institution whose recent folly and incompetence
ultimately led to Athens' catastrophic decline:

Sophokles answered, "Yes."
"Why? Did you not think it a terrible decision?"
"Yes," he said.
"So were you not doing something terrible?"
"That's right," he said. "But there was no better alternative."[32]

There was no better alternative to Athens' defeated democracy than
an aristocratic junta! This rueful admission, coming as Athens' and
Sophokles' great century winds down, lacks the high drama of the poet's
best dialogue but has its own deep sadness. And it reminds us that for
the Greeks, honest talk was truth's home ground. Nonetheless, it's brac-
ing to hear the Sophokles we know from his tragedies—a realistic, self-
aware intelligence—speak in person from an ancient text.

Confirming the facts of Sophokles' life, however, requires a leap
of faith. A number of contemporary scholars, most notably Mary
Lefkowitz, conclude that Hellenist biographers, our most abundant
source of information, had little documented material to work with and
therefore relied heavily (and uncritically) on inferences from Sophokles'
own plays or on references to a character named "Sophokles" in popular ancient dialogues and comedies. But it's still possible to develop a
portrait of the poet by piecing together the old, suspect stories with
sounder evidence unavailable to the earliest chroniclers of his life.

Sophokles first appears in Athenian national life at age fifteen,
dancing naked (according to one source) and leading boy dancers in a
hymn of gratitude to celebrate Athens' defeat of the Persian fleet in the

---

[31] Vernant and Vidal-Naquet, 43.
[32] Aristotle, *Rhetoric,* 3, 18, 1419 A 25. This is my translation of the passage, for
which I consulted the translation of J. H. Freese.

straits of Salamis.[33] He had been taught by excellent masters in music, dance, and wrestling, and won crowns competing against his age-mates in all three disciplines.

He was born c. 497–496 and died c. 406–405 in his ninety-first year, productive to the last.[34] His father Sophillus was said to have manufactured weapons (probably in a factory operated by slaves) and his mother to have been a midwife. They lived in Kolonos, a rural *deme,* or suburb, just north of Athens. His parents' social status—they may not have been aristocrats, as were other playwrights' families, but they surely had money and owned property—did not hamper his career prospects. Sophokles' talents, so formidable and so precociously developed, won him early fame as a dramatist and, in at least one instance, as an actor. He triumphed in his play *Nausicaa* as the eponymous young princess who, playing ball with her girlfriends, discovers the nearly naked Odysseus washed up on the beach.[35] Later in life Sophokles was respected as a participant in democratic governance at the highest level. Most of the ancient biographical sources attest to his good looks, his easygoing manner, his enjoyment of life, and his consistently superior luck.[36]

[33]Athens prevailed not only through superior fighting skills in close naval combat, but also through superior strategy, enticing the Persians to sail so far up a narrow bay in Salamis that their warships, squeezing closely together, lost the ability to maneuver and thus were vulnerable to a swift enveloping maneuver of the Athenian fleet. Sophokles would remember this tactic and "employ" it, as I later explain, in a social encounter.

[34] The ancient sources of information about Sophokles' life must be carefully evaluated. I have benefited from Hugh Lloyd-Jones' introduction to his translations of Sophokles' complete plays for the Loeb Classical Library Series, and from the work of Lefkowitz, Jebb, and Gould. In the end, when actually assembling my narrative account I used my own judgment and tried to indicate the degree of certainty each piece of information carries.

[35] Lloyd-Jones (1994, 11) cites the popularity of Sophokles' performance as chronicled by Stefan Radt in *Tragicorum Graecorum Fragmenta IV: Sophocles* (1977). Lloyd-Jones and Lefkowitz, however, say the story might have its origin in a comic poet's joke. But given Sophokles' attested talents as a dancer and gymnast, why shouldn't we believe he'd make a credible athletic princess? It was common practice in the early fifth century for poets to act in their own tragedies. Sophokles, who allegedly had a weak voice, was one of the first to stop the practice.

[36] The details of Sophokles' adult family life are few. He and his wife, Nicostrate, had one son, Iophon, who also wrote tragedies. He fathered another son, Ariston, with a mistress named Theoris. According to a contested passage in the *Life,* Iophon accused his father of senility a few years before Sophokles' death and took legal action to gain control of his assets. The alleged cause of the lawsuit was Iophon's jealousy of Ariston's son, Sophokles the Younger, who would posthumously produce his grandfather's *Oedipus at Kolonos* and later

An instance of this luck occurred in 468, at the start of his first Great Dionysia. Playwrights and their casts customarily appeared, uncostumed and unmasked, the day before the festival to give a preview, called the *proagon,* of the tragedies they were about to present.[37] Sophokles' major competitor on his first try at the prize was Aeschylus, not only a veteran of the Battle of Marathon but Athens' greatest living dramatist. It seems likely that some aspect of Sophokles' *proagon* presentation stirred an enormous controversy, and one that threatened the traditional judging process. Or perhaps word of the quality and nature of the four plays Sophokles was rehearsing had spread, raising expectations for the young poet and alarming Aeschylus' partisans.

The awarding of prizes at the Great Dionysia normally involved choosing by lot (from a list supplied by the Council) one judge from each of Athens' ten tribes. Critical acumen was not required to get one's name on the list, but the *choregoi* were present when it was assembled and probably had a hand in the selection. At the conclusion of the festival the ten selected judges, each having sworn that he hadn't been bribed or unduly influenced, would inscribe on a tablet the names of the three competing playwrights in order of merit. These "ballots" were placed in a large urn. The presiding official—in 468 it was the archon Apsephion—would then draw five ballots at random; "on these five tablets the issue of the contest was decided."[38] But according to an account by Plutarch, Apsephion sensed the "spirit of rivalry and partisanship . . . running high in the audience" and dispensed with the normal selection of judges by lot.[39] The enormously popular statesman Kimon[40] and nine other generals had just finished pouring the required libations to Dionysos when Apsephion prevented them from leaving and obliged all ten to take the oath and sit as judges. The distinguished generals awarded Sophokles first prize. The defeat did not faze the older dramatist, whose masterwork, *The Oresteia,* was produced a decade later.

---

win his own prize at the Dionysia. In court Sophokles reportedly defended his sanity by reciting a passage from a work in progress, the *Kolonos*—most probably the ode in praise of Athens. (It's possible that Sophokles' bitterness intensified the hatred that his character Oedipus directs at his own sons in that play.) A few months before his death Sophokles appeared with his chorus at the *proagon* of the Dionysia to mourn the death of Euripides; it seems highly unlikely that the archon would have granted a chorus to a senile Sophokles.

[37] Csapo and Slater, 110.
[38] Pickard-Cambridge, 97.
[39] Plutarch, Cimon, 9.
[40] Kimon was not only a successful general but the founder of a new Athenian colony at Skyros; recently he'd returned to Athens bringing with him the 400-year-old bones of the city's earliest hero, Theseus, which he buried and made the focus of a hero cult. His prestige most likely added weight to the judges' award of first prize to Sophokles.

Only guesswork can suggest what element in Sophokles' "debut" brought him instant success. The late Thomas Gould, in *The Ancient Quarrel between Poetry and Philosophy*, makes an intriguing assumption: the decisive innovation was the religious thrill each of Sophokles' plays contains. Gould believes that one of the plays, the lost *Triptolemos*, with a plot that combined intensely religious and patriotic elements, was part of Sophokles' winning entry.[41]

During Sophokles' half-century career as a *didaskolos* he wrote and directed about one hundred twenty plays, and was awarded first prize at least nineteen times. No record exists of his placing lower than second. Seven of his plays survive as entire works, along with a substantial fragment of a satyr play, *The Trackers*. Only two very late plays can be given exact production dates: *Philoctetes* in 409 and *Oedipus at Kolonos,* staged posthumously, in 401. Some evidence suggests that *Antigone* was produced around 442–441[42] and *Oedipus the King* in the 420s. *Ajax, Elektra,* and *The Women of Trachis* have been conjecturally dated through stylistic analysis.

Sophokles' fellow citizens respected him sufficiently to vote him into high city office on at least three occasions. He served as chief tribute-collector for Athens' overseas empire in 443–442, and his tribe voted him in as one of ten military commanders in 441–440. In 411 he was elected to a ten-man commission charged with rescuing Athenian governance from the massive defeat in Sicily, and was thereby party to the decision mentioned above that replaced Athens' democracy with a short-lived, four hundred-member oligarchy.

Aristotle, who had access we forever lack to the hundreds of fifth-century plays produced at the Dionysia, preferred Sophokles to his rivals Aeschylus and Euripides. In fact, Aristotle considered *Oedipus the King* the most perfect example of tragic form; he developed his influential (but now largely discredited) theory of tragedy from his analysis of it. Aristotle also credited Sophokles with the invention of painted scenery and the introduction of a third actor, but other early authorities dispute these claims. Sophokles himself may have written a theatrical treatise entitled *On the Chorus,* now lost. Gould believed that this work, if it ever existed, would have covered the entire range of dramatic production—writing scripts, designing scenery and costumes, training dancers and musicians—since the Athenian idiom for giving

[41] The thrill was accomplished by showing the gods inflicting undeserved suffering on sympathetic characters. Gould's theory is worked out with flair, philosophical and literary depth, and fascinating detail. *The Ancient Quarrel* also contains a lively and (mostly) judicious brief life of Sophokles. I have followed its emphases in preparing my own account.

[42] See my discussion below of a claim made by Aristophanes of Byzantium. If it is indeed true, *Antigone* must have been staged shortly before Sophokles' election.

a dramatist the wherewithal to stage four plays at the Dionysia was "to grant a chorus."

A few surviving comments attributed to Sophokles (perhaps from his lost prose work) speak to his own literary development and his mature stylistic intentions. Plutarch quotes him as saying that he needed to shake off the influence of Aeschylus before he could find his own voice.[43] He did so by learning to mock Aeschylean massiveness and, his words imply, Aeschylus' metaphoric congestion. Sophokles survived Aeschylus' intimidating example, he himself admitted, by imitating his elder's style and then laughing at the successful result. Only then could he achieve the detachment needed to break Aeschylus' spell. Sophokles' innovation was to simplify and quiet his style to convey nuances of character (ethos) and to concentrate on projecting human, rather than divine excellence (arête). A passage in Aristotle's Poetics reinforces Sophokles' claim that he made his poetry less elevated and more accessible.[44] The preferred metrical form in tragedies, writes Aristotle, was originally trochaic tetrameter, a highly syncopated meter well suited to music, dance, and elevated discourse. But the iambic trimeter used by Sophokles, which better fit the rhythms of conversational speech, replaced it. In Sophokles' hands ordinary speech became extraordinarily eloquent.

Sophokles' backstage organizational skills might be the ultimate source of a controversial claim by Aristophanes of Byzantium in the third century that "admiration for his production of Antigone" influenced his selection as one of the ten generals, or strategoi, in 441–440. Since dramatic skill alone does not readily translate into military prowess, the claim has been much doubted. Jebb and Gould, however, suggest that it was the managerial and inspirational skills on display during the production of Antigone, rather than any politically rousing sentiments in the play, that earned Sophokles this post. Writes Gould, "Here was a man who could carry anything off with wonderful success, no matter how important and complex."[45] Jebb supports the claim more pragmatically by pointing out that generals usually ran military affairs without leaving Athens, and were not always expected to conduct military campaigns. But Athens was faced with a war on Sophokles' watch as general. He and the nine other generals, including Perikles, sailed to subdue Samos, an ally in revolt, early in 440, well before the usual navigation season began.

On a diplomatic errand related to that war,[46] Sophokles attended a

[43] Moralia, 78e–79b

[44] Poetics, 1449a, 15–25.

[45] Gould 1990, 160–61.

[46] Jebb 1888, xliii–xliv. Sophokles was apparently headed to Lesbos to seek backup support for the Athenian force of triremes about to attack Samos.

dinner party on the island Chios, possibly as a guest of Ion of Chios, a playwright who had also competed in the Dionsysia, although he was not an Athenian citizen. The sustained account of that evening is rarely examined in any detail, but its details give a glimpse of a man whose playful spirit enhanced his commanding presence. The story has come down to us in Athanaeus' multivolume *Deipnosophistai,* a compendium of gossip and dinner-chat about and among ancient worthies.[47] Athenaeus quotes a passage from Ion's book, *Sojournings,* whose authenticity seems assured because its particulars fit the historical facts it contains,[48] and because it's written in Ion's native Ionian dialect. In this passage Ion records two simultaneously unfolding events—Sophokles' flirtation with the handsome lad serving wine, and that flirtation's interruption by a local schoolmaster's boorish attempt at literary criticism.

Ion notes that when drinking, Sophokles' mood was often "boyish."[49] Sophokles, indeed in good spirits that night, noticed the wine boy's blush and asked if the boy would like him to drink with pleasure: *If you do, don't be too hasty handing me the wine cup and taking it away.* When the boy reddened more intensely at Sophokles' interest, Sophokles recited a line from a poem by Phrynichos to his couch-mate: *The light of love is shining on vermillion cheeks.* The couch-mate, a schoolmaster, remarked that a poet as wise in his art as Sophokles ought to think the line very bad: *It's not a happy expression to call cheeks purple,*[50] *for if purple paint were splashed on the boy's cheek it would destroy his looks.* Sophokles immediately recited several other famous lines of poetry that fuse color with beauty to convey an emotion, and he deconstructed each one hilariously according to the schoolmaster's literary principles. As Sophokles extrapolated, the poor man's critical "paintbrush" defaced every charming metaphor in Greek poetry it touched. Hilarity ensued. One cringes for the luckless academic.

Having subdued his couch-mate, Sophokles then turned his attention back to the boy, who was trying to extract a fleck of straw floating in Sophokles' newly filled wine cup. *Blow it away instead,* said Sophokles, *for I don't want you to get your fingers wet.* (The allusion was to Homer's Dawn, whose rosy fingers the schoolmaster envisioned as sullied by red dye.) The boy blew on the wine as Sophokles slowly brought the cup closer to his mouth, and as the boy's puckered lips came into range, Sophokles kissed them. In the midst of roaring laughter Soph-

---

[47] The name of Athenaeus' massive collection of anecdotes can be loosely translated as "Philosophers at Dinner." Or, as those who dispute the authenticity of much of its contents might translate, "Sophists Cooking Things Up."

[48] Jebb, loc. cit. Even Ion's description of the evening's ambiance fits the facts: The fire in the dining room suggests the weather was still cold.

[49] During his visit to Chios Sophokles was fifty-five or fifty-six.

[50] I paraphrase here. Actually, the dye-color in Phrynichos' line was porphyry, a deep reddish-purple.

okles crowed, *Perikles, you know, says that as a military strategist I'm an excellent poet. But didn't this latest maneuver of mine turn out nicely for me?* This "Skirmish of the Windblown Winecup" resembles the triumph of military strategy that Sophokles celebrated when he was the rosy wine server's age: Themistokles' enticement of the Persian Fleet up a narrow strait at Salamis and toward the submerged rams of Athenian triremes lying in wait.

Athenaeus includes another anecdote that suggests the rough banter with which Sophokles and Euripides might have pummeled each other at dinner parties or during the Dionysia.[51] But whatever antagonism the two poets may have felt for each other, there's no doubt Sophokles deeply respected Euripides. When word arrived just prior to the start of the Dionysia in 406 that the author of *Medea, Hippolytos,* and *The Trojan Women* had died in Macedonia, Sophokles and his entire company appeared in the Odeon at the *proagon,* dressed in black, in tribute to their sardonically brilliant colleague.

Sophokles is convincingly described as universally respected, lustful, and intensely religious, qualities that did not seem incompatible to his contemporaries. Religious piety meant something quite different to an Athenian than the suppression of pleasure and the saintly demeanor it might suggest to us. His involvement in various cults, including one related to the god of health, Aesclepius, and another to the hero Herakles, surely contributed to his reputation as "loved by the gods" and "the most religious of men." But since Greek gods regularly destroyed

---

[51] This story involves a sexual encounter each poet had with a young boy outside the city walls. The youth took Sophokles' cape after their tryst and left the poet his smaller one to wear back to the city; when the same boy parted company with Euripides, no such "mistake" was made. Euripides spread the word that Sophokles' "embarrassment" showed his "low moral character," and Sophokles wrote the following poem, taking his rival to task for having a reputation as a serial adulterer.

> The Sun, Euripides, not this boy, stripped off my cape;
> but when you go out to steal another man's wife,
> beware the cold North Wind blowing through your affairs!
> For when you're caught plowing a field you don't own,
> you implicate Eros himself in your crime.

Sophokles makes a comparison here on two levels: He contrasts his completely legal pedophilia with Euripides' actionable adultery. And he uses an old fable, in which the Sun is deemed a much more potent means of removing a man's cloak than the wind, to distinguish between his own hot passion and Euripides' coldly calculating thievery. Euripides might have felt understandable irritation at the moral superiority assumed in Sophokles' famous contrast: *Euripides imitates men as they are, Sophokles as they ought to be.* (Aristotle, *Poetics,* 1460b, 35.) The anecdote and poem may be forgeries, but the skillful animus of the epigram increases the likelihood of its being genuine.

innocent people to punish their ancestors' crimes and meted out justice with far from an even hand, worshipping them was no safe or easy task. Sophokles' tragedies neither explained nor disguised the gods' brutality. In Gould's phrase, he "engineered scenes that thrilled the original audiences with emotions enriched by literal belief in divinity."[52] *To be religious* in Sophokles' case meant to stir in his audience the direct sensation that gods were present in the dramatized experience of his characters. And that experience always included "the great unmerited suffering" of his heroes.[53]

One remarkable absence in Sophokles' own life was documented suffering of any kind. His luck continued to the moment his body was placed in its tomb. As Sophokles lay dying, a Spartan army had once again invaded the Athenian countryside, blocking access to Sophokles' intended burial site beyond Athens' walls. But after Sophokles' peaceful death the Spartan general allowed the poet's burial party to pass through his lines, commanded to do so, it was widely believed, by the god Dionysos.

[52] Gould 1990, 130.
[53] Ibid., 139–40.

Oedipus the King
"Handling Trouble and Confronting Gods"

In Sophokles' time the Greeks believed that the fate of an individual was bound up with one's *daimon,* a divinity who presides over the happiness or misery of that person's life. The Greek word for happiness, *eudaimonia,* literally meaning "well daimoned," suggests that a person so blessed is divinely and perhaps permanently protected. But a daimon could just as often devastate an individual or an entire family. In *Oedipus the King* the intimate and personal divinity who strikes Oedipus blow after deadly blow is a daimon—a kind of executioner who does Fate's bidding.

Our modern skepticism—that an intelligent, arbitrary Fate controls anyone's life (except as a lazy metaphor)—leads us to ask in what sense it is true, as the events of Oedipus' life strongly suggest, that his actions have been shaped by a malign divinity. It's possible, by using a good deal of wanton ingenuity, to claim that Oedipus exercised free will and that his choices led him unaware into catastrophe. But our first and overwhelming impression prevails: the *gods* have willed Oedipus to do what he did. Oedipus and all the other characters come to this conclusion; the design and verbal texture of the play confirm it. And in the theater the constant allusion to a daimonic shaping force makes this fatedness vivid and powerful.

Although an ancient audience would know of Oedipus' background fully and familiarly from other plays and mythical sources, a modern one might know only its bare outlines. The following summary fills in the details.

> Laios, the king of Thebes, has learned from an oracle that his own son will kill him. When his wife, Jokasta, bears a son, Laios entrusts the infant to one of his herdsmen with orders that he leave the baby to die on Mt. Kithairon, exposed with its ankles pierced and pinned together. Out of pity, the herdsman gives the child to his friend, a shepherd from Korinth, who returns with the child to his city and presents it to Polybos the king. Polybos raises the child, whose swollen ankles cause him to be named Oedipus, as his son and heir.
>
> When Oedipus is a young man, a drunken guest at a feast tells him he is not Polybos' real son. Oedipus, upset by the man's claim, questions his parents about his birth, but they reassure him that he is their son. Still haunted by doubt, Oedipus goes to Delphi, where Apollo refuses to answer the question about his parentage but tells him instead that he is fated to murder his own father and to father children with his own mother. Afraid to return to Korinth and his parents, Oedipus decides to move far away. On the road to Thebes he is attacked by a traveler whom he kills; when

the other members of the party attack, he strikes them down. Unbeknownst to Oedipus, that traveler was Laios, his birth father. And one of the men left for dead survives.

On his arrival in Thebes Oedipus finds the city terrorized by the Sphinx—a monster with a lion's body, a bird's wings and a woman's head—who kills all those who fail to solve her riddle. But Oedipus solves it, and the Sphinx dies. Thebes rewards him with the throne and marriage to the recently widowed Queen Jokasta, by whom in time he has four children. When the play opens, Oedipus has been living in prosperity for about fifteen years.

With this information the audience should be able to grasp the famous web of double meanings that pervades the dialogue of *Oedipus the King*.

The play opens with an appeal by a delegation of Thebans who beg Oedipus to find a cure for the plague now killing his people, their crops, and their livestock. Oedipus promises to solve the mystery and end the plague. His passionate inquest reveals, when all the facts finally fit together, that he himself has caused the plague: Oedipus, a man who has killed his father and incestuously loved his mother, poisons and sickens Thebes with his presence. The plot that discloses the events of Oedipus' life—with sudden twists and turns, elations and despairs, deductions both mistaken and correct, clashes of will, and angry outbursts—moves toward understanding and eloquent grief. Since Aristotle's time critics have praised its economy. Yet this tightest of dramatic plots requires that Apollo and the daimon invade Oedipus' life on stage just as they invaded it before he arrived in Thebes. The gods' cruelty must be visible not only in the unspeakable actions Oedipus commits, but in the diabolical *manner* by which the daimon intervenes to reveal to Oedipus what he has done. One such intervention is Jokasta's fatal mention of the crossroads where Laios was killed, which forces Oedipus to grasp that he might well be Laios' murderer. Another is the discovery of the lone survivor of the attack, who presumably knows whether one man or many murdered his king; he turns out, by chance it seems, to be the same herdsman who gave the baby Oedipus to the Korinthian shepherd. While Oedipus pursues Laios' killers, he repeatedly alters his immediate objective as new information and circumstances influence him. He makes each alteration on rational grounds, but each twist reveals one more instance of the daimon's continuous intervention. These daimonic coincidences give the action its fatedness, but also its surprise and speed.

Modern audiences might resist the conclusion that a great play can possess such a totally fated hero, one who seems a puppet at the mercy of gods. Or they might assume that characters are compelling only when doing and saying things for which they are morally responsible—that only by such acts is character revealed. But Oedipus' actions, regardless of their fatedness, express his swift insight and ready sympathy, the impatience of his nature, and the largeness of his mental grasp—as this list of only his most prominent decisions illustrates: He goes to Delphi to resolve his questioned paternity and refuses to return to Korinth after hearing Apollo's terrifying predictions. He strikes back at the man who struck him. He risks his life to confront the Sphinx, attempts to solve her riddle, assumes leadership of Thebes when its citizens offer it to him, and accepts marriage with the widowed queen of his predecessor. When plague strikes he sends Kreon, Jokasta's brother, to Delphi for advice. He persists in the search for Laios' killers even though Tiresias, the blind prophet, Jokasta, and the old Herdsman in turn urge him to quit. And when all the truth is known, he puts out his eyes and demands exile. The Servant who reports his blinding and Jokasta's suicide points out that Oedipus took these last two actions knowing the consequences but made all his previous choices ignorant of his fate. (The self-blinding, however, is also a fated action, since Tiresias predicts it in his exit speech.) But Oedipus is no less interesting if we assume that all the actions he took were forced by the daimon.

The image of a storm endangering a city, a familiar Greek metaphor, embodies the power the daimon possesses in *Oedipus the King,* but Sophokles' use of it in this play is particularly resonant. Comparing Oedipus several times to a helmsman facing trouble in a storm, the playwright suggests the power by which human resourcefulness and freedom of action can resist a threatening divinity or an indifferent Nature. Indeed, Oedipus and all the characters except Tiresias believe Oedipus' problems are like a storm that a gifted and courageous sailor can weather. But Oedipus' superior intelligence is of no ultimate use in riding out the storm. Sophokles reveals this truth with an opposing series of images in which the daimon leaps, strikes, and plunges directly at its target. His consistent use of certain Greek words suggests that the blow Oedipus struck at Laios, the sexual mounting of Jokasta by her son, and the plunging of the pins into Oedipus' eyes are all physical aspects of one single metaphysical action: the blow that Oedipus declares Apollo "struck" at him.[1] The daimon uses Oedipus as both weapon and quarry.

The presence of the daimon, the unseen power that has shaped Oedipus' life, looms continually in the echoes, double meanings, and ironies that inhabit nearly every line of the play. As the investigator of Laios' murder, Oedipus naturally thinks of himself as the hunter; as he uncovers his own potential guilt he becomes the one who's hunted. The audience feels the daimon's effect again when Oedipus tells his people that though each of them is sick, none is so sick as he is, and again when Kreon talks about Laios' disappearance:

[1] See nn. 1371, 1419, 1431, 1516.

He told us his journey would take him
close to god. But he never came back. (114–15/129–30)[2]

The word translated as "close to god" is the noun *theoros,* which normally refers to someone who sees or takes part in a holy event or rite;
here Kreon most likely implies that Laios' destination was Delphi. But
by not naming Delphi, Sophokles can use the inclusiveness of the word
theoros to suggest that "closeness to god" might be manifest in an in-
terview at Delphi or in an encounter at a fork where three roads meet.

For the audience to experience the play fully, the director must
dramatize the intervening presence of this divinity on stage; the daimon should be physically present in gesture, voice inflection, movement, and spatial relationships.[3] We must be able to sense divinity co-
ercing the events of the present as well as events long past. Staging can
support the nuances of the script by concentrating attention on the
difference between Oedipus' apparent ability to secure his well-being
by acting wisely—and the truth: that his whole life has been and is being willed by powers he cannot see and does not suspect. Here are five
moments in the play where such reinforcement is possible; some of
these are minor, others have a larger potential impact.

(1) Oedipus responds to the sight of Kreon returning from Delphi by calling out:

O Lord Apollo,
may the luck he brings save us! Luck so bright
we can see it—just as we see him now. (80–82/90–93)

Oedipus prays here to Apollo, Delphi's presiding god, the very force
that will destroy him. An altar to Apollo is on stage; the suppliants have
approached it and perhaps laid their branches on it; Jokasta herself will
later pay it tribute. Possibly the shrine includes a statue of Apollo; statues are referred to several times in the play, once quite poignantly by

---

[2] In citing lines from the plays in the introductions I have given first the line
numbers of the Greek text and second the lines as they are numbered in my
translation. For each play I've included the range of Greek line numbers that
correspond to my translation in the running heads at the top of each page.

[3] The director Teresa Choate had the brilliant idea to introduce the daimon
directly into her Nashville, Tenn., production of the play, which was staged in
front of the concrete replica of the Parthenon located in that city's downtown.
Choate placed "Apollo," an athletically built actor entirely covered in gold
body paint, on stage throughout. As he stood relaxed, but completely still and
silent, he followed the action with his piercing eyes. At only one moment did
he move. As the Messenger from Korinth enters, Apollo's left arm flashed, and
his finger pointed, directly at the deadly new arrival.

Oedipus at line 1379/1563. Any gesture by Oedipus at line 80/90 that alerts the audience to the reality of Apollo (by involving his statue or altar, for instance), will add texture to the confidence Oedipus so mistakenly feels.

(2) When the Chorus Leader announces Tiresias' arrival he declares:

> There's the man who will convict him. (297/359)

By "him" the Leader means Laios' murderer, the focus of immediate discussion. In the ensuing argument between the king and his seer, Oedipus will provoke the recalcitrant Tiresias to accuse him of that murder and of causing the ruin of Thebes. In Oedipus' rising anger at the prophet he must sound assured of his own righteousness and certain that a rational cosmos supports his fury. The actor playing Tiresias must register something grander than retaliatory pique. We must grasp the actual horror Tiresias feels at the pollution Oedipus' body holds, and be convinced that Tiresias' anger is a response not only to Oedipus' taunts, but to his crimes. To give such a cast to his speech, Tiresias should speak *ex cathedra,* from near the altar of Apollo. If the daimon actually speaks anywhere, it is in the crescendo of Tiresias' revelation; here the naming of Oedipus' horrifying acts changes that ambiguous "him" into an indictment by the gods. Apollo's presence may be suggested by having the blind prophet aim his words directly (and eerily) at Oedipus. Much later in the play, when Oedipus himself enters blind and weak, he should evoke Tiresias' entrance. As he is led by a boy servant, Oedipus should seek the same vantage at Apollo's altar, but this time in understanding and acceptance of the truth. Apollo is in Tiresias; by physically becoming like Tiresias, Oedipus will reveal how utterly Apollo is now present in him as well.

(3) At the precise moment Jokasta "proves" to Oedipus that he could not have murdered Laios, she gives the detail that will inform Oedipus of his almost certain guilt:

> Yet, as rumor had it, foreign bandits
> killed Laios at a place where three roads meet. (716/831–32)

The daimon in those words strikes Oedipus a physical blow. Jokasta notices his distraught reaction; she asks him about it at 728/846, after Oedipus describes what he felt when she named the crossroads:

> Just now, something you said made my heart race.
> Something . . . I remember . . . wakes up terrified.
> (726–27/844–45)

The daimon has invaded Oedipus' memory, and the actor should show us by physical gesture that it is there.

(4) A few lines later, Oedipus has composed himself enough to put into a logical narrative (771–833/887–963) what he now knows: that under the surface of his threatened but successful life another set of events has been happening, events whose moral import he just now perceives. His words reveal an unexpected vulnerability. Oedipus is no longer the manly commander totally in charge. His present anxiety unearths the anxiety of years past. The actor should be able to suggest that Oedipus' great stature has diminished. His body language should reflect, however subtly, his rapidly reversing fortunes: the blow struck by the drunk's revelation; Oedipus' uneasy reassurance by his parents; the hounding accusation in his mind; his resentment at the treatment he received at Delphi; his flight from Korinth and the awful realization that he was guided by the gods to the place where three roads meet. As Oedipus remembers and acts out the killing of Laios and his men—a thrilling use of the historical present tense in the speech—the full knowledge of Apollo's presence in his hands should register in motions as slow and implacable as the daimon itself. He now kills his predecessor knowing fully what he is doing. He is the *autocheir,* the one whose hands killed, or, more freely, the red-handed one. Hands in this play are mentioned repeatedly, they are what the *miasma,* the pollution, stains. The actor's use of his hands should possess this knowledge.

(5) Of all the daimon's interventions, the one in response to Jokasta's prayer is the most vivid and unmistakable.

> Lords of my country, this thought
> came to me: to visit the gods' shrines
> with incense and a bough in my hands.
> Oedipus lets alarms of every kind
> inflame his mind . . .
>   Since he won't listen to me,
> Apollo—you're the nearest god—
> I come praying for your good will . . .
> Cleanse us, cure our sickness. (911–23/1050–61)

As Jokasta speaks the words "the nearest god," the Messenger from Korinth should arrive—the timing, and the visual élan of his entry marking him as Apollo's answer to her prayer. News the Messenger brings will indeed cleanse Thebes and cure its sickness, but the cleansing will cause also Jokasta's death and Oedipus' self-blinding. The mocking cruelty of the daimon reverses all hopeful expectation because the Messenger intends to bring good news—that Oedipus' father Polybos has died and that the people choose Oedipus to succeed him. Hearing about the death of the

man Oedipus believes is his father, he euphorically concludes not only
that the oracle predicting he would kill his father has been discredited,
but that all oracles are now shown worthless. Oedipus' elation (and the
Chorus' echo of it) should overwhelm Jokasta's nearly inarticulate misery
as she runs into the palace to hang herself. In this excess, in the surge of
Oedipus' hope almost beyond reason, the daimon makes itself felt. The
daimonic essence is to mislead, to withhold meaning, to obstruct human
knowledge until the damage is final. The counterpoint between Oedipus'
fresh hope and Jokasta's agony will show the two faces of the daimon.

At the level of human character and motivation the Korinthian
Messenger embodies the double meanings present in so much of this
play's dialogue. He intends to convey one thing—good news—but cannot prevent himself from conveying something far different and far
worse. He displays the helplessness of the human will in his small crucial way as much as Oedipus does on a larger, graver scale.

The Messenger's inability to know what will be made of his news
is analogous to the characters' limited understanding of the words they
speak in the first half of the play. The characters are oblivious to daimon-
powered events that the audience already understands by reading between the lines—the double meanings, the ironies, the allusions to
cruel fate. The gods themselves are remarkably silent, but the daimon
infests and controls much of what the characters say. Speech, so sus-
ceptible to fatal meanings its speakers cannot comprehend, becomes itself a divine instrument for humbling humankind. Awaiting Kreon's return from Delphi with impatience, Oedipus thinks ahead to how he
will respond to the oracle:

> But when he comes, I'd be the criminal
> not to do all the god shows me to do. (76–77/86–87)

But by *doing* what the god asks, by finding the killer of Laios, Oedipus
becomes the criminal *(kakos)*. Later he regrets the circumstances that
kept him from returning to his Korinthian parents:

> So far I've been very lucky—and yet,
> there's no greater pleasure
> than to look our parents in the eyes! (998–99 /1140–42)

"Seeing" his parents, however, will prove so much the reverse of happiness that he must obliterate sight itself.

Sometimes Sophokles' words hint at how a scene might be staged.
Here Oedipus faces the difficulty of finding Laios' murderer:

> . . . unless I can mesh some clue I hold
> with something known of the killer, I will
> be tracking him alone, on a cold trail. (220–21/265–67)

The word translated as "clue" is *symbolon,* and Oedipus refers to it here as a device the Greeks used to confirm kinship or the authenticity of a written message. A *symbolon* was the broken half of some larger whole, typically a potsherd that would exactly match the edge of the other half held by a friend, relative, or ally. A *symbolon* was sometimes used to identify a lost parent or child; parents who abandoned a baby might tie a *symbolon* around its neck so that, if the baby survived, it could be identified when the parents' half of the potsherd matched the child's half. By simply using the word *symbolon* Sophokles invokes the context of a child finding his lost parents.

As the action unfolds, Oedipus will fit many clues together, but the final and decisive fit occurs in the meeting on stage of two men. The Korinthian Messenger and the old Herdsman, who long ago passed the baby Oedipus to him, will link Oedipus' Korinthian life to his birth in Thebes as the son of Jokasta and Laios. Oedipus' determination has indeed meshed one clue he holds with another; by putting the pieces together he's forced to see the incest and the killing he has committed as parts of a monstrous whole. On stage Oedipus should make palpable the terrible perfection of the knowledge the two men bring by joining their hands. The Korinthian should clasp the Herdsman, a reunion in friendship the Herdsman may sharply resist but which he cannot deny or evade. They are the flesh of the *symbolon* Oedipus knew from the start he must find, a symbol whose destructive effect was indeed beyond prediction or intuition.

Oedipus is most mistaken to believe that he lives in a world in which a good and able man may count on help and approval from responsible divinities. This belief too should be reinforced by the actor's demeanor. Most powerfully dramatic is Oedipus' loss of this optimism. All through his long speech interdicting Laios' killer, Oedipus calls confidently on the gods to support his search and its righteousness:

> I warn those who would disobey me:
> god make their fields harvest dust,
> their women's bodies harvest death. (269–71/325–27)

Acting on this trust, Oedipus will make many reasonable inferences: that because he knows his nature is not that of a father-killer or mother-marryer, Tiresias' accusations must be motivated by treason; or that because Polybos is dead, the oracle predicting he would kill his father must be wrong. Because the truth is so much less likely than what Oedipus assumes ought to be probable, he is led by his confidence into more and more mistaken deductions. These mistakes cannot be seen as failures of his intelligence. In each case he follows what we would call the laws of probability. He is the political ruler whose survival depends on making decisive use of what limited facts are in hand; his astute skills in cross-examination are evident in his questioning of Kreon, Jokasta,

the Korinthian Messenger, and the old Herdsman. Even under stress
and when angry, even when fully conscious of how brutally the daimon
has betrayed him, he manages to reason clearly.

A good instance of his ability to think swiftly and make imaginative leaps can be found late in the play in his response to the news that
he is not Polybos' son, but a foundling recovered from a mountainside.
After suffering the dreadful predictions of what he would do to his parents, Oedipus suddenly finds himself parentless. His quick mind instantly adopts a new parent— *Tyche,* Luck.

> Let it burst! My seed may well *be* common!
> Even so, I still must know who I am.
> The meanness of my birth may shame
> her womanly pride. But since, in my
> own eyes, I am the child of Luck—
> *she* is the source of my well-being—
> never will I be dishonored.
> Luck is the mother who raised me; the months
> are my brothers, who've seen me through
> the low times in my life and the high ones.
> Those are the powers that made me.
> I could never betray them *now*—
> by calling off the search
> for the secret of my birth! (1076–85/1222–35)

Euphoric as this is, it fits what Oedipus at this moment knows of his life.
He knows he has been favored. He has survived dire oracles and self-
exile from Korinth; he has defeated the Sphinx and won Thebes. Now
he learns he was saved from death on the very mountain that looms
over Thebes. Luck herself, a vivid presence to a Greek of Sophokles'
time, must be his true parent. And Oedipus is right, his life has issued
from Luck, though the kind of mothering she has given him he does
not yet see. When the truth arrives, he speaks no more of this mother
Luck. He accepts Laios and Jokasta as his true father and mother, and
acknowledges what it means to be their son.

This readiness to make daring formulations is Oedipus' out-
standing quality. He is open to new evidence, he can change his mind.
And Sophokles purposely shows Oedipus changing his mind about
the largest question of all. Oedipus' sense of the reasonable has been
grounded in the belief that a person of good will, energy, and ability
will have the gods' help and therefore be better able to achieve happiness than a person who lacks these attributes. Willingness to abandon
the belief that the gods favor the good—and he abandons it at the very
moment the evidence becomes overpowering—is proof of his intelligence. Oedipus never doubts this intelligence and his own good will.
When he returns blind and frail to the stage, we will hear him refor-

mulate the nature of human life in terms of his own life. Uppermost in his mind will be marriage, his sexual acts, and the kinship binding parents and children.

If we reflect on the taboos forbidding incest and parricide, and the threat of defilement that enforces them, we will see that, whatever origins they may have in our genetic struggle for survival, these taboos express our awe for our parents. Yet this very expression of our awe, the curse upon the son who violates his filial bonds, drives Oedipus toward the realization that safety would be his only if both his parents were dead. This reverses our normal belief, from childhood, that our safety *derives* from our parents.

OEDIPUS   While [my mother] lives, I will live in fear,
             no matter how persuasive you are.
JOKASTA   Your father's tomb shines a great light.
OEDIPUS   On him, yes! But I fear her. She's alive. (985–88/1129–32)

The laws that enforce the limits and guarantee the bonds of family love are here brought into opposition to that love. The natural wish that one's parents live far into old age, that children and parents should comfort each other, yields to a more powerful imperative that a taboo not be violated. Oedipus' happiness at the death of his father, and his momentary realization that his mother's existence threatens his, is logical and draws our sympathy. Yet, we must shiver at the reversal of our normal feelings.[4] This moment reveals, as does his claim that he is the child of Luck, the troubled mental state in which Oedipus now lives, a state the actor must reveal in the voice he gives these lines.

Oedipus presses the truth out of the old Herdsman until he hears the words that end all doubt: "He was a child from the house of Laios" (1171/1318). Then Oedipus understands:

All! All! It has all happened,
it was all true. O light! May this
be the last time I look on you.
You see now what I am. I am
the child who must not be born,
I loved where I must not love,
I killed where I must not kill. (1182–85/1336–42)

Here the brute force of knowing that he has done what no one can forgive overwhelms him. His mind probes the bonds of family love that created those unforgiving acts of incest and father murder.

Oedipus' willingness to discover the worst about himself, and his understanding of it, have rightly led readers to see his honesty as heroic. But acknowledging Oedipus as heroically honest doesn't make him any

---

[4] I am indebted to the discussion of these lines in Segal 1981, 225–26.

less a victim. Like Job's, his heroism lies in his ability to accept his role as a victim. If we find this victimhood and the fatedness that caused it an embarrassment rather than something powerful and dramatic, we may be tempted to picture Oedipus as still a masterful figure both in blinding himself and in his dealings with Kreon. But neither Oedipus' words nor the effect of his requests will bear any "heroically defiant" interpretation. He remains subordinate to Kreon and to his fate. If the stage production wishes to honor the text, it must show Oedipus powerless in these final moments.

Sophokles did write a play that dramatizes the rebirth and transformation of Oedipus' power, but *Oedipus at Kolonos* depicts events (and was in fact written) far in the future. The following words of Oedipus (in our play) both foreshadow those events and reinforce his present loss of freedom:

> And yet, I know this much:
> no sickness can kill me. Nothing can.
> I was saved from that death
> to face an extraordinary evil.
> Let my fate take me now, where it will. (1455–57/1651–55)

In this speech we hear Oedipus peacefully accept the flow of Fate that has carried him to this moment and will carry him into the future. He will no longer believe that his own intelligence and actions can do more than fuse with Fate, whose design his life will fulfill. To deny that fatedness is true and central to *Oedipus the King* is to reduce the play's enveloping net of double meanings to mere stylistic enhancement. The double meanings are crucial to Sophokles' daimonic vision of human life. They point to our imperfect grasp of reality—and so phrased, they never let us forget the role of the gods in shaping it. Most of them reinforce the violent and sexual nature of Oedipus' fatedness, the source of his pollution. For instance, when Jokasta describes Laios' physical appearance to Oedipus, her words suggest both the origin of Oedipus' resemblance to the dead king and her attraction to him:

> He looked then not very different from you now. (742/860)

Oedipus' victimhood, however, is a remarkable kind, one that posed Sophokles a considerable problem. The only victimization that can be visually shown Sophokles shows us: the bloody result of Oedipus blinding himself. To feel the impact of his greater victimization— the god-caused incest and patricide—Oedipus must remain before our eyes long enough for the shock of the blood and hollow eye sockets to wear off. If we are to see beyond his blinding, he must stay on stage to tell us what his life means. Twice Oedipus rebukes the Chorus for not understanding why self-blinding, and not suicide, was the only adequate response to his anguish.

The Servant who reports Oedipus' blinding remarks on his vulnerability: "He's so weak, though, he needs to be helped" (1292/1465). If Oedipus walks on stage unaided, the chance to dramatize his physical dependency will be lost. When the Chorus first sees him emerge weak and bloody-eyed from his palace doors, their words respond not only to his appearance, but to the uncanny pollution he carries:

> Your pain is terrible to see,
> pure, helpless anguish . . .
> What god would go
> to such inhuman lengths
> to savage your defenseless life?
> I cannot look at you—
> though there's so much
> to ask you, so much to learn,
> so much that holds my eyes—
> so strong are the shivers of awe
> you send through me. (1297–1307/1470–83)

At first the Chorus conveys the expected shock and fear at the sight of a god-crushed man. But, as always, human destruction provokes fascination. The Chorus wants desperately to know what Oedipus knows, and yet they dread knowing. Their bodily motion should register the ebb and flood of their attraction.

The Chorus does in fact get the knowledge it craves from Oedipus. If we listen carefully to Oedipus' words (and to the Chorus') during the final part of the play, we will learn what beliefs and allegiances have survived. As Oedipus steps out into the sunlight, he dwells first on his trauma and frailty. He is wounded and disoriented; his world has gone black. Pain and abandonment suffuse his first speeches. Then he reacquires the human world still close by him when he hears the voice of the Chorus. Clarity and poise return as he tells the Chorus that Apollo destroyed his life, but that it was he and no one else who chose to strike out his own eyes. He discriminates precisely between what the gods have done to him and what he himself has done. Apollo may have predicted Oedipus' blindness through Tiresias, but unlike all his other evils, Oedipus' mind willed, and his hand executed, this evil. Although it was his choice, at that moment his choice was horribly limited. His thoughts now are on the consequences of what has happened, for his city, his family, and himself. Not a vestige of his joy in being "the child of Luck" remains. He knows himself "the most ruined, the most cursed, /the most god-hated man who ever lived" (1343–46/1528–29). "I have no god now," he says (1360/1544). We have seen him abandon the assumption that divinity must be good to a good man; we wonder what he does have left.

The power of his family, of blood ties, remains; Oedipus' violation of them has made them inescapable. His horror of seeing the eyes
of his parents in Hades is the first reason he gives for blinding himself.
He cannot endure the pain of watching his defiled children grow to
maturity. He has lost the right to see the sources of civic emotion in
Thebes, its statues and towers. The gods who have forced an unaware
Oedipus to commit such atrocities have chosen their emotional terrain
well. Oedipus cannot forgive himself what he has *done,* what his hands,
his seed, his body, have done. There is no escape from the hold that our
father, our mother, our children, have upon us. The understanding of
their power over us leads Oedipus to one of his finest and most painful
imaginative leaps. He names the cause of the family itself, the sexual act
in marriage, and declares it the source of humankind's devastation:

> O marriages! You marriages! You created us,
> we sprang to life, then from that same seed
> you burst fathers, brothers, sons,
> kinsmen shedding kinsmen's blood,
> brides and mothers and wives—the most loathsome
> atrocities that strike mankind. (1403–8/1591–96)

Where the bonds of love are most intense, the danger is greatest. Oedipus knows he has released and survived more of this potential misery
than any other man, but all humankind is potentially vulnerable. That
love may cause such pain is the great resource of the god Apollo, who
has defined the unique pain of Oedipus. The audience must see that
Oedipus is the victim of his loyalties—loyalties that the god uses to
force his responses and his choices. Oedipus' daimon has seized and
ravaged family love itself. The vulnerability of all human life to devastating reversal is especially concentrated within the family, where so
much love and violence exist in the same relationships, and where forbidden erotic feeling may so easily shatter its sanctioned forms. The
daimon can destroy us by loosening the fragile bonds that hold destructive forces in check.

Oedipus and Jokasta and the Chorus may alter their belief in oracles and gods moment by moment, but they never alter their intense
belief in the taboos and loyalties that derive from blood ties. The family is an ineradicable presence. With an energy equal to his unconscious
violation of his family, Oedipus asserts its conscious force in his two
long final speeches. He begs Kreon to bury Jokasta with the respect due
a kinswoman, demands exile and death for himself to lift the pollution
from the city, and he asks that exposure on Kithairon be the mode of
his death: that was what his parents had decreed for him; he now bit-
terly accepts the rightness of that decision. He foresees a barren and
lonely future for his daughters, who will not marry because they carry

his curse. Oedipus talks of these things directly to his young daughters, whom Kreon has brought to him; he takes his daughters in his arms as he speaks. We see the bodily result of the incest here; the father's arms are the brother's. Our attention focuses on what remains of this family, not on the gods. Oedipus has relinquished his authority to Kreon, repeatedly thanking him, praising him, begging him.

These are the two strongest emotional tableaux we take from the last moments: Oedipus' hugging his broken, defiled family; then Oedipus powerless, and being told he is powerless by Kreon.[5] Both images are fused as Kreon separates Ismene and Antigone from Oedipus' hands and orders the blind man to go inside. Oedipus' love is as palpable to us by the end of the play as his wrath, his intelligence, his energy, his special relation with divinity, and his monumental ill-fatedness. It is a wonderful stroke that this side of his character is uppermost in our minds as we leave the theater. It reminds us of a truth that might be lost in the fury of the drama, that the intensity of his love for his family and his city underlies the intensity of his misery, and is as much its cause as the daimon itself.

[5] Some scholars, Jebb and Knox among them, believe that Kreon's ambiguous phrase, "I never promise if I can't be sure," implies assent to Oedipus' demand for exile. (Oedipus does eventually achieve this wish in most versions of the myth.) But Oedipus has asked for immediate exile, and Kreon forces him at least temporarily inside the palace. Knox cites Kreon's problematical yielding as evidence of a larger pattern in which Oedipus, despite his blindness, weakness, and shattered confidence, manages to reassert his moral authority and dominate Kreon during this scene. I agree with Knox that Oedipus is a remarkable character in this final scene, but I do not believe this quality has to do with domination or power. Surely Kreon's words:

> You won the power once, but you couldn't
> keep it to the end of your life (1523/1731–32)

are the last words on the subject from the stage, and the final Chorus, if genuine, does not contradict them.

Oedipus the King

Delegation of Thebans, mostly young (silent)

Oedipus, King of Thebes

Priest of Zeus

Kreon, Jokasta's brother

Chorus of older Theban men

Leader (of the Chorus)

Tiresias, blind prophet of Apollo

Boy to lead Tiresias (silent)

Jokasta, Oedipus' wife

Attendants and maids (silent)

Messenger from Korinth

Herdsman, formerly of Laios' house

Servant, from Oedipus' house

Antigone and Ismene, Oedipus' daughters (silent)

SCENE   *Before the Royal Palace in Thebes. The palace has an imposing central double door. Two altars stand near it; one is to Apollo. The delegation of Thebans enters carrying olive branches wound with wool strips. They gather by the altars and stairs to the palace. The light and atmosphere are oppressive. Oedipus enters through the great doors.*

OEDIPUS My children, fresh green life
old Kadmos nurtures and protects,
why surge at me like this? Why sit here
beseeching, with your wool-strung boughs—
while the city is swollen
with howls of pain, reeking incense,
and prayers sung to the Healing God?
I thought it wrong, my sons, to hear others
speak for you, so I've come out myself.
I am called Oedipus, whose fame   <10>
the world knows.
                         Tell me, old man,
yours is the natural voice for the rest,
what is your state of mind? You're terrified?
Looking for reassurance? Be certain
I'll give you all the help I can.
I'd be a hard man if an approach
like yours failed to rouse my pity.

PRIEST You rule our land Oedipus! You can see
who comes to your altars—how varied
we are in years: children too weak-winged   <20>
to fly far, others hunched with age,
a few priests—I am a priest of Zeus—
joined by the best of our young lads.
More of us wait with wool-strung boughs
in the markets, and at Athena's two temples.
Some, at the river shrine, are watching
the embers for the glow of prophecy.
You can see our city going under,
too feeble to lift its head clear
of the angry murderous waves.   <30>
Plague blackens our flowering farmland,
sickens our cattle where they graze.
Our women in labor give birth to nothing.

A burning god rakes his fire through our town;
he hates us with fever, he empties
the House of Kadmos, enriching
black Hades with our groans and tears.
We haven't come to beg at your hearth
because we think you're the god's equal.
We've come because you are the best man   <40>
at handling trouble or confronting gods.
You came to Thebes, you freed us

from the tax we paid with our lives
to that rasping Singer. You did it with no
help from us. We had nothing to teach you.

People say—they believe!—you had a god's
help when you restored life to our city.
Oedipus, we need *now* the great power
men everywhere know you possess.
Find some way to protect us—learn it   <50>
from a god's whisper, or a man's.
This much I know: guidance
from men proven right in the past
will meet a crisis with the surest force.
Act as our greatest man! Act
as you did when you first seized fame!
We believe your nerve saved us then.
Don't let us look back on your rule and say,
He lifted us once, but then let us fall.
Put us firmly back on our feet,   <60>
so Thebes will never fall again.

You were a bird from god, you brought good luck
the day you rescued us. Be that man now!
If you want to rule us, it's better
to rule the living than a barren waste;
walled cities and ships are worth nothing
when they've been emptied of people.

OEDIPUS   I do pity you, children. Don't think I'm unaware.
I know what need brings you: this sickness
ravages all of you. Yet, sick as you are,   <70>
not one of you suffers a sickness like mine.
Yours is a private grief, you feel
only what touches you. But my heart grieves
for you, for myself, and for our city.
You've come to wake me to all this.
There was no need. I haven't been sleeping.
I have wept tears enough, for long enough;
my mind has raced down every twisting path.
And after careful thought, I've set in motion
the only cure I could find: I've sent Kreon,   <80>
my wife's brother, to Phoibos at Delphi,
to hear what action or what word of mine
will save this town. Already, counting the days,
I'm worried: what is Kreon doing?

	He takes too long, more time than he needs. But when he comes, I'd be the criminal not to do all the god shows me to do.
PRIEST	Timely words. The moment you spoke, your men gave the sign: Kreon's arriving.
OEDIPUS	O Lord Apollo may the luck he brings save us! Luck so bright we can see it—just as we see him now.

<90>

*(Kreon enters from the countryside,
wearing a laurel crown speckled with red.)*

PRIEST	He must bring pleasing news. If not, why would he wear a laurel crown dense with berries?
OEDIPUS	We'll know very soon; he's within earshot. Prince! Brother kinsman, son of Menoikeos! What kind of answer have you brought from god?
KREON	Good news. No matter how grave, troubles that turn out well are truly strokes of luck.
OEDIPUS	What did the god say? Nothing you've said so far alarms or reassures me.

<100>

KREON	Do you want me to speak in front of these men? If so, I will. If not, let's go inside.
OEDIPUS	Speak here, to all of us. I suffer more for them than for my own life.
KREON	Then I'll report what I heard from Apollo. He made his meaning very clear. He commands we drive out what corrupts us, what sickens our city. We now harbor something incurable. He says: purge it.

<110>

OEDIPUS	Tell me the source of our trouble. How do we cleanse ourselves?
KREON	By banishing a man or killing him. It's blood— kin murder—that brings this storm on our city.
OEDIPUS	Who is the man god wants us to punish?
KREON	As you know, King, our city was ruled once by Laios, before you came to take the helm.
OEDIPUS	I've heard as much. Though I never saw him.

KREON Well, Laios was murdered. Now god tells you
     plainly: with your own hands punish   <120>
     the very men whose hands killed Laios.

OEDIPUS Where do I find these men? How do I track
     vague footprints from a bygone crime?

KREON The god said: here, in our own land.
     What we look for we can capture;
     what we ignore goes free.

OEDIPUS Was Laios killed at home? Or in the fields?
     Or did they murder him on foreign ground?

KREON He told us his journey would take him
     close to god. But he never came back.   <130>

OEDIPUS Did none of his troop see and report
     what happened? Isn't there anyone
     to question whose answers might help?

KREON All killed but a single terrified
     survivor, able to tell us but one fact.

OEDIPUS What was it? One fact might lead to many,
     if we had one small clue to give us hope.

KREON They had the bad luck, he said, to meet bandits
     who struck them with a force many hands strong.
     This wasn't the violence of one man only.   <140>

OEDIPUS What bandit would dare commit such a crime . . .
     unless somebody here had hired him?

KREON That was our thought, but after Laios
     died, we were mired in new
     troubles—and no avenger came.

OEDIPUS But here was your kingship murdered!
     What kind of trouble could have blocked your search?

KREON The Sphinx's song. So wily, so baffling!
     She forced us to forget the dark past,
     to confront what lay at our feet.   <150>

OEDIPUS Then I'll go back, start fresh,
     and light up that darkness.
     Apollo was exactly right, and so were you,
     to turn our minds back to the murdered man.
     It's time I joined your search for vengeance;
     our country and the god deserve no less.

This won't be on behalf of distant kin—
I'll banish this plague for my own sake.
Laios' killer might one day come for me,
exacting vengeance with that same hand.   <160>
Defending the dead man serves *my* interest.
Rise, children, quick, up from the altar,
pick up those branches that appeal to god.
Someone go call the people of Kadmos here—
tell them I'm ready to do anything.
With god's help our good luck
is assured; without it we're doomed.

(Exit Oedipus, into the palace.)

PRIEST   Stand up, children. He has proclaimed
himself the cure we came to find.
May god Apollo, who sent the oracle,   <170>
be our savior and end this plague!

(The Theban suppliants leave; the Chorus enters.)

CHORUS   What will you say to Thebes,
Voice from Zeus? What sweet sounds
convey your will from golden Delphi
to our bright city?
We're at the breaking point,
our minds are wracked with dread.
Our wild cries reach out to you,
Healing God from Delos—
in holy fear we ask: does your will   <180>
bring a new threat, or has an old doom
come round again as the years wheel by?
Say it, Great Voice,
you who answer us always,
speak as Hope's golden child.

Athena, immortal daughter of Zeus,
your help is the first we ask;
then Artemis your sister
who guards our land, throned
in the heart of our city.   <190>
And Apollo, whose arrows
strike from far off! Our three
defenders against death: come now!
Once before, when ruin threatened,
you drove the flames of fever from our city.
Come to us now!

The troubles I suffer are endless.
The plague attacks our troops;
I can think of no weapon
that will keep a man safe.   <200>
Our rich earth shrivels what it grows;
women in labor scream, but no
children are born to ease their pain.
One life after another flies—
you see them pass—
like birds driving their strong wings
faster than flash-fire
to the death god's western shore.

Our city dies as its people die
these countless deaths, her children   <210>
rot in the streets, unmourned,
spreading more death.
Young wives and gray mothers
wash to our altars, their cries
carry from all sides, sobbing
for help, each lost in her pain.
A hymn rings out to the Healer;
an oboe answers,
keening in a courtyard.
Against all this, Goddess,   <220>
golden child of Zeus,
send us the bright shining
face of courage.

Force that raging killer, the god Ares,
to turn his back and run from our land.
He wields no weapons of war to kill us,
but burning with his fever,
we shout in the hot blast of his charge.
Blow Ares to the vast sea-room
of Amphitritê, banish him   <230>
under a booming wind
to jagged harbors in the roiling
seas off Thrace. If night
doesn't finish the god's black work,
the day will finish it.
Lightning lurks
in your fiery will,
O Zeus, our Father. Blast it
into the god who kills us.

Apollo, lord of the morning light,   <240>
draw back your taut, gold-twined
bowstring, fire the sure arrows
that rake our attackers and keep them at bay.

Artemis, bring your radiance
into battle on bright quick feet
down through the morning hills.
I call on the god whose hair
is bound with gold,
the god who gave us our name,
Bakkhos!—the wine-flushed—who answers   <250>
the maenads' cries, running
beside them! Bakkhos,
come here on fire,
pine-torch flaring.
Face with us the one god
all the gods hate: Ares!

(Oedipus has entered while the Chorus was singing.)

OEDIPUS   I heard your prayer. It will be answered
           if you trust and obey my words:
           pull hard with me, bear down on the one cure
           that will stop this plague. Help   <260>
           will come, the evils will be gone.
           I hereby outlaw the killer
           myself, by my own words, though I'm a stranger
           both to the crime and to accounts of it.

           But unless I can mesh some clue I hold
           with something known of the killer, I will
           be tracking him alone, on a cold trail.
           Since I've come late to your ranks, Thebans,
           and the crime is past history,
           there are some things that you,   <270>
           the sons of Kadmos, must tell me.

           If any one of you knows how Laios,
           son of Labdakos, died, he must
           tell me all that he knows.
           He should not be afraid to name
           himself the guilty one: I swear
           he'll suffer nothing worse than exile.
           Or if you know of someone else—
           a foreigner—who struck the blow, speak up.

I will reward you now, I will thank you always.   <280>
But if you know the killer and don't speak—
out of fear—to shield kin or yourself,
listen to what that silence will cost you.
I order everyone in my land,
where I hold power and sit as king:

don't let that man under your roof,
don't speak with him, no matter who he is.
Don't pray or sacrifice with him,
don't pour purifying water for him.
I say this to all my people: <290>
drive him from your houses.
He is our sickness. He poisons us.
This the Pythian god has shown me.
This knowledge makes me an ally—
of both the god and the dead king.
I pray god that the unseen killer,
whoever he is, and whether he killed
alone or had help, be cursed with a life
as evil as he is, a life
of utter human deprivation.   <300>
I pray this, too: if he's found at my hearth,
inside my house, and I know he's there,
may the curses I aimed at others punish me.
I charge you all—act on my words,
for my sake and the god's, for our dead land
stripped barren of its harvests,
abandoned by its gods.
Even if god had not forced the issue,
this crime should not have gone uncleansed.
You should have looked to it! The dead man   <310>
was not only noble, he was your king!
But as my luck would have it,
I have his power, his bed—a wife
who shares our seed. And had she borne
the children of us both, she might
have linked us closer still. But Laios
had no luck fathering children, and Fate
itself came down on his head.
These concerns make me fight for Laios
as I would for my own father.   <320>
I'll stop at nothing to trace his murder
back to the killer's hand.
I act in this for Labdakos and Polydoros,

for Kadmos and Agenor—all our kings.
I warn those who would disobey me:
god make their fields harvest dust,
their women's bodies harvest death.
                                      O you gods,
let them die from the plague that kills
us now, or die from something worse.
As for the rest of us, who are   <330>
the loyal sons of Kadmos:
may justice go with us,
the gods be always at our side.

CHORUS   King, your curse forces me to speak.
None of us is the killer.
And none of us can point to him.
Apollo ordered us to search,
it's up to him to find the killer.

OEDIPUS   So he must. But what man can force
the gods to act against their will?   <340>

LEADER   May I suggest a second course of action?

OEDIPUS   Don't stop at two. Not if you have more.

LEADER   Tiresias is the man whose power of seeing
shows him most nearly what Apollo sees.
If we put our questions to him, King,
he could give us the clearest answers.

OEDIPUS   But I've seen to this already.
At Kreon's urging I've sent for him—twice now.
I find it strange that he still hasn't come.

LEADER   There were rumors—too faint and old to be much help.   <350>

OEDIPUS   What were they? I'll examine every word.

LEADER   They say Laios was killed by some travelers.

OEDIPUS   That's something even I have heard.
But the man who did it—no one sees him.

LEADER   If fear has any hold on him
he won't linger in Thebes, not after
he hears threats of the kind you made.

OEDIPUS   If murder didn't scare him, my words won't.

LEADER   There's the man who will convict him:
god's prophet, led here at last.   <360>

God gave to him what he gave no one else:
the truth—it's living in his mind.

(Enter Tiresias, led by a Boy.)

OEDIPUS   Tiresias, you are master of the hidden world.
You can read earth and sky, you know
what knowledge to reveal and what to hide.
Though your eyes can't see it,
your mind is well aware of the plague
that afflicts us. Against it, we have no
savior or defense but you, my Lord.
If you haven't heard it from messengers,   <370>
we now have Apollo's answer: to end
this plague we must root out Laios' killers.
Find them, then kill or banish them.
Help us do this. Don't begrudge us
what you divine from bird cries, show us
everything prophecy has shown you.
Save Thebes! Save yourself! Save me!
Wipe out what defiles us, keep
the poison of our king's murder
from poisoning the rest of us.   <380>
We're in your hands. The best use a man
makes of his powers is to help others.

TIRESIAS   The most terrible knowledge is the kind
it pays no wise man to possess.
I knew this, but I forgot it.
I should never have come here.

OEDIPUS   What? You've come, but with no stomach for this?

TIRESIAS   Let me go home. Your life will then
be easier to bear—and so will mine.

OEDIPUS   It's neither lawful nor humane   <390>
to hold back god's crucial guidance
from the city that raised you.

TIRESIAS   What you've said has made matters worse.
I won't let that happen to me.

OEDIPUS   For god's sake, if you know something,
don't turn your back on us! We're on our knees.

TIRESIAS   You don't understand! If I spoke
of my grief, then it would be yours.

OEDIPUS	What did you say? You know and won't help?
	You would betray us all and destroy Thebes? <400>
TIRESIAS	I'll cause no grief to you or me. Why ask
	futile questions? You'll learn nothing.
OEDIPUS	So the traitor won't answer.
	You would enrage a rock.
	Still won't speak?
	Are you so thick-skinned nothing touches you?
TIRESIAS	You blame your rage on *me?* When you
	don't see how she embraces you,
	this fury you live with? No, you blame me.
OEDIPUS	Who wouldn't be enraged? Your refusal
	to speak dishonors the city. <410>
TIRESIAS	It will happen. My silence can't stop it.
OEDIPUS	If it must happen, you should tell me now.
TIRESIAS	I'd rather not. Rage at that, if you like,
	with all the savage fury in your heart.
OEDIPUS	That's right. I *am* angry enough to speak
	my mind. I think you helped plot the murder.
	Did everything but kill him with your own hands.
	Had you eyes, though, I would have said
	you alone were the killer.
TIRESIAS	That's your truth? Now hear mine: <420>
	honor the curse your own mouth spoke.
	From this day on, don't speak to me
	or to your people here. You are the plague.
	You poison your own land.
OEDIPUS	So. The appalling charge has been at last
	flushed out, into the open. What makes you
	think you'll escape?
TIRESIAS	I have escaped.
	I foster truth, and truth guards me.
OEDIPUS	Who taught you this truth? Not your prophet's trade.
TIRESIAS	You did. By forcing me to speak. <430>
OEDIPUS	Speak what? Repeat it so I understand.
TIRESIAS	You missed what I said the first time?
	Are you provoking me to make it worse?

OEDIPUS   I heard you. But you made no sense. Try again.

TIRESIAS   You killed the man whose killer you now hunt.

OEDIPUS   The second time is even more outrageous.
            You'll wish you'd never said a word.

TIRESIAS   Shall I feed your fury with more words?

OEDIPUS   Use any words you like. They'll be wasted.

TIRESIAS   I say: you have been living unaware   <440>
            in the most hideous intimacy
            with your nearest and most loving kin,
            immersed in evil that you cannot see.

OEDIPUS   You think you can blithely go on like this?

TIRESIAS   I can, if truth has any strength.

OEDIPUS   Oh, truth has strength, but you have none.
            You have blind eyes, blind ears, and a blind brain.

TIRESIAS   And you're a desperate fool—throwing taunts at me
            that these men, very soon, will throw at you.

OEDIPUS   You survive in the grip of black   <450>
            unbroken night! You can't harm me
            or any man who can see the sunlight.

TIRESIAS   I'm not the one who will bring you down.
            Apollo will do that. You're his concern.

OEDIPUS   Did you make up these lies? Or was it Kreon?

TIRESIAS   Kreon isn't your enemy. You are.

OEDIPUS   Wealth and a king's power,
            the skill that wins every time—
            how much envy, what malice they provoke!
            To rob me of power—power I didn't ask for,   <460>
            but which this city thrust into my hands—
            my oldest friend here, loyal Kreon, worked
            quietly against me, aching to steal my throne.
            He hired for the purpose this fortuneteller—
            conniving bogus beggar-priest!—a man
            who knows what he wants but cannot seize it,
            being but a blind groper in his art.
            Tell us now, when or where did you ever
            prove you had the power of a seer?
            Why—when the Sphinx who barked black songs   <470>
            was hounding us—why didn't you speak up

and free the city? Her riddle wasn't the sort
just anyone who happened by could solve:
prophetic skill was needed. But the kind
you learned from birds or gods failed you. It took
Oedipus, the know-nothing, to silence her.
I needed no help from the birds,
I used my wits to find the answer.
I solved it—the same man for whom you plot
disgrace and exile, so you can   \<480>
maneuver close to Kreon's throne.
But your scheme to rid Thebes of its plague
will destroy both you and the man who planned it.
Were you not so frail, I'd make you
suffer exactly what you planned for me.

LEADER   He spoke in anger, Oedipus—but so
did you, if you'll hear what we think.
We don't need angry words. We need insight—
how best to carry out the god's commands.

TIRESIAS   You may be king, but my right   \<490>
to answer makes me your equal.
In this respect, I am as much
my own master as you are.
You do not own my life.
Apollo does. Nor am I
Kreon's man. Hear me out.
Since you have thrown my blindness at me
I will tell you what your eyes don't see:
what evil you are steeped in.
                           You don't see
where you live or who shares your house.   \<500>
Do you know your parents?
                       You are their enemy
in this life and down there with the dead.
And soon their double curse—
your father's and your mother's—
will lash you out of Thebes
on terror-stricken feet.
Your eyes, which now see life,
will then see darkness.
Soon your shriek will burrow
in every cave, bellow   \<510>
from every mountain outcrop on Kithairon,
when what your marriage means strikes home,
when it shows you the house

that took you in. You sailed
a fair wind to a most foul harbor.
Evils you cannot guess
will bring you down to what you are.
To what your children are.
Go on, throw muck at Kreon,
and at the warning spoken through my mouth.   <520>
No man will ever be
ground into wretchedness as you will be.

OEDIPUS   Should I wait for him to attack me more?
May you be damned. Go. Leave my house
now! Turn your back and go.

TIRESIAS   I'm here only because you sent for me.

OEDIPUS   Had I known you would talk nonsense,
I wouldn't have hurried to bring you here.

TIRESIAS   I seem a fool to you, but the parents
who gave you birth thought I was wise.   <530>

OEDIPUS   What parents? Hold on. Who was my father?

TIRESIAS   Today you will be born. Into ruin.

OEDIPUS   You've always got a murky riddle in your mouth.

TIRESIAS   Don't you outsmart us all at solving riddles?

OEDIPUS   Go ahead, mock what made me great.

TIRESIAS   Your very luck is what destroyed you.

OEDIPUS   If I could save the city, I wouldn't care.

TIRESIAS   Then I'll leave you to that. Boy, guide me out.

OEDIPUS   Yes, let him lead you home. Here, underfoot,
you're in the way. But when you're gone,   <540>
you'll give us no more grief.

TIRESIAS   I'll go. But first I must finish
what you brought me to do—
your scowl can't frighten me.
The man you have been looking for,
the one your curses threaten, the man
you have condemned for Laios' death:
I say that man is here.
                         You think he's an immigrant,
but he will prove himself a Theban native,
though he'll find no joy in that news.   <550>

A blind man who still has eyes,
a beggar who's now rich, he'll jab
his stick, feeling the road to foreign lands.

(Oedipus enters the palace.)

He'll soon be shown father and brother
to his own children, son and husband
to the mother who bore him—she took
his father's seed and his seed,
and he took his own father's life.
You go inside. Think through
everything I have said.   <560>
If I have lied, say of me, then—
I have failed as a prophet.

(Exit Tiresias.)

CHORUS What man provokes
the speaking rock of Delphi?
This crime that sickens speech
is the work of *his* bloody hands.
Now his feet will need to outrace
a storm of wild horses, for
Apollo is running him down,
armed with bolts of fire.   <570>
He and the Fates close in,
dread gods who never miss.

From snowfields
high on Parnassos
the word blazes out to us all:
track down the man no one can see.
He takes cover in thick brush,
he charges up the mountain
bull-like to its rocks and caves,
going his bleak, hunted way,   <580>
struggling to escape the doom
Earth spoke from her sacred mouth.
But that doom buzzes low,
never far from his ear.

Fear is what the man who reads birds
makes us feel, fear we can't fight.
We can't accept what he says
but have no power to challenge him.
We thrash in doubt, we can't see
even the present clearly,   <590>

much less the future.
And we've heard of no feud
embittering the House
of Oedipus in Korinth
against the House of Laios here,
no past trouble and none now,
no proof that would make us blacken
our king's fame, as he seeks
to avenge our royal house
for this murder not yet solved.   <600>

Zeus and Apollo make no mistakes
when they predict what people do.
But there is no way to tell
whether an earthbound prophet sees
more of the future than we can—
though in knowledge and skill
one person may surpass another.
But never, not till I see the charges
proved against him,
will I give credence   <610>
to a man who blames Oedipus.
All of us saw his brilliance
prevail when the wingèd virgin
Sphinx came at him: he passed the test
that won the people's love.
My heart can't find him guilty.

(Kreon enters.)

KREON   Citizens, I hear that King Oedipus
has made a fearful charge against me.
I'm here to prove it false.
If he thinks anything I've said or done   <620>
has made this crisis worse, or injured him,
then I have no more wish to live.
This is no minor charge.
It's the most deadly I could suffer,
if my city, my own people—you!—
believe I'm a traitor.

LEADER   He could have spoken in a flash
of ill-considered anger.

KREON   Did he say *I* persuaded the prophet to lie?

LEADER   That's what he said. What he meant wasn't clear.   <630>

KREON   When he announced my guilt—tell me,
         how did his eyes look? Did he seem sane?

LEADER   I can't say. I don't question what my rulers do.
         Here he comes, now, out of the palace.

         (Oedipus enters.)

OEDIPUS So? You come here? You have the nerve
         to face me in my own house? When you're exposed
         as its master's murderer?
         Caught trying to steal my kingship?
         In god's name, what weakness did you see
         in me that led you to plot this?   <640>
         Am I a coward or a fool?
         Did you suppose I wouldn't notice
         your subtle moves? Or not fight back?
         Aren't you attempting something
         downright stupid—to win absolute power
         without partisans or even friends?
         For that you'll need money—and a mob.

KREON   Now you listen to me.
         You've had your say, now hear mine.
         Don't judge until you've heard me out.   <650>

OEDIPUS You speak shrewdly, but I'm a poor learner
         from someone I know is my enemy.

KREON   I'll prove you are mistaken to think that.

OEDIPUS How can you prove you're not a traitor?

KREON   If you think mindless presumption
         is a virtue, then you're not thinking straight.

OEDIPUS If you think attacking a kinsman
         will bring you no harm, you must be mad.

KREON   I'll grant that. Now, how have I attacked you?

OEDIPUS Did you, or did you not, urge me   <660>
         to send for that venerated prophet?

KREON   And I would still give you the same advice.

OEDIPUS How long ago did King Laios . . .

KREON   Laios? Did what? Why speak of him?

OEDIPUS . . . die in that murderous attack?

KREON   That was far back in the past.

OEDIPUS	Did this seer practice his craft here, then?
KREON	With the same skill and respect he has now.
OEDIPUS	Back then, did he ever mention my name?
KREON	Not in my hearing. <670>
OEDIPUS	Didn't you try to hunt down the killer?
KREON	Of course we did. We found out nothing.
OEDIPUS	Why didn't your expert seer accuse me then?
KREON	I don't know. So I'd rather not say.
OEDIPUS	There is one thing you can explain.
KREON	What's that? I'm holding nothing back.

OEDIPUS   Just this. If that seer hadn't conspired with you,
he would never have called me Laios' killer.

KREON   If he said that, *you heard him,* I didn't.
I think you owe me some answers.   <680>

OEDIPUS   Question me. I have no blood on my hands.

KREON   Did you marry my sister?

OEDIPUS   Do you expect me to deny that?

KREON   You both have equal power in this country?

OEDIPUS   I give her all she asks.

KREON   Do I share power with you both as an equal?

OEDIPUS   You shared our power and betrayed us with it.

KREON   You're wrong. Think it through rationally, as I have.
Who would prefer the anxiety-filled
life of a king to one that lets him sleep at night—   <690>
if his share of power still equaled a king's?
Nothing in my nature hungers for power—
for me it's enough to enjoy a king's rights,
enough for any prudent man. All I want,
you give me—and it comes with no fear.
To be king would rob my life of its ease.
How could my share of power be more pleasant
than this painless pre-eminence, this ready
influence I have? I'm not so misguided
that I would crave honors that are burdens.   <700>
But as things stand, I'm greeted and wished well

on all sides. Those who want something from you
come to me, their best hope of gaining it.
Should I quit this good life for a worse one?
Treason never corrupts a healthy mind.
I have no love for such exploits.
Nor would I join someone who did.
Test me. Go to Delphi yourself.
Find out whether I brought back
the oracle's exact words. If you find   <710>
I plotted with that omen-reader, seize me
and kill me—not on your authority
alone, but on mine, for I'd vote my own death.
But don't convict me because of a wild thought
you can't prove, one that only you believe.
There's no justice in your reckless confusion
of bad men with good men, traitors with friends.
To cast off a true friend is like suicide—
killing what you love as much as your life.
Time will instruct you in these truths, for time   <720>
alone is the sure test of a just man—
but you can know a bad man in a day.

LEADER   That's good advice, my lord—
             for someone anxious not to fall.
             Quick thinkers can stumble.

OEDIPUS   When a conspirator moves
             abruptly and in secret against me,
             I must out-plot him and strike first.
             If I pause and do nothing, he
             will take charge, and I will have lost.   <730>

KREON   What do you want? My banishment?

OEDIPUS   No. It's your death I want.

KREON   Then start by defining "betrayal" . . .

OEDIPUS   You talk as though you don't believe me.

KREON   How can I if you won't use reason?

OEDIPUS   I reason in my own interest.

KREON   You should reason in mine as well.

OEDIPUS   In a traitor's interest?

KREON   What if you're wrong?

OEDIPUS   I still must rule.   <740>

KREON	Not when you rule badly.
OEDIPUS	Did you hear him, Thebes!
KREON	Thebes isn't yours alone. It's mine as well!
LEADER	My Lords, stop this. Here's Jokasta leaving the palace—just in time to calm you both. With her help, end your feud.

(Enter Jokasta from the palace.)

JOKASTA	Wretched men! Why are you out here so reckless, yelling at each other? Aren't you ashamed? With Thebes sick and dying you two fight out some personal grievance? Oedipus. Go inside. Kreon, go home. Don't make us all miserable over nothing.	<750>
KREON	Sister, it's worse than that. Oedipus your husband threatens either to drive me from my own country, or to have me killed.	
OEDIPUS	That's right. I caught him plotting to kill me, Lady. False prophecy was his weapon.	
KREON	I ask the gods to sicken and destroy me if I did anything you charge me with.	
JOKASTA	Believe what he says, Oedipus. Accept the oath he just made to the gods. Do it for my sake too, and for these men.	<760>
LEADER	Give in to him, Lord, we beg you. With all your mind and will.	
OEDIPUS	What do you want me to do?	
LEADER	Believe him. This man was never a fool. Now he backs himself up with a great oath.	
OEDIPUS	You realize what you're asking?	
LEADER	I do.	
OEDIPUS	Then say it to me outright.	<770>
LEADER	Groundless rumor shouldn't be used by you to scorn a friend who swears his innocence.	
OEDIPUS	You know, when you ask this of me you ask for my exile—or my death.	

LEADER	No! We ask neither. By the god outshining all others, the Sun— may I die the worst death possible, die godless and friendless, if I want those things. This dying land grinds pain into my soul— grinds it the more if the bitterness <780> you two stir up adds to our misery.
OEDIPUS	Then let him go, though it means my death or my exile from here in disgrace. What moves my pity are your words, not his. He will be hated wherever he goes.
KREON	You are as bitter when you yield as you are savage in your rage. But natures like your own punish themselves the most— which is the way it should be. <790>
OEDIPUS	Leave me alone. Go.
KREON	I'll go. You can see nothing clearly. But these men see that I'm right. *(Kreon goes off.)*
LEADER	Lady, why the delay? Take him inside.
JOKASTA	I will, when you tell me what happened.
LEADER	They had words. One drew a false conclusion; the other took offense.
JOKASTA	Both sides were at fault?
LEADER	Both sides.
JOKASTA	What did they say? <800>
LEADER	Don't ask that. Our land needs no more trouble. No more trouble! Let it go.
OEDIPUS	I know you mean well when you try to calm me, but do you realize where it will lead?
LEADER	King, I have said this more than once. I would be mad, I would lose my good sense, if I lost faith in you—you who put our dear country back on course when you found her wandering, crazed with suffering. <810>

Steer us straight, once again,
with all your inspired luck.

JOKASTA   In god's name, King, tell me, too.
What makes your rage so relentless?

OEDIPUS   I'll tell you, for it's you I respect, not the men.
Kreon brought on my rage by plotting against me.

JOKASTA   Go on. Explain what provoked the quarrel.

OEDIPUS   He says I murdered Laios.

JOKASTA   Does he know this himself? Or did someone tell him?

OEDIPUS   Neither. He sent that crooked seer to make the charge   <820>
so he could keep his own mouth innocent.

JOKASTA   Then you can clear yourself of all his charges.
Listen to me, for I can make you believe
no man, ever, has mastered prophecy.
This one incident will prove it.
A long time back, an oracle reached Laios—
I don't say Apollo himself sent it,
but the priests who interpret him did.
It said that Laios was destined to die
at the hands of a son born to him and me.   <830>
Yet, as rumor had it, foreign bandits
killed Laios at a place where three roads meet.

(Oedipus reacts with sudden intensity to her words.)

But the child was barely three days old
when Laios pinned its ankle joints together,
then had it left, by someone else's hands,
high up a mountain far from any roads.
That time Apollo failed to make Laios die
the way he feared—at the hands of his own son.
Doesn't that tell you how much sense
prophetic voices make of our lives?   <840>
You can forget them. When god wants
something to happen, he makes it happen.
And has no trouble showing what he's done.

OEDIPUS   Just now, something you said made my heart race.
Something . . . I remember . . . wakes up terrified.

JOKASTA   What fear made you turn toward me and say that?

OEDIPUS   I thought you said, Laios was struck down
where three roads meet.

JOKASTA	That's the story they told. It hasn't changed.
OEDIPUS	Tell me, where did it happen? <850>
JOKASTA	In a place called Phokis, at the junction where roads come in from Delphi and from Daulis.

OEDIPUS	How long ago was it? When it happened?
JOKASTA	We heard the news just before you came to power.
OEDIPUS	O Zeus! What did you will me to do?
JOKASTA	Oedipus, you look heartsick. What is it?
OEDIPUS	Don't ask me yet. Describe Laios to me. Was he a young man, almost in his prime?
JOKASTA	He was tall, with some gray salting his hair. He looked then not very different from you now. <860>
OEDIPUS	Like me? I'm finished! It was aimed at me, that savage curse I hurled in ignorance.
JOKASTA	What did you say, my Lord? Your face scares me.
OEDIPUS	I'm desperately afraid the prophet sees. Tell me one more thing. Then I'll be sure.
JOKASTA	I'm so frightened I can hardly answer.
OEDIPUS	Did Laios go with just a few armed men, or the large troop one expects of a prince?
JOKASTA	There were five only, one was a herald. And there was a wagon, to carry Laios. <870>
OEDIPUS	Ah! I see it now. Who told you this, Lady?
JOKASTA	Our slave. The one man who survived and came home.
OEDIPUS	Is he by chance on call here, in our house?
JOKASTA	No. When he returned and saw that you had all dead Laios' power, he touched my hand and begged me to send him out to our farmlands and sheepfolds, so he'd be far away and out of sight. I sent him. He was deserving—though a slave— of a much larger favor than he asked. <880>
OEDIPUS	Can you send for him right away?
JOKASTA	Of course. But why do you need him?

OEDIPUS   I'm afraid, Lady, I've said too much.
               That's why I want to see him now.

JOKASTA   I'll have him come. But don't I have the right
               to know what so deeply disturbs you, Lord?

OEDIPUS   So much of what I dreaded has come true.
               I'll tell you everything I fear.
               No one has more right than you do,
               to know the risks to which I'm now exposed.   <890>
               Polybos of Korinth was my father.
               My mother was Merope, a Dorian.
               I was the leading citizen, when Chance
               struck me a sudden blow.
               Alarming as it was, I took it
               much too hard. At a banquet,
               a man who had drunk too much wine
               claimed I was not my father's son.
               Seething, I said nothing. All that day
               I barely held it in. But next morning   <900>
               I questioned mother and father. Furious,
               they took their anger out on the man
               who shot the insult. They reassured me.
               But the rumor still rankled, it hounded me.
               So with no word to my parents,
               I traveled to the Pythian oracle.
               But the god would not honor me
               with the knowledge I craved.
                                          Instead,
               his words flashed other things—
               horrible, wretched things—at me: <910>
               I would be my mother's lover,
               I would show the world children
               no one could bear to look at, I
               would murder the father whose seed I am.
               When I heard that, and ever after,
               I traced the road back to Korinth
               only by looking at the stars. I fled
               to somewhere I'd never see outrages
               like those the god promised, happen to me.
               But my flight carried me to just the place   <920>
               where, you tell me, the king was killed.
               Oh, woman, here is the truth. As I approached
               the place where three roads joined,
               a herald, a colt-drawn wagon, and a man
               like the one you describe, met me head on.

The man out front and the old man himself
began to crowd me off the road.
The driver, who's forcing me aside,
I smash in anger.
       The old man watches me,
he measures my approach, then leans out   <930>
lunging with his two-spiked goad
dead at my skull. He's more than repaid:
I hit him so fast with the staff
this hand holds, he's knocked back
rolling off the cart. Where he lies, face up.
Then I kill them all.

But if this stranger and Laios . . . were the same blood,
whose triumph could be worse than mine?
Is there a man alive the gods hate more?
Nobody, no Theban, no foreigner,   <940>
can take me to his home.
No one can speak with me.
They all must drive me out.
I am the man—no one else—
who laid this curse on myself.
I make love to his wife with hands
repulsive from her husband's blood.
Can't you see that I'm evil,
my whole nature, utter filth?
Look, I must be banished. I must   <950>
never set eyes on my people, never
set foot in my homeland, because . . .
I'll marry my own mother,
kill Polybos my father,
who brought me up and gave me birth.
If someone said things like these
must be the work of a savage god,
he'd be speaking the truth. O you
pure and majestic gods! Never,
never, let the day such things happen   <960>
arrive for me. Let me never see it.
Let me vanish from men's eyes
before that doom comes down on me.

LEADER   What you say terrifies us, Lord. But don't lose hope
until you hear from the eyewitness.

OEDIPUS   That is the one hope I have left—to wait
for this man to come in from the fields.

JOKASTA   When he comes, what do you hope to hear?

OEDIPUS   This: if his story matches yours,
            I will have escaped disaster.   <970>

JOKASTA   What did I say that would make such a difference?

OEDIPUS   He told you Laios was killed by bandits.
            If he still claims there were several,
            then I cannot be the killer. One man
            cannot be many. But if he says: one man,
            braving the road alone, did it,
            there's no more doubt.
            The evidence will drag me down.

JOKASTA   You can be sure that was the way
            he first told it. How can he take it back?   <980>
            The entire city heard him, not just me.
            Even if now he changes his story,
            Lord, he could never prove that Laios'
            murder happened as the god predicted.
                                              Apollo

            said plainly: my son would kill Laios.
            That poor doomed child had no chance
            to kill his father, for he was killed first.
            After that, no oracle ever
            made me look right, then left, in fear.

OEDIPUS   You've thought this out well. Still, you must   <990>
            send for that herdsman. Don't neglect this.

JOKASTA   I'll send for him now. But come inside.
            Would I do anything to displease you?

            (Oedipus and Jokasta enter the palace.)

CHORUS   Let it be my good luck
            to win praise all my life
            for respecting the sky-walking laws
            born to stride
            through the light-filled heavens.
            Olympos
            alone was their father,   <1000>
            no human mind could conceive them;
            those laws
            neither sleep nor forget—
            a mighty god lives on in them
            who does not age.

A violent will
fathers the tyrant,
and violence, drunk
on wealth and power,
does him no good;   <1010>
he scales the heights—
until he's thrown
down to his doom,
where quick feet are no use.
But there's another fighting spirit
I ask god never to destroy—
the kind that makes our city thrive.
That god will protect us
I will never cease to believe.

But if a man   <1020>
speaks and acts with contempt—
flouts the law, sneers
at the stone gods in their shrines—
let a harsh death punish
his doomed indulgence.
Even as he wins he cheats,
he denies himself nothing,
his hand reaches for things
too sacred to be touched.
When crimes like these, which god hates,   <1030>
are not punished—but *honored*—
what good man will think his own life
safe from god's arrows piercing his soul?
Why should I dance to *this* holy song?

If prophecies don't show the way
to events all men can see,
I will no longer honor
the holy place untouchable:
Earth's navel at Delphi.
I will not go to Olympia   <1040>
nor the temple at Abai.
You, Zeus who hold power, if Zeus
lord of all is really who you are,
look at what's happening here:
prophecies made to Laios fade,
men ignore them;
Apollo is nowhere
glorified with praise;
the gods lose force.

(Jokasta enters from the palace carrying a suppliant's branch and some smoldering incense. She approaches the altar of Apollo near the palace door.)

JOKASTA   Lords of my country, this thought   <1050>
              came to me: to visit the gods' shrines
              with incense and a bough in my hands.
              Oedipus lets alarms of every kind
              inflame his mind. He won't let past
              experience calm his present fears,
              as a man of sense would.
              He's at the mercy of everybody's
              terrifying words. Since he won't listen to me,
              Apollo—you're the nearest god—

(Enter Messenger from the countryside.)

              I come praying for your good will. Look,   <1060>
              here is my branch. Cleanse us, cure our sickness.
              When we see Oedipus distraught, we all shake,
              as though sailing with a fearful helmsman.

MESSENGER   Can you point out to me, strangers,
              the house where King Oedipus lives? Better
              yet, tell me if you know where he is now.

LEADER   That's the house where he lives, stranger. He's inside.
              This woman is his wife and mother . . . of his children.

MESSENGER   I wish her joy, and the family joy
              that comes when a marriage bears fruit.   <1070>

JOKASTA   And joy to you, stranger, for those kind words.
              What have you to tell us? Or to ask?

MESSENGER   Great news, Lady, for you and your mate.

JOKASTA   What news? Who sent you to us?

MESSENGER   I come from Korinth.
              You'll rejoice at my news, I'm sure—
              but it may also make you grieve.

JOKASTA   What? How can it possibly do both?

MESSENGER   They're going to make him king. So say
              the people who live on the isthmus.   <1080>

JOKASTA   Isn't old Polybos still in power?

MESSENGER   No longer. Death has laid him in the tomb.

JOKASTA	You're saying, old man, Polybos has died?
MESSENGER	Kill me if that's not the truth.

(Jokasta speaks to a servant girl, who then runs inside.)

JOKASTA	Girl, run to your master with the news.

You oracles of the gods! Where are you now?
The man Oedipus feared he would kill,
the man he ran from, that man's dead.
Chance killed him. Not Oedipus. Chance!

(Oedipus enters quickly from the palace.)

OEDIPUS	Darling Jokasta, my loving wife,	<1090>
	why did you ask me to come out?	

JOKASTA	Listen to what this man has to say.
	See what it does to god's proud oracle.

OEDIPUS	Where's he from? What's his news?

JOKASTA	From Korinth. Your father isn't . . .
	Polybos . . . is no more . . . he's dead.

OEDIPUS	Say it, old man. I want to hear it from your mouth.

MESSENGER	If plain fact is what you want first,
	have no doubt he is dead and gone.

OEDIPUS	Was it treason, or did disease bring him down?	<1100>

MESSENGER	A slight push tips an old man into stillness.

OEDIPUS	Then some sickness killed him?

MESSENGER	That, and the long years he had lived.

OEDIPUS	Oh, yes, wife! Why should we scour Pythian smoke	
	or fear birds shrieking overhead?	
	If signs like these had been telling the truth	
	I would have killed my father. But he's dead.	
	He's safely in the ground. And here I am,	
	who didn't lift a spear. Or did he	
	die of longing for me? That might	<1110>
	have been what my killing him meant.	
	This time, Polybos' death has dragged	
	those worthless oracles with him to Hades.	

JOKASTA	Didn't I tell you that before?

OEDIPUS	You did. But I was still driven by fear.

JOKASTA   Don't let these things worry you anymore.

OEDIPUS   Not worry that I'll share my mother's bed?

JOKASTA   Why should a human being live in fear?
              Chance rules our lives!
              Who has any sure knowledge of the future?   <1120>
              It's best to take life as it comes.
              This marriage with your mother—don't fear it.
              In their very dreams, too, many men
              have slept with their mothers.
              Those who believe such things mean nothing
              will have an easier time in life.

OEDIPUS   A brave speech! I would like to believe it.
              But how can I if my mother's still living?
              While she lives, I will live in fear,
              no matter how persuasive you are.   <1130>

JOKASTA   Your father's tomb shines a great light.

OEDIPUS   On him, yes! But I fear her. She's alive.

MESSENGER   What woman do you fear?

OEDIPUS   I dread that oracle from the god, stranger.

MESSENGER   Would it be wrong for someone else to know it?

OEDIPUS   No, you may hear it. Apollo told me
              I would become my mother's lover, that I
              would have my father's blood on these hands.
              Because of that, I haven't gone near Korinth.
              So far, I've been very lucky—and yet,   <1140>
              there's no greater pleasure
              than to look our parents in the eyes!

MESSENGER   Did this oracle drive you into exile?

OEDIPUS   I didn't want to kill my father, old man.

MESSENGER   Then why haven't I put your fears to rest,
              King? I came here hoping to be useful.

OEDIPUS   I would give anything to be free of fear.

MESSENGER   I confess I came partly for that reason—
              to be rewarded when you've come back home.

OEDIPUS   I will never live where my parents live.   <1150>

MESSENGER   My son, you can't possibly know what you're doing.

OEDIPUS	Why is that, old man? In god's name, tell me.
MESSENGER	Is it because of them you won't go home?
OEDIPUS	I am afraid Apollo spoke the truth.
MESSENGER	Afraid you'd do your parents unforgivable harm?
OEDIPUS	Exactly that, old man. I am in constant fear.
MESSENGER	Your fear is groundless. Do you understand?
OEDIPUS	How can it be groundless if I'm their son?
MESSENGER	But Polybos was no relation to you.
OEDIPUS	What? Polybos was not my father? <1160>
MESSENGER	No more than I am. Exactly the same.
OEDIPUS	How the same? He fathered me and you didn't.
MESSENGER	He didn't father you any more than I did.
OEDIPUS	Why did he say, then, that I was his son?
MESSENGER	He took you from my hands as a gift.
OEDIPUS	He loved me so much—knowing I came from you?
MESSENGER	He had no children. That moved him to love you.
OEDIPUS	And you? Did you buy me? Or find me somewhere?
MESSENGER	I found you in the wooded hollows of Kithairon.
OEDIPUS	Why were you wandering way out there? <1170>
MESSENGER	I had charge of the sheep grazing those slopes.
OEDIPUS	A migrant hired to work our flocks?
MESSENGER	I saved your life that day, my son.
OEDIPUS	When you picked me up, what was wrong with me?
MESSENGER	Your ankles know. Let them show you.
OEDIPUS	Ahh! Why do you bring up that ancient wound?
MESSENGER	Your ankles had been pinned. I set you free.
OEDIPUS	From birth I've carried the shame of those scars.
MESSENGER	That was the luck that named you, Oedipus.
OEDIPUS	Did my mother or my father do this to me? <1180> Speak the truth for god's sake.

MESSENGER	I don't know. The man who gave you to me will know.
OEDIPUS	You took me from someone? You didn't happen on me yourself?
MESSENGER	I took you from another shepherd.
OEDIPUS	Who was he? Tell me as plainly as you can.
MESSENGER	He was known as someone who worked for Laios.
OEDIPUS	The same Laios who was once king *here?*
MESSENGER	The same. This man worked as his shepherd.
OEDIPUS	Is he alive? Can I see him? <1190>
MESSENGER	Someone from here could answer that better.
OEDIPUS	Does anyone here know what has become of this shepherd? Has anyone seen him in town or in the fields? Speak up now. The time has come to make everything known.
LEADER	I believe he means that same herdsman you've already sent for. Your wife would be the best one to ask.
OEDIPUS	Lady, do you recall the man we sent for? Is that the man he means? <1200>
JOKASTA	Why ask about him? Don't listen to him. Ignore his words. Forget he said them.
OEDIPUS	With clues like these in my hands, how can I fail to solve the mystery of my birth?
JOKASTA	For god's sake, if you care about your life, give up your search. Let my pain be enough!
OEDIPUS	You'll be fine! What if my mother was born from slaves—from three generations of slaves— how could that make you lowborn?
JOKASTA	Listen to me: I beg you. Don't do this. <1210>
OEDIPUS	I cannot listen. I must have the truth.
JOKASTA	I'm thinking only of what's best for you.
OEDIPUS	*What's best for me* exasperates me now.
JOKASTA	You poor child! Never find out who you are.

OEDIPUS   Someone, bring me the herdsman. Let
           that woman glory in her precious birth.

JOKASTA   Oh you poor doomed child! That is the only name
           I can call you now. None other, forever!

           (Jokasta runs into the palace.)

LEADER   Why has she left like that, Oedipus,
           driven off by a savage grief? I'm afraid   <1220>
           something horrendous will break this silence.

OEDIPUS   Let it burst! My seed may well *be* common!
           Even so, I still must know who I am.
           The meanness of my birth may shame
           her womanly pride. But since, in my
           own eyes, I am the child of Luck—
           she is the source of my well-being—
           never will I be dishonored.
           Luck is the mother who raised me; the months
           are my brothers, who've seen me through   <1230>
           the low times in my life and the high ones.
           Those are the powers that made me.
           I could never betray them *now*—
           by calling off the search
           for the secret of my birth!

CHORUS   By the gods of Olympos, if I have
           a prophet's range of eye and mind—
           tomorrow's moonlight
           will shine on you, Kithairon.
           Oedipus will honor you—   <1240>
           his native mountain,
           his nurse, his mother. Nothing
           will keep us from dancing
           then, mountain joyful to our king!
           We call out to Phoibos Apollo:
           be the cause of our joy!

           (Chorus turns toward Oedipus.)

           My son, who was your mother?
           Which nymph bore you to Pan,
           the mountain rover?
           Was it Apollo's bride   <1250>
           to whom you were born
           in the grassy highlands?
           Or did Hermes, Lord of Kyllene,

or Bakkhos of the mountain peaks,
take you—a sudden joy—
from nymphs of Helikon,
whose games he often shares?

OEDIPUS   Old men, if it's possible
to recognize a man I've never met,
I think I see the herdsman we've been waiting for.   <1260>
Our fellow would be old, like the stranger approaching.
Those leading him are my own men.
But I expect you'll know him better.
Some of you will know him by sight.

(Enter Herdsman, led by Oedipus' servants.)

LEADER   I do know him. He is from Laios' house,
a trustworthy shepherd if he ever had one.

OEDIPUS   Korinthian, I'll ask you to speak first:
is this the man you mean?

MESSENGER   You're looking at him.

OEDIPUS   Now you, old man. Look at me.   <1270>
Answer every question I ask you.
Did you once come from Laios' house?

HERDSMAN   I did. I wasn't a bought slave,
I was born and raised in their house.

OEDIPUS   What was your job? How did you spend your time?

HERDSMAN   My life I have spent tending sheep.

OEDIPUS   In what region did you normally work?

HERDSMAN   Mainly Kithairon, and the country thereabouts.

(Oedipus gestures toward the Messenger.)

OEDIPUS   That man. Do you recall ever seeing him?

HERDSMAN   Recall how? Doing what? Which man?   <1280>

(Oedipus goes to the Messenger and puts his hand on him.)

OEDIPUS   This man right here. Have you ever seen him before?

HERDSMAN   Not that I recognize—not right away.

MESSENGER   It's no wonder, master. His memory's faded,
but I'll revive it for him. I'm sure he knows me.
We worked the pastures on Kithairon together—

he with his two flocks, me with one—
for three whole grazing seasons, from early spring
until Arcturos rose. When the weather turned cold
I'd drive my flocks home to their winter pens,
he'd drive his away to Laios' sheepfolds.   <1290>
Do I describe what happened, old friend? Or don't I?

HERDSMAN   That's the truth, but it was so long ago.

MESSENGER   Do you remember giving me a boy
            I was to raise as my own son?

HERDSMAN   What? Why ask me that?

MESSENGER   There, my friend, is the man who was that boy.

            (He nods toward Oedipus.)

HERDSMAN   Damn you! Shut up and say nothing.

OEDIPUS   Don't attack him for his words, old man.
            Yours beg to be punished far more than his.

HERDSMAN   Tell me, royal master, what've I done wrong?   <1300>

OEDIPUS   You didn't answer him about the boy.

HERDSMAN   He's trying to make something out of nothing.

OEDIPUS   Speak of your own free will. Or under torture.

HERDSMAN   Dear god! I'm an old man. Don't hurt me.

OEDIPUS   One of you, bind his arms behind his back.

            *(Servants approach the Herdsman
            and start to seize his arms.)*

HERDSMAN   Why this, you doomed man? What else must you know?

OEDIPUS   Did you give him the child, as he claims you did?

HERDSMAN   I did. I wish that day I had died.

OEDIPUS   You will die if you don't speak the truth.

HERDSMAN   Answering you is what will get me killed.   <1310>

OEDIPUS   I think this man is deliberately stalling.

HERDSMAN   No! I've said it once. I gave him the boy.

OEDIPUS   Was the boy from your house? Or someone else's?

HERDSMAN   Not from my house. Someone gave him to me.

OEDIPUS   The person! Name him! From what house?

HERDSMAN   Don't ask me that, master. For god's sake, don't.

OEDIPUS   If I have to ask one more time, you'll die.

HERDSMAN   He was a child from the house of Laios.

OEDIPUS   A slave? Or a child born of Laios' blood?

HERDSMAN   Help me! I am about to speak terrible words.   <1320>

OEDIPUS   And I to hear them. But hear them I must!

HERDSMAN   The child was said to be Laios' own son.
             Your lady in the house would know that best.

OEDIPUS   *She* gave the child to you?

HERDSMAN   She gave him, King.

OEDIPUS   To do what?

HERDSMAN   I was to let it die.

OEDIPUS   Kill her own child?

HERDSMAN   She feared prophecies.

OEDIPUS   What prophecies?

HERDSMAN   That this child would kill his father.

OEDIPUS   Why, then, did you give him to this old man?

HERDSMAN   Out of pity, master. I hoped this man   <1330>
             would take him back to his own land.
             But that man saved him for this—
             the worst grief of all. If the child
             he speaks of is you, master, now you
             know: your birth has doomed you.

OEDIPUS   All! All! It has all happened,
             it was all true. O light! May this
             be the last time I look on you.
             You see now what I am. I am
             the child who must not be born,   <1340>
             I loved where I must not love,
             I killed where I must not kill.

             (Oedipus runs into the palace.)

CHORUS   Men and women who live and die,
             I set no value on your lives.

Which one of you ever, reaching
for blessedness that lasts,
finds more than what *seems* blest?
You live in that seeming
a while, then it vanishes.
Your fate teaches me this, Oedipus,   <1350>
yours, you suffering man, the story
god spoke through you: never call
any man fortunate.

O Zeus, no man drew a bow like this man!
He shot his arrow home,
winning power, pleasure, wealth;
he killed the virgin Sphinx,
who sang the god's dark oracles;
her claws were hooked and sharp.
He fought off death in our land;   <1360>
he towered against its threat.
Since those times I've called you my king,
honoring you mightily, my Oedipus,
who wielded the great might of Thebes.

But now—nobody's story
has the sorrow of yours,
O my so famous Oedipus—
the same great harbor
welcomed you
first as child, then as father   <1370>
tumbling upon your bridal bed.
How could the furrows your father plowed, doomed
man, how could they suffer so long in silence?

Time, who sees all, caught you
living a life you never willed.
Time damns this marriage that is
no marriage, where the fathered child
fathered children himself.
O son of Laios, I wish
I'd never seen you! I fill my lungs,   <1380>
I sing with all my power
the plain truth in my heart.
Once you gave me new breath,
O my Oedipus!—but now
you close my eyes in darkness.

(Enter Servant from the palace.)

SERVANT   You've always been our land's most honored men.
               If you still have a born Theban's love
               for the House of Labdakos, you'll be crushed
               by what you're about to see and hear.
               No rivers could wash this house clean—   <1390>
               not the Danube, not the Rion—
               it hides so much evil that now
               is coming to light. What happened here
               was not involuntary evil, it was willed.
               The griefs that punish us the most
               are those we've chosen for ourselves.

LEADER   We already knew more than enough
               to make us grieve. Do you have more to tell?

SERVANT   It is the briefest news to say or hear.
               Our royal lady Jokasta is dead.   <1400>

LEADER   That pitiable woman. How did she die?

SERVANT   She killed herself. You will be spared the worst—
               since you weren't there to see it.
               But you will hear, exactly as I can
               recall it, what that wretched woman suffered.
               She came raging through the courtyard
               straight for her marriage bed, the fists
               of both her hands clenched in her hair.
               Once in, she slammed the doors shut and called out
               to Laios, so long dead; she remembered   <1410>
               his living sperm of long ago, who killed Laios,
               while she lived on to breed with her son
               more ruined children.
                                       She grieved for the bed
               she had loved in, giving birth
               to all those doubled lives—
               husband fathered by husband,
               children sired by her child.
               From this point on I don't know how she died—
               Oedipus burst in shouting,
               distracting us from her misery.   <1420>
               We looked on, stunned, as he plowed through us
               raging, asking us for a spear,
               asking for the wife who was no wife
               but the same furrowed twice-mothering earth
               from whom he and his children sprang.
               He was frantic, yet some divine hand
               drove him toward his wife—none of us near him did.

As though someone were guiding him, he lunged,
with a savage yell, at the double doors,
wrenching the bolts from their sockets.   <1430>
He burst into the room. We saw her there:
the woman above us, hanging by the neck,
swaying there in a noose of tangled cords.
He saw. And bellowing in anguish
he reached up, loosening the noose that held her.
With the poor lifeless woman laid out on the ground
this, then, was the terror we saw: he pulled
the long pins of hammered gold clasping her gown,
held them up, and punched them into his eyes,
back through the sockets. He was screaming: <1440>
"Eyes, now you will not, no, never
see the evil I suffered, the evil I caused.
You will see blackness—where once
were lives you should never have lived to see,
yearned-for faces you so long failed to know."
While he howled out these tortured words—
not once, but many times—his raised hands
kept beating his eyes. The blood kept coming,
drenching his beard and cheeks. Not a few wet drops,
but a black storm of bloody hail lashing his face.   <1450>

What this man and this woman did
broke so much evil loose! That evil joins
the whole of both their lives in grief.
The happiness they once knew was real,
but now that happiness is in ruins—
wailing, death, disgrace. Whatever misery
we have a name for, is here.

LEADER   Has his grief eased at all?

SERVANT   He shouts for someone to open the door bolts:

"Show this city its father-killer," he cries,   <1460>
"Show it its mother . . ." He said the word, I can't.
He wants to banish himself from the land,
not doom this house any longer
by living here, under his own curse.
He's so weak, though, he needs to be helped.
No one could stand up under a sickness like his.
Look! The door bolts are sliding open.
You will witness a vision of such suffering
even those it revolts will pity.

(Oedipus emerges from the slowly opening
palace doors. He is blinded, with blood
on his face and clothes, but the effect
should arouse more awe and pity than shock.
He moves with the aid of a servant.)

LEADER   Your pain is terrible to see,   <1470>
                pure, helpless anguish,
                more moving than anything
                my eyes have ever touched.
                                              O man of pain,
                where did your madness come from?
                What god would go
                to such inhuman lengths
                to savage your defenseless life?

                (Moans.)

                I cannot look at you—
                though there's so much
                to ask you, so much to learn,   <1480>
                so much that holds my eyes—
                so strong are the shivers of awe
                you send through me.

OEDIPUS   Ahhh! My life
                screams in pain.
                Where is my misery
                taking me?
                How far does my voice fly,
                fluttering out there
                on the wind?   <1490>
                O god, how far have you thrown me?

LEADER   To a hard place. Hard to watch, hard to hear.

OEDIPUS   Darkness buries me in her hate, takes me
                in her black hold.
                Unspeakable blackness.
                It can't be fought off,
                it keeps coming,
                wafting evil all over me.
                Ahhh!
                Those goads piercing my eyes,   <1500>
                those crimes stabbing my mind,
                strike through me—one deep wound.

LEADER   It is no wonder you feel

nothing but pain now,
both in your mind and in your flesh.

OEDIPUS   Ah friend, you're still here,
faithful to the blind man.
I know you are near me. Even
in my darkness I know your voice.

LEADER   You terrify us. How could you   <1510>
put out your eyes? What god drove you to it?

OEDIPUS   It was Apollo who did this.
He made evil, consummate evil,
out of my life.
But the hand
that struck these eyes
was my hand.
I in my wretchedness
struck me, no one else did.
What good was left for my eyes to see?   <1520>
Nothing in this world could I see now
with a glad heart.

LEADER   That is so.

OEDIPUS   Whom could I look at? Or love?
Whose greeting could I answer
with fondness, friends?
Take me quickly from this place.
I am the most ruined, the most cursed,
the most god-hated man who ever lived.

LEADER   You're broken by what happened, broken   <1530>
by what's happening in your own mind.
I wish you'd never learned the truth.

OEDIPUS   May he die, the man
who found me in the pasture,
who unshackled my feet,
who saved me from that death for a worse life,
a life I cannot thank him for.
Had I died then, I would have caused
no great grief to my people and myself.

LEADER   I wish he had let you die.   <1540>

OEDIPUS   I wouldn't have come home to kill my father,
no one could call me lover
of her from whose body I came.

I have no god now.
I'm son to a fouled mother,
I fathered children in the bed
where my father once gave me
deadly life. If ever an evil
rules all other evils
it is my evil, the life   <1550>
god gave to Oedipus.

LEADER   I wish I could say you acted wisely.
                You would have been better off dead than blind.

OEDIPUS   There was no better way than mine.
                No more advice! If I had eyes, how could
                they bear to look at my father in Hades?
                Or at my devastated mother? Not even
                hanging could right the wrongs I did them both.
                You think I'd find the sight of my children
                delightful, born to the life mine must live?   <1560>
                Never, ever, delightful to my eyes!
                Nor this town, its wall, gates and towers;
                nor the sacred images of our gods.
                I severed myself from these joys when I
                banished the vile killer—myself!—
                totally wretched now, though I was raised
                more splendidly than any Theban.
                But now the gods have proven me
                defiled, and of Laios' own blood.
                And once I've brought such disgrace on myself,   <1570>
                how could I look calmly on my people?
                I could not! If I could deafen my ears
                I would. I'd deaden my whole body,
                go blind and deaf to shut those evils out.
                The silence in my mind would be sweet.
                O Kithairon, why did you take me in?
                Or once you had seized me, why didn't you
                kill me instantly, leaving no trace of my birth?
                O Polybos and Korinth, and that palace
                they called the ancient home of my fathers!   <1580>
                I was their glorious boy growing up,
                but under that fair skin
                festered a hideous disease.
                My vile self now shows its vile birth.
                                                    You,
                three roads, and you, darkest ravine,
                you, grove of oaks, you, narrow place

where three paths drank blood from my hands,
my fathering blood pouring into you:
Do you remember what I did while you watched?
And when I came here, what I did then?   <1590>
O marriages! You marriages! You created us,
we sprang to life, then from that same seed
you burst fathers, brothers, sons,
kinsmen shedding kinsmen's blood,
brides and mothers and wives—the most loathsome
atrocities that strike mankind.
I must not name what should not be.
If you love the gods, hide me out there,
kill me, heave me into the sea,
anywhere you can't see me.   <1600>
Come, take me. Don't shy away. Touch
this human derelict. Don't fear me, trust me.
No other man, only myself,
can be afflicted with my sorrows.

LEADER   Here's Kreon. He's come when you need him,
to take action or to give you advice.
He is the only ruler we have left
to guard Thebes in your place.

OEDIPUS   Can I say anything he'll listen to?
Why would he believe me?   <1610>
I wronged him so deeply.
I proved myself so false to him.

(Kreon enters.)

KREON   I haven't come to mock you, Oedipus.
I won't dwell on the wrongs you did me.

(Kreon speaks to the attendants.)

Men, even if you've no respect
for a fellow human being, show some
for the life-giving flame of the Sun god:
don't leave this stark defilement out here.
The earth, the holy rain, the light, can't bear it.

Quickly, take him back to the palace.   <1620>
If these sorrows are shared
only among the family,
that will spare us further impiety.

OEDIPUS   Thank god! I feared much worse from you.
Since you've shown me, a most vile man,

                    such noble kindness, I have one request.
                    For your sake, not for mine.

KREON   What is it? Why do you ask me like that?

OEDIPUS   Expel me quickly to some place
                    where no living person will find me.   <1630>

KREON   I would surely have done that. But first
                    I need to know what the god wants me to do.

OEDIPUS   He's given his command already.
                    I killed my father. I am unholy. I must die.

KREON   So the god said. But given
                    the crisis we're in, we had better
                    be absolutely sure before we act.

OEDIPUS   You'd ask about a broken man like me?

KREON   Surely, by now, you're willing to trust god.

OEDIPUS   I am. But now I must ask for something   <1640>
                    within your power. I beg you! Bury her
                    who's lying inside—as you think proper.
                    Give her the rites due your kinswoman.
                    As for me, don't condemn my father's city
                    to house me while I'm still alive.
                    Let me live out my life on Kithairon,
                    the very mountain—
                    the one I've made famous—
                    that my father and mother chose for my tomb.
                    Let me die there, as my parents decreed.   <1650>
                    And yet, I know this much:
                    no sickness can kill me. Nothing can.
                    I was saved from that death
                    to face an extraordinary evil.
                    Let my fate take me now, where it will.

                    My children, Kreon. My sons.
                    They're grown now. They won't need your help.

                    They'll find a way to live anywhere.
                    But my poor wretched girls, who never
                    ate anywhere but at my table;   <1660>
                    they've never lived apart from me.
                    I fed them with my own hands.
                                              Care for them.
                    If you're willing, let me touch them now,
                    let me give in to my grief.

Grant it Kreon, from your great heart.
If I could touch them, I would
imagine them as my eyes once saw them.

*(The gentle sobbing of Oedipus' two daughters
is heard offstage. Soon two small girls enter.)*

What's this?
O gods, are these my children sobbing?
Has Kreon pitied me?   <1670>
Given me my own dear children?
Has he?

KREON   I have. I brought them to you
because I knew how much joy,
as always, you would take in them.

OEDIPUS   Bless this kindness of yours. Bless your luck.
May the gods guard you better than they did me.
Children, where are you? Come to me.
These are your brother's hands, hands
of the man who created you, hands that caused   <1680>
my once bright eyes to go dark.
He, children, saw nothing, knew nothing,
he fathered you where his own life began,
where his own seed grew. Though I can't
see you, I can weep for you . . .

(Oedipus takes his daughters in his arms.)

when I think how bitter your lives will be.
I know the life that men will make you live.
What public gatherings, what festivals
could you attend? None! You would be sent home
in tears, without your share of holy joy.   <1690>
When the time comes to marry, my daughters,
what man will risk the revulsion—
the infamy!—that will wound you
just as it wounded your parents?
What evil is missing? Your father killed
his father, he had children with the mother
who bore him, fathered you
at the source of his own life.
                              Those are the insults
you will face. Who will marry you?
No one, my children. You will grow old   <1700>
unmarried, living a dried-up childless life.
Kreon, you're all the father they have now.

The parents who conceived them are both lost.
Keep these two girls from rootless wandering,
unmarried and helpless. They are your kin.
Don't bring them down to what I am.
Pity them. They are so young, and but for you,
alone. Touch my hand, kind man,
make that touch your promise.

(Kreon touches him.)

Children, had you been old enough   <1710>
to comprehend, I would have taught you more.
Now, all I can do is ask you to pray:
that you live only where you're welcomed;
that your lives be happier than mine was,
the father from whose seed you were born.

KREON   Enough grief. Go inside now.

OEDIPUS   Bitter words, which I must obey.

KREON   Time runs out on all things.

OEDIPUS   Grant my request before I go.

KREON   Speak.   <1720>

OEDIPUS   Banish me from my homeland.

KREON   Ask god to do that, not me.

OEDIPUS   I am the man the gods hate most.

KREON   Then you will have your wish.

OEDIPUS   You consent?

KREON   I never promise if I can't be sure.

OEDIPUS   Then lead me inside.

KREON   Come. Let go of your children now.

OEDIPUS   Don't take them from me.

KREON   Give up your power, too.   <1730>
            You won the power once, but you couldn't
            keep it to the end of your life.

(Kreon leads Oedipus into the palace.)

CHORUS   Thebans, that man is the same Oedipus
            whose great mind solved the famous riddle.
            He was a most powerful man.

Which of us seeing his glory, his prestige,
did not wish his luck could be ours?
Now look at what wreckage the seas
of savage trouble have made of his life.
To know the truth of a man, wait   <1740>
till you see his life end.
On that day, look at him.
Don't claim any man is god's friend
until he has passed through life
and crossed the border into death—
never having been god's victim.   <1746>

(All leave.)

Oedipus at Kolonos
"His Death Was a Cause for Wonder"

By setting *Oedipus at Kolonos* on the edge of a sacred grove blessed with flowers, grape vines, nightingales, shade trees, and clearings suitable for dancing, Sophokles invokes the physical place where men and gods converge, the solemn ground where the human and divine pay their respects to each other. The Greek word for such kindness (or favor) is *charis,* the grace extended by men and gods to the worthy, the needy, the damaged, and the miserable. Sophokles thus gives *charis* a visible presence on stage—and an imaginative one in the audience's mind—that becomes more significant as the drama unfolds.

In the Grove of the Eumenides Oedipus will find the *charis* Apollo promised him at Delphi—almost as an afterthought—when as a troubled young man he received the worst news any Greek ever heard from a god.[1] Within the grove's precincts the aged Oedipus will be transformed from a defiled exile into a welcomed hero. As John Gould put it, "Nowhere else in Greek tragedy does the primitively mysterious power of boundaries and thresholds, the 'extraterritoriality' of the sacred make itself felt with the fierce precision that Sophokles achieves in the [*Kolonos'* first choral ode]."[2] And we do sense immediately the primitive dread aroused by the grove's divine inhabitants: Oedipus, accompanied by Antigone, hides in the trees as the Chorus sweeps onstage. The Old Men denounce the invisible intruder, scour the grove for signs of him, and sing their terror of the all-seeing Eumenides, whom they warily address as "Kindly Ones." To escape the goddesses' withering glance the chorus members walk with their own eyes lowered. Since speech is forbidden, the prayers they mouth are silent.

Oedipus responds to the Old Men's warnings by leaving this sacred place and surrendering himself. He won't reenter the grove until play's end. Meanwhile, by dramatizing Oedipus' claims to the gods' *charis,* Sophokles explores a subject of particular fascination to him—heroes and their deaths as paradigms for the fully empowered human spirit.

Sophokles' final surviving work, the last of his two dramas about Oedipus, brings his hero's story to a thrilling conclusion, one we would not have predicted for the ruined man at the end of *Oedipus the King.* In addition to chronicling Oedipus' reversal of fortune, the *Kolonos* also conveys the wise old citizen playwright's last reflections on themes keenly important to him: the damage that lives wrecked in one generation inflict on the next; the difference between moral guilt and religious defilement; the responsibilities of parents and children to each other; the miseries of old age; and the greatness of Athens.

The *Kolonos,* which was produced posthumously at the Theater

---

[1] That this promise of haven in the sacred grove of the Eumenides was made to Oedipus during his first visit to Delphi is suggested at 46/54 and 452–54/488–90. Another possible allusion comes in *Oed King* (1455–57/1652–55).

[2] John Gould, "Hikiteia," *Journal of Hellenic Studies* 93 (1973): 90.

of Dionysos in 401 by Sophokles the Younger,[3] coincides with Athens' darker endgame—the final defeat by Sparta that closed its century-long era of political innovation, military hegemony, and theatrical genius. Sophokles celebrates Athens' past and its timeless moral and mythical glory throughout the play—most brilliantly in one choral ode, a song of gratitude to the "mother city, / for the great gifts the gods have given her" (710–11/775–76). A few incidents in the plot might also allude to the mother city's decline. Polyneikes' reckless and self-obsessed campaign against Thebes recalls Athens' own military debacles stretching back to the invasion of Sicily in 415. Theseus' unsentimental appreciation of Oedipus, as well as his swift dispatch of troops that rout Kreon's attempt to abduct Oedipus' daughters, remind us that skilled and gracious men, like Perikles, once led Athens.

The play's linear narrative structure has been criticized for lacking the vertiginous plot turns and ironic double meanings of *Oedipus the King.* Nor does the *Kolonos* possess the swiftness, tension, and tragic impact of *Antigone.* But the *Kolonos* appropriately unfolds to reveal Oedipus' dormant greatness. Cumulative scenes of accusation and defense test and confirm Oedipus' strengths and his sangfroid: his stubbornness, his quick analytic intelligence, his love for his caring daughters, his rhetorical flair, his sense of his own value to others, his unflinching moral fury. The play's sheer length affords Sophokles the scope to develop and nuance his vision of an eternally embattled hero.

While modern readers will have no trouble relating to most of Oedipus' convictions and obsessions—belief that he's innocent of willful murder and incest; confidence that he'll achieve the good death the gods have promised—much in the *Kolonos* might puzzle us. But if we're aware of the Greek religious and social practices at work in the play, the larger and enduring issues these engage will come into focus. This introduction and the notes are intended to supply what's needed.

Our word for what an invincible power does to people is "fate"; the equivalent Greek word is *tyche* (pronounced too-káy). Both words point to life-altering events that happen outside a person's control. But to possess the full context of *tyche*—which may be also translated as "luck" or "destiny"—we must imagine *tyche* as a force that put constant pressure on the mind, a force beyond both comprehension and appeal. It is no wonder, considering that the ordinary Greek believed *tyche* governed the events of his life,[4] that plots which precipitate disaster, as do those of *Oedipus the King* and *Medea,* and those with upbeat outcomes, such as Euripides' *Alkestis* or Aeschylus' *Eumenides,* were equally popu-

---

[3] The poet's grandson, whose own plays were produced in the Great Dionysia in the fourth century.
[4] See the Guard's formulation at *Antigone,* 235–36/267–68: ". . . I'm of the opinion / nothing but my own fate can cause me harm."

lar with Athenian audiences and playwrights. A theatrical plot was no more likely to be censured for its credulity-straining twists than a man's action-packed life would have been interpreted as meaningless happenstance. Both a play's and a life's plot revealed the gods at work and therefore implicitly conveyed the divinities' moral encouragement or warning.

Just as the concept of the daimon explains why Oedipus' seemingly rational choices ruin his life in *Oedipus the King*,[5] the nature of the hero and hero cults illuminates his death's significance in the *Kolonos*. *Oedipus the King* shows the gods—or their proxy, the personal daimon who shapes the events of Oedipus' life—using savage duplicity to destroy him. The *Kolonos,* on the other hand, reveals the gods' change of heart, their ultimate, if long withheld, concern and grace—their *charis*. Both Oedipus dramas thus share the goal of understanding and radically reinterpreting past events in the hero's life that were predicted and, apparently, ordained by the gods. The earlier Oedipus' intellect was helpless against the divine malevolence of his daimon. But in the *Kolonos* Oedipus' justifications, conscious choices, and cogent analyses are rewarded and finally blessed.

The later play reacts to and departs from the earlier play with its first word. The *Kolonos* begins with *"Teknon,"* meaning "child"; *Oedipus the King* with *"O tekna,"* meaning "[My] children." With plural and singular forms of the same word Sophokles marks Oedipus' enormous loss of power between middle and old age. In *Oedipus the King, O tekna*'s context in a formal address assures his fellow citizens that in a time of plague and despair Oedipus assumes responsibility for all Thebans; he will seek to restore their well-being with a father's passion. *Teknon,* used as a term of endearment in the *Kolonos,* reminds Antigone that she's obliged to help her weary father; he is now utterly dependent on her alone. Indeed, our first sight of Oedipus in the *Kolonos* reveals exactly the broken and homeless man that Tiresias, in *Oedipus the King,* predicted he would become: blind, old, and weary, wandering the roads, supporting himself with a stick.

Oedipus also announces in this final drama a new way of thinking about the defilement that parricide and incest have brought upon him. He is convinced that though he must always remain a damaged person, the acts themselves were free of moral guilt. He harbors as well an unrealized belief, first formulated in these lines from *Oedipus the King,* that the gods have spared him for some great future role or mission:

> [N]o sickness can kill me. Nothing can.
> I was saved from that death
> to face an extraordinary evil.
> Let my fate take me now, where it will. (1455–58/1652–55)

[5] See introduction to *Oed King* for a full discussion of *daimon*.

Oedipus may have based this conviction—that the evil he suffers is part of a larger pattern—on a section of the original Delphic prophecy that was never mentioned in *Oedipus the King:* the promise that Oedipus' suffering life will end in benign death. In the *Kolonos* Oedipus recalls this lost prophecy while praying to the Kindly Ones:

> When the god condemned me to such grief,
> he assured me my long life would end here—
> that I'd find a haven, and be taken in
> by vengeful goddesses . . . (87–90/96–99)

Sophokles orchestrates virtually every scene in the *Kolonos* to clarify and complete these two overriding and unresolved issues. Is Oedipus divinely justified in believing himself morally innocent of the parricide and incest he committed? What does the oracle that promises him a benign death mean in all its fullness? Sophokles pursues each question by deepening the context in which he confronts it, and by dramatizing the answers, both of which evolve through several stages and fuse into one extraordinary final image: Oedipus transformed into a *heros.*

To fifth-century Greeks the word *heros* (the singular form) had a meaning quite distinct from our own. We use the word "heroes" to refer to people who place themselves at considerable risk or exertion to accomplish, often for the common good, something splendid, dangerous, or self-sacrificing. The Greeks used the word to refer to men and women on whom the gods had bestowed extraordinary honor and power at the moment of their deaths. Theseus, who killed the Minotaur and started Athens on its path to glory; Iphigenia, whose life was sacrificed to produce a fair wind for the Argive army as it sailed to Troy; and Orestes, who killed his own mother to avenge her murder of his father Agamemnon, were mythical heroes around whose tombs enduring cults arose. Hero cults also honored some real people: Brasidas, a Spartan general who three times defeated Athenian armies in northern Greece; Kleomedes, an Olympic boxing champion who became a deranged mass-murderer of schoolchildren;[6] and Sophokles himself, who sponsored the cult of Aesklepius, the god of healing, in Athens—possibly by installing the god's statue, or his priest, in his own house.[7] The

---

[6] Kleomedes' heroization occurred under duress. After he killed his Olympic boxing opponent, his victory was stripped from him. In anger he pulled the pillars of a school down, killing the pupils. He hid from the families of the dead children in a large trunk in the temple of Athena but disappeared by the time they broke into it. The town asked the oracle at Delphi how they should proceed. "Honor him as a hero," the oracle advised.

[7] During the fifth century the heroizing of ones' dead family members proliferated, but standards deteriorated. There are hundreds of records of ordinary Greeks whose families designated them as *heroes* but who lacked the mythical stature of those discussed in this introduction.

presence of a *heros'* corpse or bones in the earth conferred benefits on the locality; that the tombs of heroes were prized and their bones fought over and sometimes stolen by rival cities that coveted their inherent magical powers are amply attested throughout the classical era.[8]

One standard component of a *heros'* nature was an unusual capacity for anger and violence.[9] Our own contemporary attitudes toward those who achieve fame by harming others are more ambivalent than those of fifth-century Greeks. We condemn unsanctioned violence as dangerous to civil society; we work to limit and control it. Yet we are quick to accept sanctioned violence against avowed enemies when the survival of our nation or ourselves is at stake. The difference between our own and ancient Greek attitudes toward heroic violence is our requirement that it be justified in moral or at least expedient terms. A Greek *heros'* fury could be appreciated simply as an impressive phenomenon, a thing of awe and beauty in itself. If violence needed justification, there was the universal requirement that a good man helps his friends and harms his enemies. Not until the advent of Socrates (in person in the fifth century) and of Plato's books (in the fourth) was this common wisdom challenged.

Though to us a hero's fury could well damn him as immoral, to the ancient Greeks a *heros'* anger—his *menis,* a most privileged word and concept in Greek culture—could make him immortal. *Menis,* in fact, begins Greek literature. It is the first word in the first line of the earliest epic poem, the *Iliad: menin aieda thea* ("Wrath, goddess, sing the wrath . . ."*).

When we first see Oedipus in the *Kolonos* he is not a *heros* full of fury but an exhausted exile. As a younger man Oedipus was convinced of his guilt in killing his father and fathering children with his mother; he blinded himself, then pleaded with Kreon to allow his exile from Thebes. Kreon demurred, saying he must consult Apollo before taking such drastic action. We discover at the beginning of the *Kolonos* that Kreon, long after Oedipus had reconciled himself to living out his life in Thebes, abruptly banished him against his will. On the road for years, and now in search of the grove Apollo named as his final resting place, Oedipus is about to present himself, and Antigone as well, since she accompanies and cares for him, as suppliants to the Athenians.

Both exile and supplication were formal conditions, governed by law and custom. Exile was often punishment for some political or personal wrongdoing. It severed people from their homelands, from the roots in city and family life that fed and supported them. Supplication

---

[8] The Athenian statesman Kimon, for instance, brought home the bones of the mythical hero Theseus from Skyros in the mid-fifth century.
[9] The most thorough and engaging modern account of heroic anger is found in Knox 1964. The discussion of heroic anger in Sophoklean tragedy has been carried even further by Gould 1990.

was an important institution, a religiously protected humanitarian appeal for specific assistance or for safe haven, usually invoked by people in desperate trouble. Protection from enemies might be sought, for instance, within a god's temple or sacred precinct, or from a king or powerful citizens. The suppliant's right to make the appeal and the supplicated authority's obligation to hear the appeal were both believed to be monitored and enforced by the gods in whose temple or in whose name the appeal was made.[10]

That Sophokles brings Oedipus to the Athenian deme[11] of Kolonos—Sophokles' own deme—and to the sacred grove of the Eumenides is fitting. The hero cult of the mythical Oedipus located his burial site in Kolonos. But Athens and the goddesses who now preside over the grove figure in another Greek play, the third in Aeschylus' *Oresteia* trilogy, staged more than fifty years before the *Kolonos.* That play, the *Eumenides,* ends in Athens, where Orestes is tried and acquitted for the murder of his mother by the judges of the Areopagus.[12] This acquittal embodies Aeschylus' vision of a world transformed from a culture of revenge—in which primordial goddesses, the Erinys or Furies, are responsible for compelling blood kin to avenge the murder of their relatives—into a world governed by the rule of law. Aeschylus relieves these goddesses of this grim duty and gives them a new name, the Eumenides, or "Kindly Ones." They now operate in a civilized society and share with law courts the job of enforcing prohibitions against kin murder. But since they're still charged with looking after family success and cohesion, they continue to frighten and punish.

In the *Eumenides* Orestes is acquitted with the decisive vote of Athena, Athens' patron goddess. In the *Kolonos,* Oedipus' analogous acquittal takes place in his own mind. He defends his innocence three times in the play, arguing each time with increasing force and vehemence; he was ignorant, he says, at the moment he acted, of the identity of the man he killed and the woman who bore him children, and therefore free of moral guilt.[13]

> Before the law
> my hands are clean.
> My actions were driven
> not by malice,
> but by ignorance. (546–48/599–603)

[10] See Theseus' and Antigone's insistence (1179–80/1290–94 and 1181–1203/1294–1316) that Oedipus hear Polyneikes' appeal.

[11] A deme was a political subdivision of Athens.

[12] See *Kolonos* n. 44–50.

[13] What remains and cannot be eradicated is defilement; we see Oedipus acknowledge that he is literally untouchable when he withdraws his impulse to touch Theseus in gratitude for rescuing his daughters (1130–34/1239–44).

The *Kolonos* works as a sequence of *agons,* or painful confrontations, in which Oedipus vanquishes all adversaries on his way to a triumphal end in the Eumenides' sacred grove. It also functions as a progression of enhancements that gradually prepares him for his final transformation. A closer look at several scenes shows each one building on its predecessor, each registering an aspect of Oedipus' improving *tyche* and his claim to the status of a *heros.*

The *Kolonos'* first episode (1–116/1–126) prepares us for the Chorus' and Theseus' subsequent entrances, but it also introduces most of the drama's central themes. The Stranger who happens upon the travelweary father and daughter, and who warns them not to invade the sacred grove, also confirms that this grove is the very place named in the oracle that Apollo gave to Oedipus long ago at Delphi. As soon as Oedipus hears the word "Eumenides" he swears he'll never leave the ground he's on; the name "Kindly Ones" is his personal and fateful sign: "It all fits: *here* is where I meet my fate" (46/54).

Hearing this, the Stranger correctly assumes this sign must be a god-sanctioned one that places Oedipus under divine protection and elevates him immediately from his vulnerable homeless status. The Stranger also identifies the horseman Kolonos (whose statue is on stage) as the community's founder; he refers to him as a *theos,* a word whose primary meaning is "god" but which also may mean a godlike *heros.* Within the play's opening minutes Oedipus has been introduced to two sets of local deities, gods and heroes, whose ranks he will eventually join. The entire drama has been prefigured within the first hundred lines.

At the end of the next episode, after Oedipus has grudgingly revealed his identity to the Old Men and tried to calm their resulting alarm, Ismene arrives in a glow of reunion soon darkened by the sharp breach between Oedipus' love for his caring daughters and his hatred of his neglectful sons. He praises his daughters for their masculine courage and castigates his absent sons as unmanly shirkers. But Ismene challenges the accusation. The brothers, in fact, are at each other's throats, about to fight a pitched battle for the throne of Thebes. Equally startling, however, are the new oracles Ismene brings and her account of how these oracles have panicked Thebes. One oracle states that Oedipus has become indispensable to the Thebans—if they bury his body just outside their territory, his remains (apparently backed by his hovering and still potent ghost) will defend them against enemy assault. "[Y]ou will hold Thebes' life in your hands," Ismene tells him (392/427).

Oedipus wonders how his corpse could possess such power. "The gods who tore you down will restore you," she explains (394/429). He bristles ruefully at the deities' tardy change of heart, but seems to accept it:

> Does little good to restore an old man
> after they have laid waste his youth. (395/430–431)

When Oedipus presses Ismene to define exactly what his buried self will possess that Thebans must fear, she utters the crucial word: "Your *rage*, when they're deployed around your tomb" (411/448). Within seconds, Oedipus unleashes his rage against his two sons. May his sons kill each other, he wishes, in remorseless retaliation for their past refusal to prevent his banishment. Then, in a stunning blaze of authority, he asks the gods to let him control the outcome of the coming siege of Thebes. "Gods, don't interfere with this brawl you've ordained!" (421/458ff.).

It doesn't take Oedipus long to connect this new oracle, which reveals the immortal power of his fury, with the much older oracle that led him to the grove of the Kindly Ones.

> . . . when I heard the oracles
> this girl brought, I recalled some prophecies—
> ones Phoibos Apollo has now fulfilled. (452–54/488–490)

He understands that the gods who destroyed him long ago in Thebes will empower him in a new way, in a different field of action—within a *heros'* grave. "To remain a man" will now mean to possess after death the primary attribute of all *heroes,* the ability to harm enemies. Oedipus then tells the Old Men he's ready to join Athens—not as a burden but as their defender. The power Thebes fears in him will make him just as valuable to Athens as he would be to Thebes, and his burial in the Grove of the Kindly Ones will unite the prophecies of two oracles widely separated in time.[14]

From here on Oedipus presents himself unapologetically to the Athenians as a gift. Clearly he's an unnerving gift, defiled and dangerous, as the Old Men let him know. In due course he'll win them over. By swiftly making sense of the perplexing information in the new oracles— as we know from *Oedipus the King,* he's skilled at solving riddles— Oedipus demonstrates that once again he brings immediate value to the city that welcomes him.

A curious (but critical) event occurs just after Oedipus, now confident of his new powers, offers to protect Athens against its enemies. The Old Men urge him to perform an atonement ritual that asks the Kindly Goddesses to forgive him for invading their grove and to grant him their protection (461–92/499–531). The ritual involves pouring pure water, collecting and bundling olive branches, and saying a brief prayer. If he doesn't perform the ritual exactly as they specify—or send someone to do it in his behalf—he'll be in serious trouble, the Old Men warn. Oedipus listens and questions them intently, perhaps showing

[14] Herakles similarly dovetails two distinct oracles in Sophokles' *The Women of Trachis.*

mild impatience, but he falls in with the religious observance. He allows himself none of the brash tone, familiar address, or slight edge of presumption that infused his initial prayers to the Goddesses: "don't be unkind / either to me or to Apollo" (86–87/94–95); "do as Apollo bids" (102/110); "Respond to me, / delightful daughters of primeval darkness" (106/114–15). Throughout the purification catechism he remains gratefully attentive. Though the significance of each ritual detail might now be lost, the purpose served by Sophokles' elaboration of it is clear: the Old Men have accepted Oedipus into their religious world; they repay his promised protection of Athens with their Eumenides-placating instructions. But as Oedipus becomes more acquiescent to the gods, he grows angrier and more alienated from his human relationships.[15]

When the Leader begins to badger Oedipus about his incestuous marriage, we might wonder at his undignified inquisitiveness. But this worthy gentleman is simply less circumspect than the rest of the characters, almost all of whom invoke Oedipus' defiling acts when they interact with him—even when seeking his help.[16] Theseus alone seems above such tactics; to this seasoned warrior-king Oedipus' wounds and sufferings are badges of honor. The Chorus Leader is understandably persistent in forcing Oedipus to dwell on his parricide and incest. He and his fellow Athenians, full of prurient but entirely human curiosity, want to know what that famous Oedipal anguish felt like in all its rawness. The Old Men—and we—hear it from the sufferer's own mouth:[17]

> Thebes married me, who suspected nothing,
> to a woman who would destroy me. . . . (525–26/568–69)

> And those daughters I fathered . . .
>   —twin scourges . . .
> were born from the birthpangs
> of our shared mother. (530–33/574–77)

> I suffered an indelible torment . . . (537/582)

As the Old Men discover, Oedipus' torment and the effects of defilement remain keen. Such misery weighs down one side of Oedipus' balance scale (to adopt the Greeks' metaphor for assessing the gravity of rival forces in one person's life); but in the end the gods will weigh in to lift Oedipus up.

Oedipus, who entered Kolonos a suppliant, will now receive suppliants himself only to reject them—first Kreon and then his own eldest son Polyneikes. Kreon attempts to manipulate Oedipus into re-

[15] See *Kolonos* n. 503.
[16] Antigone, for instance, reminds Oedipus that evil begets evil, as his parents' fate proves; therefore Oedipus should be reluctant to reject Polyneikes' appeal.
[17] In excerpting Oedipus' admissions, I have omitted the Leader's interruptions.

turning home to Thebes by using his misfortunes against him (728–1043/795–1144). *You're in miserable shape,* says Kreon, *your squalor disgraces you and your family, you're degrading your daughter, you would be better off under your family's roof, so leave Athens now and come home with me.* Oedipus' savage responses—informed by his superior insight and rhetoric—remind us that his mind was always his sharpest weapon. Oedipus is back in form. His sense of timing—and Time itself—in this discourse is impressive: our needs change, our wounds heal, our lives move on, he says.[18] A home (and eventually a tomb) in Athens has become his passionate desire. His argument against Kreon won, Oedipus ends his speech by demonstrating what makes him so valuable: his fury. That fury, he promises all within earshot, will be deadly to his own sons; their graves in Thebes will be their only patrimony. He soon has his chance to deliver that message directly to Polyneikes, who arrives in Kolonos just as Theseus returns from rescuing Oedipus' kidnapped daughters and sending Kreon back toward Thebes.

Misguided and doomed as Polyneikes is, there is something initially appealing about him as he comes onstage. The last of the characters to challenge Oedipus, he immediately owns up to neglecting shamefully his father's welfare and nurture. He admits past failure, doesn't appear to be crudely manipulative, and states his desperate situation frankly: his attempt to win Thebes back depends on the good will of this blind old man—the father whom he turned out of Thebes to die on the roads.

Oedipus had reluctantly agreed, at the request of Antigone, to hear Polyneikes' plea. But Polyneikes' luck has expired. Like Kreon, Polyneikes repeatedly undermines his own pretensions. He equates himself with Oedipus—don't they both share the shame of exiled suppliants? Cannot they make common cause to defeat their enemies and regain what has been wrongfully taken from each? But their situations are not comparable. Oedipus brings Theseus and Athens, in exchange for their generous welcome, a gift of robust value. Polyneikes, in pursuing his lust for power, offers his father nothing in exchange but the grief (or pleasure) of seeing his other son killed. The ingrained fecklessness in Polyneikes' character, his blindness to others' feelings and interests, dooms him.

In these last few scenes Oedipus has conducted himself as a passionate but imperfect human being. He utterly despises Polyneikes and his plea; his sole measure of both his sons' worthiness remains their failure to protect and nurture him. But suddenly Oedipus begins to act with godlike force and assurance. He kills his sons in his imagination—

[18] Oedipus personifies Time, or *Kronos*. Time is a companion who teaches acquiescence (7–8/7–8); later Time is fickle, first a betrayer, then a restorer of trust (607–20/665–78).

with conviction and without remorse. His earlier wish that both sons die, begun as a prayer, escalates to full-throated, raging prophecy. Finally, he summons Ares, the god of war, to carry out the curse he delivers. Thus Sophokles foreshadows Oedipus' ultimate transformation:

> [Y]ou'll never win this war on your homeland;
> you won't survive to skulk back to the plains
> of Argos. By your brother's hand you will
> die—as you'll kill the man who threw you out.
> That is my curse: and I ask the blackest
> paternal darkness of the underworld
> to become your new home in Tartaros;
> I summon the spirits native to this place;
> I summon Ares the Destroyer, who has
> inflamed your minds with murderous hatred! (1385–92/1514–23)

The ferocity he once turned inward he now turns on his sons.[19] Such fury recalls the ancient road rage with which Oedipus shed his own father's blood. In this passage from *Oedipus the King,* he recalled the murder of Laios with present-tense vividness:

> The old man watches me,
> he measures my approach, then leans out
> lunging with his two-spiked goad
> dead at my skull. He's more than repaid:
> I hit him so fast with the staff
> this hand holds, he's knocked back
> rolling off the cart. Where he lies, face up.
> Then I kill them all. (806–13/929–36)

The two situations differ, of course. Oedipus was unaware of Laios' identity as he struck him the fatal blow, while now, an old man himself, he knows exactly whom he would kill and why. He never ponders whether it is just to will his sons' death. During his *agon* with Kreon, Oedipus claims to know the future better than his Theban adversary because his sources are better: "Apollo . . . and Zeus." By invoking the power of Ares in prophesying his sons' deaths, Oedipus already seems possessed of a Zeus-like power over the god of war. He's driven by the *heros'* credo: to destroy ones' enemies, even if the enemies happen to be his own flesh and blood.

Oedipus' fury activated the curse on the house of Labdakos,

---

[19] Oedipus' lack of remorse, his savage treatment of Polyneikes, remains the most troubling, antipathetic feature of the *Kolonos,* despite our understanding of the pent-up emotion behind it (and our knowledge that such emotion was reinforced by a fifth-century Athenian law requiring children to care for their parents in old age).

which as a young man he tried so disastrously to evade.[20] Now it dooms his daughters as well. Antigone will die as her principled stubbornness reinforces the ancient curse. Ismene survives, though she declares in *Antigone* that hers will not be much of a life with her sister gone. Oedipus has, once again, killed them all—his sons deliberately, his daughters as collateral damage.

If the *Kolonos* were about a tyrant whose pretension to godlike powers demanded his destruction, such proud claims would put Oedipus in mortal danger. In this play Sophokles does not so judge Oedipus; he affirms his *heros'* belief that the gods speak directly to him and will respond to his wishes. The Messenger will quote the exact words a godly voice used to beckon Oedipus from life into death (1627–28/1780–83). Oedipus is mortal, he will die, but the long postponement of his death— during which he suffered physical and spiritual deprivation as well as incurable remorse for the damage he inflicted on his parents, children, and city—has earned him in the end a *heros'* death. Earlier in the play Kreon failed to see (perhaps understandably) that the usual rules governing the human condition do not apply to Oedipus:

> Anger doesn't diminish
> as we age. It consumes us till we die.
> Only the dead are immune from anguish. (954–55/1038–40)

But anger proves to be something Oedipus does take with him to Hades.

The implication that Oedipus absorbs godlike characteristics, first embedded in the lethal prophecies hurled by father at son, is further expressed through Sophokles' uncanny ability to make ordinary human actions radiate divinity. Oedipus, leading his sighted companions, strides off to his secret destination within the grove needing no eyes to find his way and no walking stick to support him.[21] Then the Messenger describes in detail Oedipus' transformation from man to *heros:* the gods' thunderous approval; their direct and repeated words urging Oedipus to come to them; his unprecedented mode of departure from this world to the next; the implicit cleansing of his lifelong defilement.

There's no doubt Oedipus still feels the painful defilement he carries from his crimes against his parents; his awareness of his defiled condition stops him, for instance, from grasping Theseus' hand.[22] No soul-searching or lawyerly justification can end the suffering that the Old Men are so crudely curious about—the "incurable anguish" Oedipus feels for killing his father and sleeping with his mother. In Sophokles' rendering of Oedipus' majestic and miraculous death he addresses this

---

[20] Labdakos was a former king of Thebes and the father of Laios. For details of the curse see introduction to *Oed King*.
[21] See *Kolonos* n. 927.
[22] See footnote 13 above.

outward defilement and inner "indelible torment" with imagery subtler—but more shocking, perhaps—than that which he uses to describe Oedipus' gradual acquisition of godlike qualities. Before we can fully understand this imagery we must return to the *Eumenides,* the final play in Aeschylus' *Oresteia* trilogy.

Oedipus' legal argument—that he was innocent of blame for his parents' death—has a counterpart in the *Eumenides:* Apollo's remarkable justification for Orestes' killing his mother, Klytemnestra.[23] The god declares that we all have but one parent, the father who mounts the woman and plants his human seed; the mother who carries the child and gives birth is not a true parent. Ergo, killing a mother is not kin murder of the same magnitude as killing a male parent.[24] Though Apollo's argument now seems preposterous—the authority of ancient myth is no match for the certainties of modern genetics—in the play it persuaded half the Areopagus' jury and Athena to acquit Orestes. The argument made sense to the Athenians; a century later Aristotle still invoked it.

Immediately after he has killed his mother in the *Libation Bearers,* the second play of Aeschylus' trilogy, the foul, snake-haired Furies, who demand that kin murderers be pursued and punished, pay Orestes a visit. But they "appear" only to him—not to the dancers on stage or to the audience—as a manifestation of his inner torment and guilt.[25] Early in the *Eumenides* the goddesses are made visible to all. They emerge from Apollo's temple at Delphi (where Orestes had gone to be outwardly cleansed of the physical defilement incurred by his parricide) and follow him to Athens, where Athena will offer them their newly diminished role. They accept, shedding their black cloaks, and reappear (in a processional joined by Athenian citizens at the end of the play) as Kindly Ones in cloaks of crimson—a color, we are told, suggestive of good will and harmony. The Kindly Ones, it seems, will no longer automatically make kin murderers their quarry; in Aeschylus' vision they will need a court's concurrence to do so. The "makeover" of the Furies into Kindly Ones, a spectacular counterpart to Oedipus' transformation from old, blind beggar to triumphant *heros,* is the only outward sign in the *Eumenides* that Orestes has been relieved of his self-loathing. He does, however, make a promise directly relevant to Oedipus' own heroic power:

[23] After Klytemnestra killed Orestes' father, Agamemnon, Apollo demanded that Orestes avenge his father's death by killing his mother.

[24] "The mother is no parent of that which is called / her child, but only the nurse of the new-planted seed / that grows. The parent is he who mounts." (Aeschylus, *Eumenides,* 658–60, p. 158.)

[25] Oedipus' Furies are visible on stage throughout the *Kolonos* as the daughters he loves, permanent reminders, he says, of his incest. They will stay with him until he leaves for Hades.

> I shall go home now, but before I go I swear
> to this your country and to this your multitude . . .
> that never man who holds the helm of my state shall come
> against your country in the ordered strength of spears,
> but though I lie then in my grave, I still shall wreak
> helpless bad luck and misadventure upon all
> who stride across the oath that I have sworn . . .[26]

Orestes rewards the Athenians for providing the political instrument of his exoneration with a promise almost identical to the one Oedipus makes in the *Kolonos*. The ghosts of both *heroes* will defend Athens against its enemies—Orestes' from his future grave in Argos, Oedipus' from within Athens' own territory. The similarities between the two characters become more apparent when we see how the gods grant Oedipus an end to the "incurable anguish" of incest and parricide he feels through most of the play. They do this by calling him home— "You there. Oedipus! / . . . Why do we hesitate? / You've waited far too long" (1627–28/1781–83)—and by controlling the nature of his entry into Hades.

The prophecy Apollo made to the young Oedipus—that when his suffering has ceased and he is at the point of death, safe haven awaits him in a grove of the Eumenides—parallels the change of Orestes' Furies from hounding tormentors into protectors of the family. Both Oedipus and Orestes live through a dynamic in which a crime changes who they are for the better. Fury drove Oedipus to commit acts that fulfilled Apollo's original prophecy. A great peacefulness—and a transformation of self-destructive fury into a harnessed rage that protects what Oedipus values, his adopted city Athens—will attend his entry into Hades and his emergence into his afterlife as a *heros*.

But Oedipus' transformation in the Grove of the Kindly Ones involves more than his fury. His crimes against his mother and father are forgiven and reimagined in a way that extends beyond any legal justification. Sophokles lets us glimpse (more than see) this transformation through the eyes of the Messenger, a witness who does not have a close-up view—only Theseus has that privilege—but one who imagines fully what he partially sees. Here the Messenger recounts the death of Oedipus:

> But the exact nature
> of the death Oedipus died, no man
> but Theseus could tell you. Zeus didn't
> incinerate him with a lightning blast,
> no sudden squall blew inland from the sea.
> So it was either a god spiriting

[26] Aeschylus, *Eumenides*, 762–69, p. 162.

> him away, or else the Earth's lower world—
> her deep foundations—opening to him,
> for he felt nothing but welcoming kindness.
>
> When this man vanished, there was no sorrow,
> he suffered no sickness; his death, like no
> other man's, was a cause for wonder. (1656–65/1812–23)

The Messenger takes it upon himself to note what Oedipus' death was not—no violent punishing by Zeus, no lightning blast, no abduction by hurricane. Sorrow, suffering, sickness—none is present. It was indeed a death that blessed and suggested forgiveness, a death administered in all its gentleness by the Earth mother, Gaia. She opened to him, allowing him no sense of violation, "for he felt nothing but welcoming kindness" (1662/1820). It was as if dying into Hades reenacted Oedipus' sexual union with Jokasta, the cause of the intolerable pain he carried throughout his life, and transformed it into an act of healing.

The Messengers' speeches in *Oedipus the King* and *Antigone* also use sexual imagery to deliver news at climactic moments, although the imagery in these earlier plays is more graphic and violent than in the *Kolonos*, where a joyful mood is wholly ascendant. In *Antigone* Haimon's lifeblood spurts onto Antigone's pale corpse as he falls and embraces her:

> Then this raging youth—with no warning—turned
> on himself, tensed his body to the sword,
> and drove half its length deep into his side.
> Still conscious, he clung to her with limp arms,
> gasping for breath, spurts of his blood pulsing
> onto her white cheek.
>   Then he lay there, his dead
> body embracing hers, married at last,
> poor man—not up here, but somewhere
> in Hades . . . (1234–41/1368–76)

In *Oedipus the King* the Messenger uses verbs with a similar sexual thrust to explain how Oedipus enters Jokasta's bedroom:[27]

> As though someone were guiding him, he lunged,
> with a savage yell, at the double doors,
> wrenching the bolts from their sockets.
> He burst into the room. We saw her there:
> the woman above us, hanging by the neck,
> swaying there in a noose of tangled cords.

[27] The Greek verbs *hallesthai*, "lunged at," and *piptein*, "burst," give a precise picture of the violence done to the door, but they strongly suggest that the violence is sexual (Gould 1970, 144).

He saw. And bellowing in anguish
he reached up, loosened the noose that held her.
(1260–67/1428–35)

It is characteristic of Sophokles' lifelong imaginative honesty to describe Oedipus' painless death with an image that conveys turbulence
and release, an image fully appropriate to Oedipus' escape from com-
promised life to powerful afterlife. If we look at the specific words
Sophokles uses, his intent becomes ever clearer. The Greek verb I translate as "opening to him" derives from *diastano*—which means to tear
apart, to break through—and is often used to describe both the sexual
and childbearing functions of the vagina.[28] Gaia's welcome of Oedipus
occurs within her deepest foundations, where birth and copulation are
joined in *charis* as they were joined in horror during Oedipus' life.

The play pauses in equilibrium at this moment, but as soon as the
Messenger finishes we plunge back into the contentious earthly life of
the survivors. Ismene and Antigone marvel at their father's death, disagree, almost quarrel, and then grieve so passionately that the Leader
and Theseus reproach them for not accepting the divine blessings inherent in their father's death. The two men urge the daughters to calm
themselves and accept this new reality; they agree to send the women
home to Thebes.[29]

Conflict and its resolution animate all drama and the *Kolonos,* up
to this point, shows us conflict in abundance. But Sophokles leaves us
with an implied question and a problem to contemplate in the Messenger's testy exit lines:

If anyone listening doesn't believe me,
I have no interest in persuading him
that I am not some credulous fool. (1665–66/1824–26)

Should we believe this miracle? Did the Messenger address any religious skeptics in the Theater of Dionysos?

The Messenger's description raises a further question. If we accept the beauty of Oedipus' death, should we also accept its moral implications? And what are these? Sophokles has first shown us an older

---

[28] Segal 1981, 400, implicitly acknowledges this meaning of *diastano,* calling
the parting of the earth a "mysterious good will and patient, parturient divi-
sion of the lower world."

[29] In these final, literally anticlimactic moments Sophokles connects the *Kolonos*
to *Antigone,* the first Oedipus play to be produced. In that play the two sisters
resume their clash of wills; Antigone will fulfill the dangerous promise she
made in the *Kolonos:* to bury Polyneikes. Our thoughts jump, as Sophokles
must have intended them to do, ahead to Antigone—on the morning after
Eteokles and Polyneikes have killed each other—as she stands outside Oedipus' old palace at Thebes, in the predawn chill, and waits for Ismene.

Oedipus, to adapt Yeats' phrase, "forgiving himself the lot"—all the actions that poisoned his life in his own mind and in the minds of his contemporaries. In the course of the Messenger's speech Sophokles shows us Zeus, Hermes, Persphone, the Eumenides—both the Olympian and the earthy or "chthonic" deities—hovering about the sacred grove as Oedipus enters it, suggesting they approve his painless death.[30]

If Athenian playwrights were teachers who embedded their wisdom in their dramas—and their official name, *didaskoloi,* asserts they were—Sophokles' final lesson says at least this much: Oedipus' own legal and philosophic self-scrutiny convinced him in the inner world of his conscience that he was innocent of crimes he committed unknowingly. The gods had already punished him savagely for these actions; they do not punish him as he dies. Just as surely, the gods do not punish him for the brave voyage of self-examination that leads to his self-forgiveness. Zeus' thunder announcing a magical death inspires awe. No less awesome is Zeus' silence when Oedipus declares the right to be the final judge of his own moral sanctity. The gods who congregate in the grove of the Eumenides do not dispute that right; they confirm it. Perhaps Sophokles intended the thunder winging Oedipus toward his death to resonate in his Athenian audience with this news: the gods, with all their *charis,* now applaud the human mind's freedom to forgive itself.

[30] The Olympians in this instance are Zeus and Hermes (who keeps a fleet foot in both realms); the chthonic divinities are Hades, Persephone, and the Furies/ Kindly Ones.

Oedipus at Kolonos

CHARACTERS	Oedipus
	Antigone
	Stranger
	Old Men of Kolonos (Chorus)
	Leader (of the Chorus)
	Ismene
	Ismene's Servant (silent)
	Theseus
	Theseus' Men (silent)
	Kreon
	Kreon's Soldiers (silent)
	Polyneikes
	Messenger

SCENE	*In the countryside a mile and a quarter northwest of the Acropolis in Athens. A sacred grove is at stage rear. Olives, grape vines, crocus, and narcissus bloom within it; birds sing and fountains splash. A path leads over the gentle rise down into the grove's depths. A natural stone bench sits upstage just inside the grove. A rock ledge running across the slope has a flat sitting place at its lower downstage end; near it is a statue of the hero Kolonos. Entering from the road to Thebes on spectators' left, Antigone guides her father, the aged Oedipus, onstage. Both are dusty and weary. Oedipus carries a staff and a traveler's pouch.*

OEDIPUS	Daughter, I'm old and blind. Where are we now, Antigone? Have we come to a town?
	(Calling out.) Who will indulge Wandering Oedipus today—with some food and a place to sleep?
	I ask little, I'm given less, but it's enough. The blows I've suffered have taught me acquiescence. So has Time, my enduring companion. So has my noble birth.
	Daughter, if you see somewhere \<10\> to rest—on public land, or in a grove set aside for the gods— guide me to it, sit me down there. Then we'll determine where we are. We're strangers here. We must listen to the locals and do what they say.
ANTIGONE	My poor exhausted father! Oedipus, the towers guarding the city seem far off. I have the feeling we're in some holy place— \<20\> there's so much olive and laurel and grape vine running wild. Listen. Deep inside, it's packed with nightingales! Rest on this ledge. For an old man, this has been a long trek.
OEDIPUS	Ease the blind man down. Be my lookout.
ANTIGONE	No need to tell me! I've been doing this awhile.
	(Oedipus sits on a stone outcrop just inside the grove.)
OEDIPUS	Now, can you tell me where we are?
ANTIGONE	Athens, but I don't know which part.
OEDIPUS	Travelers on the road told us that much.
ANTIGONE	Shouldn't I go ask what this place is called? \<30\>
OEDIPUS	Do that, child. If this place can support life.
ANTIGONE	But people *do* live here. No need to search. I see a man nearby. Right over there.
OEDIPUS	Is he headed in our direction?
	(Enter Stranger who strides toward them.)

ANTIGONE   *(Whispering.)*
            No. He's already close. Whatever seems
            called for, say it to him now. He's here.

OEDIPUS   Stranger, this girl—whose eyes see for us both—
            tells me that you've arrived opportunely,
            to help us resolve our quandary . . .

STRANGER   Hold it.
            Before you start asking *me* questions,   <40>
            get off that rock! You're on forbidden ground.

            (Antigone helps Oedipus rise slowly to his feet.)

OEDIPUS   What kind of ground? Belonging to which gods?

STRANGER   It's off limits. No one's allowed to live here.
            It's sacred to fearsome goddesses—
            daughters of Darkness and the Earth.

OEDIPUS   By what respectful name do you call them—
            since I'm about to offer them a prayer?

STRANGER   People here call them the Kindly Ones—
            the goddesses who see everything.
            Other places might give them harsher names.   <50>

OEDIPUS   Then let them be kind to *this* suppliant!
            I'll never leave this sacred ground.

STRANGER   Why do you say that?

OEDIPUS   It all fits: *here* is where I meet my fate.

STRANGER   Well then, I won't presume to drive you out.
            Not till I get permission from the city.

            (Stranger prepares to leave.)

OEDIPUS   For god's sake, man! Don't scorn me because I
            look like a tramp. I need to know something.

STRANGER   Then say what you need. I won't hold back.

OEDIPUS   This place we've entered—what do they call it?   <60>

STRANGER   I'll say only what I know *personally.*
            This entire grove is holy and belongs
            to grim Poseidon. Prometheus the firegod
            also has a shrine here. That rock ledge
            you're on is our country's brass-footed threshold.
            It anchors Athens. The horseman over there—

(Stranger gestures toward an equestrian statue.)

is Kolonos, who settled the farmland
hereabouts. We've all taken his name. That's
the story, stranger. Kolonos isn't
so much a legend as a presence we feel.   <70>

| OEDIPUS | Then people do live around here? |
| STRANGER | Of course! They're named after that hero there. |

(Stranger nods toward the statue of Kolonos.)

OEDIPUS	You have a king? Or do the people rule?
STRANGER	We have a king who governs from Athens.
OEDIPUS	Whose eloquence and strength brought him to power?
STRANGER	Theseus. Old King Aigeus' son.
OEDIPUS	I wonder . . . could someone from here go find him?
STRANGER	To take a message? Bring him back? What for?
OEDIPUS	To be hugely repaid for a small kindness.
STRANGER	Tell me, how can a blind man be of use? <80>
OEDIPUS	All my words have a vision of their own.

STRANGER Look, friend, don't do anything reckless.
Your bearing tells me you're from noble stock,
but it's clear you're down on your luck.
Stay put, right where I found you, while I go
let the men in town know what's happened.
Never mind Athens—*we* will decide
whether you stay here or move on.

(Exit Stranger.)

OEDIPUS	Has the stranger left, child?
ANTIGONE	He's gone, father. You can speak freely. <90>
	It's quiet now. I'm the only one here.

(Oedipus takes a posture of prayer.)

OEDIPUS Ladies whose eyes we dread, since your grove
is the first in this land where I've come to pray,
don't be unkind
either to me or to Apollo.
When the god condemned me to such grief,
he assured me my long life would end here—

that I'd find a haven, and be taken in
by vengeful goddesses, to be a source
of strength to those who welcomed me, and a curse   <100>
to those who drove me out. The god promised
he'd show a sign—an earthquake, some thunder
or lightning flamed from Zeus's own hand.

It must have been, Ladies, a trustworthy
omen from you that led me to this place.
Why else would you be the first deities
I've met on my travels? I—a sober man—
find my way to you, who spurn wine. What else
could have brought me to this rough stone bench?

Please, Goddesses, do as Apollo bids: <110>
grant me a clear path to my life's end—unless
I seem in some way beneath your concern,
profaned as I am by the worst evils
a man may endure. Respond to me,
delightful daughters of primeval darkness!
And help me Athens, most
honored city in Greece,
homeland of Pallas Athena! Pity
this feeble ghost of the man Oedipus.
My body hasn't always looked like this.   <120>

ANTIGONE   Shhh, be quiet now. Some old men—they look
            ancient!—have come searching for you.

OEDIPUS   I'll be quiet. Get me to the trees,
            off the road, so I can hear what they say.
            What we learn will help us
            decide our best course of action.

            (Antigone guides Oedipus up the slope and into the grove.
            Chorus of Old Men enters. Gracefully they probe along
            the grove's edge in a coordinated dancing movement
            while singing their entry song.)

OLD MEN   Look for him,
            though we don't know
            who he is, or where
            he's hiding now.   <130>
            He's bolted for cover,
            totally brazen!
            Search the whole grove.
            Look sharp, look everywhere.

The old fellow's
a foreigner, an intruder;
no native would invade
prohibited grounds
of virgins so violent,
so uncontrollable—   <140>
their very names
we fear to say out loud.
We walk in their midst,
eyes lowered, not breathing
a word, though our lips
mouth silent prayers.

LEADER   We've heard the report:
Someone with no respect
for the goddesses has arrived.
But looking across the sacred glen   <150>
I don't see him or his hiding place.

(Oedipus steps forward from the foliage.)

OEDIPUS   I'm here. The man you're looking for. I see
with my ears, as people say of the blind.

LEADER   Ahhh! Ahhh!
The sight of you, the sound of your voice, appalls us.

OEDIPUS   Don't look at me as though I'm some outlaw.

LEADER   Keep us safe, Zeus. Who is this ancient man?

OEDIPUS   Not someone whose life you might envy—
you men charged with guarding your country!
Isn't that obvious? Why else   <160>
would I walk as I do, dependent
on other people's eyes, and tethered,
large as I am, to this frail creature?

LEADER   Were you born blind?
You must have led a long
bleak life. Take our advice:
Don't add one more curse
to your miseries. You've gone
too far! Please step back!
Don't go stumbling   <170>
through that green glade
where speech is forbidden,
where we pour

clear water from a bowl,
blending it
with honey-sweet libations.

Watch yourself,
stranger with such
horrendous luck—
stand back, walk away!   <180>
Move further back!
Do you hear me? If you
have something to tell us,
get off that sacred ground!
Speak only
where talk is allowed.
Until then, keep quiet.

OEDIPUS   Daughter, what should we do?

ANTIGONE   Respect their customs, father.
Defer and obey as required.   <190>

OEDIPUS   Give me your hand, then.

ANTIGONE   Here, feel mine.

*(Oedipus, with Antigone supporting him, very
cautiously approaches the cluster of elders.)*

OEDIPUS   I'm going to trust you, strangers. Don't
betray me when I leave this holy ground.

LEADER   Nobody will force you to leave
this resting place against your will.

(Oedipus pauses in his progress.)

OEDIPUS   Further?

LEADER   Keep going.

OEDIPUS   More?

LEADER   Keep him moving, girl, you can see the path.

ANTIGONE   Come on, father.   <200>
Keep stepping
into the dark
as I lead you.

LEADER   You are, old man, a stranger
in a strange land.
Accustom yourself

to hating what our city
despises and revering
what it loves.

OEDIPUS   Guide me, child, to some spot   <210>
where I can speak and listen
without offending the gods.
Let's not fight the inevitable.

LEADER   Stop right there. Don't move
beyond that rock ledge.

OEDIPUS   Stop here?

LEADER   That's far enough, I'm telling you!

OEDIPUS   May I sit down?

LEADER   Yes. Edge sideways and squat down on that rock.

(Antigone holds Oedipus and guides his steps.)

ANTIGONE   Father, let me do this. Take one   <220>
easy step after another . . .

OEDIPUS   Oh, my.

ANTIGONE   . . . leaning your tired body
on my loving arm.

OEDIPUS   I'm sorry for my weakness.

(Antigone sits him on the rock ledge downstage.)

LEADER   Poor fellow, now that you're at ease,
tell us who you are in the world.
Who would want to be moved about
in such excruciating pain?
Tell us where you live.

OEDIPUS   Strangers, I have no home! But please don't . . . <230>

LEADER   What don't you want us to ask, old man?

OEDIPUS   Don't! Just don't ask who I am.
No questions, no more probing.

LEADER   Is there a reason?

OEDIPUS   The horror I was born to.

LEADER   Go on.

OEDIPUS   *(Whispering.)*
Child, what should I tell them?

LEADER	Speak up, stranger: tell us your bloodlines. Start with your father.
OEDIPUS	What's going to happen to me, child?
ANTIGONE	You've been pushed to the brink. Better tell them.
OEDIPUS	All right, I'll say it. There's no way to hide it.

<240>

LEADER	You both take too much time. Go on, speak.
OEDIPUS	You've heard of Laios' son . . .
OLD MEN	*Aaaaah!*
OEDIPUS	. . . and the house of Labdakos . . .
OLD MEN	O Zeus!
OEDIPUS	. . . and doomed Oedipus?
LEADER	That's who you are?
OEDIPUS	Don't fear my words . . .
OLD MEN	Aaagghhh! Aaagghhh!

(As their cries of apprehension overwhelm Oedipus'
previous words, the Old Men en bloc turn away from him.)

OEDIPUS	. . . because I am a broken man.
OLD MEN	Aaagghhh! Aaagghhh!
OEDIPUS	What's going to happen, child?
LEADER	Get out of here! Leave our country!

<250>

OEDIPUS	And the promise you made me? How do you plan to honor that?
LEADER	When someone who's been wronged defends himself by striking back, fate doesn't punish him. And when deception is used to counter deceit, it should cause pain, not gratitude. Stand up! Now! Get off that seat! Leave this land as fast as you can walk, so you won't burden our city with your deadly contagion.

<260>

ANTIGONE	Strangers, so full of holy sentiments! You can't abide my agèd father's presence, can you? Because you've heard the rumors about those actions he took in ignorance. Think how unhappy it makes me

to plead with you on my father's behalf.
Strangers, I am looking at you with eyes
that aren't blind, and I beg *you* to see *me*
as though I were your family—and to feel
responsible for this afflicted man.   <270>
Our miserable lives depend on you
as if you all were gods. Give us the help
that we've stopped hoping for!

I'm begging you, in the name
of whatever you hold dear—
whether it's your child or your wife,
your fortune or your god!
                    However hard
you look, you'll never find a man who can
escape his own fate-driven actions.

LEADER   We pity both of you, daughter—   <280>
you and your father Oedipus.
You've led unfortunate lives.
But we fear the gods, we fear their anger,
if we say more than we've already said.

OEDIPUS   What good are fame and glory, if they just
trickle away and accomplish nothing?
Men call Athens the most god-fearing city,
a safe haven for persecuted strangers,
their best hope when they need a helping hand.
But how do these virtues benefit me   <290>
when you force me to climb down these ledges
and depart from your country? Does my *name*
frighten you? My appearance? Or my past deeds?
I performed every one of those actions,
you should know, but I willed none. You want me
to speak of my relations with my father
and mother—is that the source of your fear?

I have no doubt it is exactly that.
Yet, tell me: how is my *nature* evil—
if all I did was to return a blow?   <300>
How could I have been guilty, even if
I'd known where my actions would take me
while I was living them? But those who tried
to murder me—*they knew* what they were doing.

My friends, the gods inspired you to drive
me off that ledge. So respect these same gods—

and grant me the refuge that you've offered.
Don't act *now* as though gods don't exist.
They protect those who fear them,
but they also destroy those who don't.   <310>
And no godless mortal ever escapes.

Let the gods show you the way: Don't blacken
Athens' reputation by taking part
in crimes of irreverence! I am
a suppliant to whom you promised
safety. Don't break that promise. And don't
shun me because of my disfigured face.
I've come here a devout and sacred man,
and I'll prove myself useful to your people.
When the man who holds power arrives,   <320>
whoever that may be, I will tell him
everything. Until then, do me no harm.

LEADER   We're impressed by the way you think, old man.
How could we not be? You speak with force.
We don't take you lightly, but we'd prefer
to have our rulers deal with this problem.

OEDIPUS   Where then, my friends, is this leader of yours?

LEADER   He's now in Athens, his home city. The same
person who sent us went on to find him.

OEDIPUS   Do you think he'll have sufficient   <330>
concern and regard for a blind old man
to travel all the way out here himself?

LEADER   He will come as soon as he hears your name.

OEDIPUS   And how will he hear my name?

LEADER   It's a long road,
but it's busy with foot traffic. News spreads
quickly. Don't worry. He'll recognize your name,
then come immediately to this place.
Your story's widely known, old man. Even
if he's asleep and wakes slowly,
word you're here will bring him in a hurry.   <340>

OEDIPUS   His coming will help Athens, and help me.
A good man is always his own best friend.

*(Antigone looks offstage, brightens, and then
calls out loudly.)*

ANTIGONE	O Zeus! What do I say now, father? Or even think?
OEDIPUS	What do you see, Antigone?
ANTIGONE	*(Raising her voice.)*

A woman riding

a young Sicilian horse. Wearing a hat
from Thessaly to keep sun off her face.
What can I say? Is she, or isn't she?
Am I hallucinating? Yes? No?
I can't tell yet. Yes! YES!
There's no one else it could be.   <350>
As she comes closer, I can see her
smiling at me. It's my sister Ismene!

OEDIPUS	What's that you're shouting, girl?
ANTIGONE	*(Still shouting)*

That I see your daughter and my sister!
You'll recognize her as soon as she speaks.

*(Enter Ismene, having just dismounted from a
small horse. She is accompanied by her Servant.)*

ISMENE	Father! Sister! It's wonderful to say those names!

It was so hard to find you. Now that I have,
I can hardly see you through my tears.

OEDIPUS	You've come, child?
ISMENE	I hate to see you like this, father.
OEDIPUS	But you've joined us.
ISMENE	Not without some trouble. <360>
OEDIPUS	Touch me, daughter.
ISMENE	Each of you take a hand.

(All three join hands and hold them a while.)

OEDIPUS	My daughters. Sisters.
ISMENE	Two wretched lives!
OEDIPUS	Hers and mine?
ISMENE	Yes. And mine as well.
OEDIPUS	Why did you come, child?
ISMENE	I care about you, father.

OEDIPUS   Then you missed me?

ISMENE   I did. And I bring news
               I wanted you to hear from me.
               I also brought our last faithful servant.

OEDIPUS   Our family's menfolk, your brothers—
               where are they when we need them?

ISMENE   They are . . . wherever they are. Grim times for them.   <370>

OEDIPUS   Those two boys imitate the Egyptians
               in how they think and how they run their lives.
               Egyptian men stay in their houses weaving
               while their women are out earning a living.
               Your brothers, who should be here helping me,
               are back home keeping house like little girls,
               while you two shoulder your father's hardships.

               Antigone has been traveling with me
               since she outgrew the care a child needs.
               She gained enough strength to be an old man's   <380>
               guide, picking her way barefoot through forests,
               hungry, rain-drenched, sun-scorched.
                                               Home comforts
               took second place to caring for her father.
               And you, Ismene, slipped out of Thebes
               undetected so many times—to bring
               the latest oracles to your father.
               And you were my eyes inside Thebes, while I
               was being banished. Ismene, what's the news
               you've brought? Why have you come?
               I'm sure you haven't traveled here empty-   <390>
               handed. Is there something I should fear?

ISMENE   Father, I'd rather not describe
               the trouble I had trying to find you.
               Just let it be! Retelling it
               would only revive all the misery.

               It's the real trouble your miserable sons are in—
               it's their wrath I've come to tell you about.
               They were keen, at first, to let Kreon rule,
               so as not to pollute the city, well
               aware the curse we inherit from way back   <400>
               still holds your house in a death grip.
               But spurred on by a god, and by their own
               disturbed minds, my brothers—three times cursed!—

began battling each other for dominance
and the king's throne in Thebes.
                      Now that hot-head,
Eteokles, your youngest, has stripped
Polyneikes, your first-born, of all power
and driven him out of the country.
Polyneikes was, from the reports I hear,
exiled to Argos. There he married power,   <410>
gaining friends willing to fight his battles—
determined to make Argos glorious
if it can conquer Thebes,
or to lift Thebes' reputation
sky high should Argos lose.
It isn't just loose talk, father,
it has become horrible fact.
When will the gods lighten
your troubles? I wish I knew.

OEDIPUS	Do you hold out some hope that the gods <420> might take notice and end my suffering?
ISMENE	I do, father. I have new oracles.
OEDIPUS	What are they? What do they say, daughter?
ISMENE	That your own people will someday need you, living—and dead—to ensure their survival.
OEDIPUS	How could a man like me save anyone?
ISMENE	They say: you will hold Thebes' life in your hands.
OEDIPUS	When I'm nothing . . . how can I still be a man?
ISMENE	The gods who tore you down will restore you.
OEDIPUS	Does little good to restore an old man <430> after they have laid waste his youth.
ISMENE	Listen! The gods *will* transform you, and Kreon *will* come here earlier than you might think.
OEDIPUS	Has he a plan, child? Tell me.
ISMENE	To station you at the Theban frontier, but prevent you from crossing over.
OEDIPUS	Why would they keep me from crossing?
ISMENE	If they don't pay your tomb proper respect it could cause them serious trouble.

OEDIPUS	They shouldn't need a god to tell them that.	\<440\>
ISMENE	It's still the reason they want you nearby, not off someplace where you'd be in charge.	
OEDIPUS	Then will they bury me in Theban earth?	
ISMENE	Father, that's not allowed. You killed your father.	
OEDIPUS	Then they must never have me in their power!	
ISMENE	If they don't, things will go badly for Thebes.	
OEDIPUS	What will cause things to go badly, daughter?	
ISMENE	Your rage, when they're deployed around your tomb.	
OEDIPUS	Who told you, child, what you have just told me?	
ISMENE	Sacred envoys sent to the Delphic hearth.	\<450\>
OEDIPUS	Did the god truly say this about me?	
ISMENE	All the returning envoys swore he did.	
OEDIPUS	Did either of my sons hear them say it?	
ISMENE	They heard it and they both knew what it meant.	
OEDIPUS	With this knowledge, did those scoundrels put the kingship ahead of helping me?	
ISMENE	It hurts me to say this, father. Yes, they did.	

OEDIPUS

Gods, don't interfere with this brawl you've ordained!
But give me the right to decide how it ends—
this battle toward which my sons lift up spears   \<460\>
and on which they're now dead set. May my son
in power, who wields the scepter, lose it;
may my exiled son never make it home.
When I was driven shamefully from Thebes
they made no move to stop it or help me.
They were spectators to my banishment;
they heard me proclaimed a homeless outcast!

You might think that Thebes acted properly,
that it gave me what I once craved. That's wrong.
On the far-off day when my fury seethed,   \<470\>
a death by stoning was my heart-felt wish.
But there was no one willing to grant it.
Later, when my suffering diminished,
I realized my rage had gone too far
in punishing my mistakes. Only then

did the city decide to force me out—
after all those years. And my own two sons,
who could have saved their father, did nothing.
It would have taken just one word. But I
wandered off into permanent exile.   <480>

My two unmarried girls fed me as best
they could. They sheltered and protected me,
my only family. But my sons traded
their father for power and a kingdom.

You can be certain I'll give them no help
in fighting their battles, and they will gain
nothing from having been rulers of Thebes.
I know that because, when I heard the oracles
this girl brought, I recalled some prophecies—
ones Phoibos Apollo has now fulfilled.   <490>

I'm ready. Let them send Kreon to find me—
or anyone who's powerful in Thebes.
If you strangers, together with those
intimidating goddesses who live
among you, are willing to enlist me,
you'll get a champion in the bargain,
someone who will defend your country
against its enemies, and damage his own.

LEADER   You've earned our pity, Oedipus,
           both you and your daughters here.   <500>
           And because you've offered to defend us,
           I'm going to give you some advice.

OEDIPUS   Whatever my host wants done, I'll do.

LEADER   Ask atonement from the goddesses you first
           met here, and whose ground you've invaded.

OEDIPUS   By what means? Tell me how to do it, friends.

LEADER   Dip water from a stream that flows year round,
           wash your hands in it, then bring some here.

OEDIPUS   And when I've brought this pure water, what then?

LEADER   You'll find bowls made by a skilled craftsman.   <510>
           Adorn their handles and their rims.

OEDIPUS   With branches or wool cloths—and then what?

LEADER   Gather fresh-cut fleece from a she-lamb.

OEDIPUS   How shall I end the ritual?

LEADER   Face the sunrise and pour an offering.

OEDIPUS   From the bowls you've just described?

LEADER   Spill some from each bowl, then empty the last.

OEDIPUS   Tell me what to put in the bowls.

LEADER   No wine. Just pure water sweetened with honey.

OEDIPUS   After I've drenched the ground under the trees?   <520>

LEADER   Using both hands, set out three bundles of nine
           olive twigs each, while you recite this prayer.

OEDIPUS   That's it—get to the heart of the matter.

LEADER   Pray that the goddesses called the Gracious Ones
           protect the suppliant, in their kindness,
           and grant him a safe refuge. That's your prayer,
           or someone else's who will pray for you.
           Don't raise your voice, pray quietly,
           and, without looking back, leave.
           Do as I've said, and I'm sure you'll succeed.   <530>
           If you don't, stranger, I'm afraid for you.

OEDIPUS   Daughters, have you heard what our friend here said?

ANTIGONE   We heard. What would you like us to do?

OEDIPUS   I lack the eyes—and the strength—to go myself.
           My double loss. One of you must do it.
           It is possible for one living soul
           to pay a debt that's owed by ten thousand,
           provided it's done with conviction.
           One of you go—but don't leave me alone.
           My body's too weak to move without help.   <540>

ISMENE   I'll carry out the ritual, but someone
           must show me the right place to perform it.

LEADER   Go around to the far side of the grove.
           If you need anything else, there's a man
           living nearby who will point you the way.

ISMENE   I'll go now, sister. You stay with father.
           Helping a parent who can't help himself
           should never seem a burden.

           (Exit Ismene and her Servant.)

LEADER	Unpleasant it may be, stranger, to stir up
	a long dormant grief. Yet there is something <550>
	I would like to hear straight from you.
OEDIPUS	What's your concern?
LEADER	That bitter, incurable anguish—
	the kind you had to wrestle with.
OEDIPUS	Out of consideration for a guest,
	don't dwell on my unfortunate past.
LEADER	Your story's widely told, my friend.
	I'd like to hear the truth of it.
OEDIPUS	*(Brusque hissing sound.)*
	Ssstop!
LEADER	Hear me out, let me speak!
OEDIPUS	*(Aspirated.)*
	Whhhy? <560>
LEADER	You owe me this. I've granted all you've asked.
OEDIPUS	I suffered anguish, friends,
	suffered what my own
	blind actions caused.
	But let the gods testify:
	I chose to do none.
LEADER	Then how did this happen?
OEDIPUS	Thebes married me, who suspected nothing,
	to a woman who would destroy me.
LEADER	Was she your mother, as I've heard, <570>
	who shared your infamous marriage bed?
OEDIPUS	She was. Your words feel
	harsh as death in my ears.
	And those daughters I fathered . . .
LEADER	What are you saying now?
OEDIPUS	—twin scourges—
LEADER	O Zeus!
OEDIPUS	. . . were born from the birthpangs
	of our shared mother.
LEADER	They're your daughters, and . . .

OEDIPUS   Yes! They're my sisters.

OLD MEN   *(Low whispering)*
                 So sorry. So sorry. So sorry.

OEDIPUS   Oh yes! A thousand evils   <580>
                 surge back, all through me.

LEADER   Then you suffered . . .

OEDIPUS   I suffered an indelible torment.

LEADER   . . . when you committed . . .

OEDIPUS   Never!

LEADER   How did you not?

OEDIPUS   I was presented with a gift—
                 one that would break my heart—
                 to repay me for all the help
                 I gave Thebes. It was a gift
                 I should never have accepted.   <590>

LEADER   Horrible. And then? You killed . . . ?

OEDIPUS   Why this? What are you asking me?

LEADER   . . . your father?

OEDIPUS   You open one old wound after another.

LEADER   Murderer!

OEDIPUS   Yes, I killed him! But I have . . .

LEADER   You have what?

OEDIPUS   . . . Justice on my side.

LEADER   How could that be?

OEDIPUS   Let me tell you. The men
                 I fought and killed
                 would have killed me.
                 Before the law
                 my hands are clean.   <600>
                 My actions were driven
                 not by malice,
                 but by ignorance.

                 (One of Theseus' Men enters, whispers to the Leader, and then exits.)

LEADER   Aigeus' son, our king, has arrived, willing
                 to do all you have asked of him.

(Enter Theseus, who walks up and examines Oedipus.)

THESEUS   For years I've heard that you had done
bloody damage to your eyes—so I thought
it could be you, son of Laios. What I learned
on my way here made me far more certain.
And to see you now at your journey's end   <610>
removes all doubt. Your clothes, your ravaged face,
tell me your name. Oedipus, I
truly pity you. And I will help you.
You and this poor girl have come here
suddenly—why? To request a favor
from Athens and from me? If so, ask it.
You would need to tell me an appalling
story indeed before I'd turn you down.
Remember, I was also raised in exile,
combating threats to my life of a kind   <620>
no other man has ever had to face.
I would never refuse a homeless man—
which you are—my help. I'm also mortal,
like you, with no greater assurance
than you have that I'll be alive tomorrow.

OEDIPUS   There's little I need add, Theseus.
In those few gracious words
you've said correctly who I am, and who
my father was, and what country I'm from—
so nothing remains. Except to tell you   <630>
what most concerns me. Then I'll be silent.

THESEUS   Go on. Say what you mean. I must know.

OEDIPUS   I came to offer you my disfigured
body as a gift. Though not pleasant
to look at, it will generate benefits
beauty could not.

THESEUS   This advantage
you claim to have brought us—what is it?

OEDIPUS   In time you will know. But not for a while.

THESEUS   Your . . . enhancement—when will it be revealed?

OEDIPUS   After I'm dead and you have buried me.   <640>

THESEUS   You ask me to oversee your last rites,
but say nothing of your life before then.

OEDIPUS   Grant my wish. Everything else will follow.

THESEUS	This favor you're asking seems a small one.
OEDIPUS	Take care. This is no trivial matter.
THESEUS	Then you anticipate trouble. From your sons?
OEDIPUS	King, my sons want to return me to Thebes.
THESEUS	If that's your desire, why would you refuse?
OEDIPUS	*(Loudly and with fury.)*
	Because, when I wished to stay, *they* refused!

THESEUS   Fool! When you're in trouble, rage never helps.   <650>

OEDIPUS   Wait till you've heard me out. Then chastise me.

THESEUS   Go on. I shouldn't speak without the facts.

OEDIPUS   Theseus, I have suffered terribly.

THESEUS   You mean the ancient curse on your family.

OEDIPUS   No. Not that story every Greek has heard.

THESEUS   Then what superhuman pain *do* you suffer?

OEDIPUS   Here's what my two sons did to me.
They banished me from my homeland. I can't
return because I killed my own father.

THESEUS   If that's the case, why would Thebes want you back?   <660>

OEDIPUS   God's voice will *compel* them to take me back.

THESEUS   Oracles must have frightened them. Of what?

OEDIPUS   That Fate will strike them down in your country.

THESEUS   And what could cause such hatred between us?

OEDIPUS   Gentle son of Aigeus, only the gods
never grow old and die. All-powerful
Time ravages the rest. Just as the earth
decays, so does the body's strength. When trust
between people dies, betrayal begins.
A spirit of respect can never last   <670>
between two friends, or between two cities,
because sooner or later resentment
kills all friendships. Though sometimes they revive.

The weather now is sunny between Thebes
and Athens—but Time in due course will bring
on a war sparked by a minor grievance—

endless days and nights in which Theban spears
shatter the peace they had promised to keep.

Then my dead body, slumbering, buried,
deathly cold, will drink their hot blood—if Zeus   <680>
is still Zeus, if Apollo spoke the truth.
But since there's no pleasure in pronouncing
words that should never be said, I will stop.

Keep *your* word and you'll never be sorry
you welcomed Oedipus to your city—unless
the gods abort their promises to me.

LEADER   From the beginning, King, this man has shown
             he has the nerve to keep every promise
             he's made to our country—and he'll keep more.

THESEUS   Who would refuse the kindness of a man   <690>
             like this? We welcome him to our home fires.
             As our wartime ally he's earned the right.
             Now he comes asking our gods to help him,
             an act with no small implication
             for Athens and myself. I value
             what he brings. Reject his offers?
             Never! I'll settle him in our land
             with the rights of a citizen.
             If it's the stranger's desire to live *here,*

             (Turning toward Leader.)

             I will charge *you* with his protection.   <700>
             Or he may wish to join me.
                                        Oedipus,
             it's your decision. I'll respect your choice.

OEDIPUS   O Zeus, do your utmost for this man.

THESEUS   What is your pleasure? To live in my house?

OEDIPUS   If that were allowed. But *here* is the place . . .

THESEUS   Here? What will you do here? I'm not opposed . . .

OEDIPUS   . . . where I will punish those who drove me out.

THESEUS   Then the great gift you meant—is your presence?

OEDIPUS   Yes. If you keep the pledges you gave me.

THESEUS   Don't doubt me. I will never betray you.   <710>

OEDIPUS	I won't demand an oath from you—as though you were a man who couldn't be trusted.
THESEUS	But that's all I can offer you: my word.
OEDIPUS	How then will you act . . .
THESEUS	What is your worst fear?
OEDIPUS	That troops will come.
THESEUS	My men will deal with them.
OEDIPUS	Take care that when you leave me . . .
THESEUS	Please. Don't tell me what to do.
OEDIPUS	How can I *not* be afraid?
THESEUS	My heart isn't pounding.
OEDIPUS	You don't know what they threaten . . .

THESEUS   I know this:
No men will seize you unless I allow it.   <720>
And if they brag how simple it will be
to kidnap you, I think the sea they're crossing
will prove too vast and too rough for their skills.
For now, take courage. Aside from any
assurance *I've* given, it was *Apollo*
who sent you. While I'm gone,
my word will protect you.

(*Exit Theseus.*)

OLD MEN   You've come, stranger, to shining Kolonos
abounding with horses
and earth's loveliest farms.   <730>
Here the Nightingale
sings her long clear trills
under green forest trees
laden with apples and berries.
In the wine-dark ivy she sings,
in the forbidden
thickets of goddesses
untroubled by hot sun
or the chill blast of winter.

She sings in the clearings   <740>
where Dionysos dances
among the everloving

maenads who raised him.
Here, drinking dew from the sky
morning after morning,
narcissi flourish;
their heavenly blossoms
crown two immortals,
Persephone and Demeter; sunlight
illumines the golden crocus.   <750>

Bountiful fountains send Kephisos
cascading down the mountain.
He never stops flowing, greening
all that grows, pouring daily
his pure waters
through the valley's nurturing hills.
Nor do the Muses,
singing in harmony, or the Goddess of Love
with golden reins in her hands,
stay away long.   <760>

A tree not found in Asia,
or on the Dorian Island of Pelops,
lives here, a tree born from itself,
a tree no one plants.
A terror to enemy spears,
the gray-green olive
grows freely on our land,
nourishing our children.
Neither the young men nor the old
will shatter and destroy it,   <770>
for Zeus of the Olive Groves,
and Athena with seagreen eyes,
guard it with tireless glare.

And now with all our strength we sing
our gratitude to our mother city,
for the great gifts the gods have given her:
that peerless glory of our land,
the strength of stallions, the speed of colts—
and the rolling power of the sea.
It was you, son of Kronos,   <780>
who gave Kolonos our throne,
and you, Lord Poseidon,
who taught us to harness, out on these roads,
the fury of horses, taught us to drive

the long-limbed oar that pulses us
over salt seas, in pursuit
of fifty Nereids' skittering feet.

(Antigone's attention is drawn offstage left.)

ANTIGONE   You've praised your land beyond all others—
prove now you can act on those glowing words.

OEDIPUS   What makes you say that to them, daughter?   <790>

ANTIGONE   Kreon's arriving, father, backed by troops.

OEDIPUS   Can I trust these kind old men to protect me?

LEADER   Don't worry, you're in good hands. I may have aged,
but this country has lost none of its strength.

(Enter Kreon, escorted by his armed Soldiers.)

KREON   You men must be the local nobility.
I detect some fear showing in your eyes
at my arrival. Don't be alarmed.
There's no need for hostile murmuring.
I haven't come intending to use force.
I'm an old man; yours is a powerful city,   <800>
if ever there was one in Greece. So yes—
I was sent here, on account of my age,
to reason with that man, and bring him home.
No single person sent me—all Thebes did.
Kinship demands I show greater concern
for his troubles than do my countrymen.

(Turning to face Oedipus.)

You've suffered for too long, Oedipus.
Please hear me out, then we can both go home.
It's high time your fellow Kadmeans
took you back. More than anyone else, I   <810>
share your sorrows, old man, now that I see
how you live in your miserable exile—
drifting in constant want, with only this girl
as your servant.
                     I never thought her life
would sink to such gross squalor, but it has:
tending to you, to your personal needs,
living in poverty. And at her age,
with no experience of men, she's ripe
for the first vulgar lout who comes along.

Those are harsh judgments, aren't they, alas,   <820>
on you and on me? On our whole family.

Since there's no way to hide your obvious
degradation, Oedipus, please agree
to placate our family gods by coming
home to the house and city of your fathers.
Thank Athens for her kindness as you leave,
for she deserves it. But your birthplace must,
if you would do the right thing, have the final
claim on you. Long ago, she nurtured you.

OEDIPUS   You! You'll try anything! You have based your   <830>
insidious arguments on the most
ethical grounds. But why make the attempt?
Why try to slide a noose around my neck?
That would cause me unendurable pain.

Some time ago, when I was tormented
by self-inflicted agony and wanted
with all my heart to be banished from Thebes,
you refused me. Later, when my grief eased
and I wished to remain home, you drove me
from my house, off the land, into exile,   <840>
without one thought of this kinship you claim.

Now this time, seeing the friendly welcome
this town and her people have given me,
you try to abduct me—your harsh purpose
sheathed in amiable words. Is there joy
in kindness that's imposed against our will?
Suppose someone refuses to help you—
though you've begged him for help. But once
you possess what your heart craves—then he
offers to give what you no longer want.   <850>
Would that be kindness? Fulfillment like that
is worthless—as are your offers to me.
They sound good, but in fact they're evil.

Let me explain your motives to these men,
so they'll see just how treacherous you are.

You have sought me out—not to take me home—
but to plant me outside your borders,
so that your city will emerge unscathed
from any invasion launched against it.

You won't get *that,* but you'll get something else: <860>
this part of me—my *spirit*—ravaging
your country. And it will rage there always:
My sons will inherit from their father
only enough of my homeland to die in!

Don't you see? I know the future of Thebes
better than you do. A great deal better,
because my sources are better: Apollo,
for instance, and his father, Zeus himself.
Your lying mouth has come here spitting out
all those words, your tongue's keener than a blade.   <870>
But your guile hurts you far more than it helps.

I don't think I've persuaded you. So leave!
Let me live here! Poor as I am, I won't
live in want if I'm at peace with myself.

KREON   In our exchange, who do you think suffers
             more, *me* by your views, or *you* by your own?

OEDIPUS   All that matters to me is that you've failed
             to change my mind, or the minds of these men.

KREON   Growing old hasn't improved your judgment,
             friend. It's perpetuated your disgrace.   <880>

OEDIPUS   Your tongue's extremely quick. But a good man
             never pleads a dishonorable cause.

KREON   Making noise doesn't prove you're making sense.

OEDIPUS   As if *you* spoke briefly, and to the point?

KREON   Not pointedly enough to pierce your mind.

OEDIPUS   Go! I speak for these men and for myself.
             Don't keep me under hostile surveillance
             in a land that's destined to be my home.

(Kreon gestures toward the Old Men and his Soldiers.)

KREON   I ask *these* men—not you—and I ask my . . .
             comrades here, to note the tone you're taking   <890>
             with a kinsman. If I ever seize you . . .

OEDIPUS   Who could seize me against my friends' will?

KREON   I swear you'll suffer even if we don't.

OEDIPUS   How do you plan to back up your bluster?

KREON   I've already seized one of your daughters
                 and removed her. I'll take the other soon.

OEDIPUS   My god.

KREON   Soon you'll have greater cause to say, "My god."

OEDIPUS   You took Ismene?

KREON   And I'll soon take this one.

                 (Kreon indicates Antigone.)

OEDIPUS   What will *you* do, my hosts—my friends?   <900>
                 Fail me by not banishing
                 this blaspheming thug?

LEADER   *(To Kreon.)*
                 Stranger, go. There's no way to justify
                 what you're attempting, or what you've just done.

KREON   *(To his Soldiers.)*
                 It's time we take this girl away by force
                 if she puts up the slightest resistance.

ANTIGONE   I don't know where to run. Are there men
                 or gods willing to help me?

LEADER   What are you doing, stranger?

KREON   I'll leave him, but I will take *her*. She's mine.

OEDIPUS   You men in power here!

LEADER   Stranger, there's no   <910>
                 justification for what you're doing,

KREON   I can justify it.

LEADER   How can you do that?

KREON   I'm taking what belongs to me.

                 (Kreon grabs Antigone.)

OEDIPUS   Stop him, Athens!

LEADER   What is this, stranger? Let the daughter go—
                 or you'll discover who holds power here.

KREON   Stand back!

LEADER   Not from you! Not while you do this!

KREON   Touch me, and you're at war with Thebes.

OEDIPUS   All of this I foresaw.

LEADER   Release the girl.

KREON   Don't issue orders when you have no power.

LEADER   I warn you, let her go.

KREON   And I warn you: leave!   <920>

LEADER   *(Yelling offstage)*
               Over here, citizens! Join our fight! My city,
               our city, is attacked! Come help us!

ANTIGONE   They're dragging me away! Friends! FRIENDS!

OEDIPUS   Tell me where you are, child.

ANTIGONE   . . . I . . . can't . . . get . . . free!

OEDIPUS   Reach out to me, daughter.

ANTIGONE   They are too strong.

KREON   *(To his Soldiers.)*
               Take her away from here.

OEDIPUS   I'm so weak! So weak!

               (Kreon's Soldiers drag Antigone off stage.)

KREON   Now you won't have two daughters for crutches.
               But since you want to lay waste your country
               and its people—who have ordered me to do this,
               though I'm still their king—go ahead,   <930>
               fight for victory! You'll find that nothing
               you're doing now, nothing you've ever done,
               has done you any good—you've turned
               your back on those who love you, while they've tried
               to head off your self-destructive fury.

LEADER   Stop where you are, stranger.

               (Leader grabs hold of Kreon.)

KREON   Keep your hands off me.

LEADER   When you've brought back his daughters!

KREON   That will cost Thebes a much steeper ransom.
               I'll take something worth more than these two girls.   <940>

LEADER   What are you threatening?

               (Leader lifts his hands from Kreon.)

KREON   To seize that man there.

LEADER   Those are shocking words.

KREON   But ones I'll make good.

LEADER   You might—unless our king stops you.

OEDIPUS   That is outrageous! So you would seize me?

KREON   Silence!

OEDIPUS   *NO!*
                        Goddesses, don't gag
              the curse rising in my throat—on you, scum,
              who have stolen my dear defenseless eyes,
              gone like the sight I once possessed.
              Let the Sun, who sees all there is, give you,
              and every member of your family,   <950>
              an old age as miserable as my own.

KREON   You people who live here, do you see that?

OEDIPUS   They see us both. They know you have caused me
              real harm, while I've struck back with mere breath.

KREON   I will not curb my rage! Though I'm alone,
              though age enfeebles me, I will take him.

              (Kreon takes hold of Oedipus.)

OEDIPUS   He's done it.

LEADER   Stranger, what arrogance possessed you?
              You think you can accomplish this?

KREON   I *will* accomplish it.   <960>

LEADER   Then I'll cease to believe Athens is a city.

KREON   The weak overcome the powerful
              if they have justice on their side.

OEDIPUS   Did you hear him?

LEADER   Zeus, back me up! He can't enforce his boast.

KREON   But Zeus knows that I can. And you don't know.

LEADER   That's an outrage!

KREON   An outrage you can't stop.

LEADER   You men who govern us! Come here! Be quick!
              These men are heading for the border.

(Enter Theseus and his Men. Kreon releases Oedipus and steps back.)

THESEUS
What makes you shout? What's wrong?
Are you so panicked that you'll disrupt   <970>
my sacrifice to the seagod of Kolonos?
Speak up! Tell me the whole story, so I'll
know why I've run here so fast my legs ache.

OEDIPUS
I recognize your voice, friend. That man
over there has done me serious harm.

THESEUS
What harm? Which man?

OEDIPUS
Kreon. He's right there, you see him. He's taken
two of my children—the two I have left.

THESEUS
What are you saying?

OEDIPUS
                                            I've told you what he did.

THESEUS
Someone run to my people at the altars.   <980>
Order every man there to leave the sacrifice
and converge at the crossroads. Go on foot,
or loosen your horses' reins and make them
gallop. Stop those girls from leaving town,
so I won't look useless to this stranger,
caught off guard by a desperate act. Go now!

And as for that man standing over there—
if I could punish him for what he's done
there is no way he would ever go free.
As things stand, he's protected by the laws   <990>
that authorized his visit to Athens.

(To Kreon.)

But we won't turn you loose until you bring
the girls here, where I can see them. Your actions
shame me, your family, and your country.

You've come to a city that loves justice.
We will do nothing contrary to law,
even though you flout our laws—invading
our territory, grabbing what you please,
keeping it by force. Do you think no men,
only slaves, live here? That I don't matter?   <1000>
It's not your breeding that makes you
a vile man. Thebes does not breed criminals.
She wouldn't support you, not if she knew
you were plundering what belongs to me—

and to the gods—using force to abduct
helpless suppliants.
                      If I had crossed
your borders, no matter how just my cause,
I would first ask your ruler's agreement,
whoever he might be, before I dragged
anybody off. I'd know how a stranger   <1010>
should deal with your country's citizens.
But you've given your city a bad name
it doesn't deserve. And as you've grown old
the years have blighted your intelligence.

I said before, and I say now: Someone
must bring the girls back. Unless you'd like
to take up permanent residence here.
These aren't just words. They speak my mind.

LEADER   Do you see what's become of you, stranger?
              We thought at first that you were honest—like   <1020>
              your people. Now we see the harm you cause.

KREON   I didn't take these actions assuming,
              as you would have it, that this city lacked
              brave or intelligent men. I took them
              because I assumed that its people
              were not so taken with my relatives
              as to feed and house them against my will.
              I was sure you people wouldn't shelter
              a morally toxic father-killer,
              a man whose wife bore children to her son.   <1030>

              I knew that the Council of Mount Ares
              convenes in your city, and believed it
              much too wise to let vagrants enter Athens.
              I trusted my conviction when I seized him.
              Nor would I have abducted him
              if he hadn't laid curses on my kinfolk.
              I am a man maligned! I have a right
              to strike back. Anger doesn't diminish
              as we age. It consumes us till we die.
              Only the dead are immune from anguish.   <1040>

              Do what you want with me.
              Though I'm nothing, mine is a just cause.
              I may be old, but I'll attempt
              to pay you back blow for blow.

OEDIPUS   You have no shame! Tell me, does your nonsense
about a weak old man best fit you? Or me?
You charge me with murder, incest, disgrace—
misfortunes I suffered, but none of which
I chose. Maybe it pleased the gods to hate
my ancestors. Examine my whole life.   <1050>
You can accuse me of no personal
wrongdoing, no crime whose expiation
impelled me to harm myself and my kin.

Tell me this. If the oracle of god
had decreed my father must die
at the hands of his own son, how
could you possibly think it just
to blame me? I wasn't even born!
No father had begotten me,
no mother had conceived me.   <1060>

And if, born to this miserable fate
as I most surely was, I traded blows
with my father in combat, and killed him,
not knowing what I was doing, or to whom—
how could you condemn that ignorant act?

As for my mother—you disgrace yourself
when you force me to speak of her marriage.
She was your sister, and our marriage
happened in just the way I'll now describe.
Given what's come from your vulgar mouth,   <1070>
there is no reason to shut mine.

Yes!—she bore me. And that wrecked both our lives.
I didn't know the truth, neither did she.
She give birth to me, and then she give birth
to children I fathered—to her shame.

I'm certain of one thing: it is your own
free choice to condemn us. But was my will
free when I married her? No! Nor do I
have any choice but to speak of it now.
Neither my marriage, nor the killing   <1080>
of my father—actions you keep on
throwing in my face—can be called crimes.

Of all my questions, answer just this one:
If, right now, a man standing beside you—
righteous you—tried to kill you, would you ask
whether or not the would-be murderer

was your father, or would you strike him down?
If your life mattered to you, I believe
you'd fight your assassin, before you asked
yourself whether you were doing the right thing.   <1090>

Into such cataclysms the gods led me.
If my father's spirit came back to life,
I don't think he would disagree.

But you! Because you're not a moral man,
because you're willing to say anything,
because to you it's all the same—
speech that's vulgar and speech that's not—
you slander and defame me
in the presence of these good men.

You're quite happy to flatter Theseus—   <1100>
and Athens, for being such a well-run state.
Yet, in the midst of your adulation,
you have forgotten that if any city
knows the best way to venerate the gods,
it is Athens above all. So you try
to snatch me from this country, abuse me,
an old man, a suppliant! And worst of all
you seize my daughters! For all these reasons
I ask the goddesses living over there
for their help—provide me with friends!—so you   <1110>
may learn what kind of men defend this city.

LEADER   He's a good man, King. His destiny
            may horrify us, but he's earned our help.

THESEUS   Enough discussion! The perpetrators
            and their captives are on the move, while we,
            the injured parties, just stand here.

KREON   What will you force a weak old man to do?

THESEUS   You can show me their route. I'll go with you.
            If you're holding the girls we're searching for
            nearby, you'll take me there yourself—but if   <1120>
            your men have galloped off with their prizes,
            that will save us some trouble, for my horsemen
            will ride them down. Your men, thank god,
            could never outrun mine to the frontier.
            Let's go! Listen to me: the snake's defanged.
            Fate's caught the marauder in her trap.
            Whatever you win by cunning, you will lose.

You'll also lose your partners in this outrage.
I doubt you would have dared to attack us
unless you had some armed accomplices—   <1130>
perhaps you were counting on some traitor.
I'd better look to it—or else one lone
man could overthrow the whole city.
Do you hear what I'm saying? Or will you
ignore my words like the warnings you had
while you were planning this atrocity?

KREON   You're on home ground, so nothing you can say
disturbs me. Back in Thebes I'll know what to do.

THESEUS   Threaten me all you like—but start walking.
Oedipus, stay here. I'm sure you'll be safe.   <1140>
And I promise you this: unless I'm killed
I'll bring both of your daughters back alive.

OEDIPUS   May the gods bless your kindness, Theseus.
Bless your devotion to our welfare.

(Exit Theseus and his Men, escorting Kreon.)

OLD MEN   Oh let us be there,
to see the enemy
turn and fight! Bronze banging
bronze on the Pythian shore
or on torch-lit beaches
where two great queens—lips sworn   <1150>
to unbreakable silence
by the priests of Eumolpos—
nurture and watch over
funeral rites for the dead.
Out where Theseus,
the battle-igniter, and two
young girls, captive sisters,
converge at our borders,
surrounded by shouting
soldiers sure they have won.   <1160>

Or will the thieves be run down
in pastures west of the snowy
rock in the town of Oea,
as they flee on fast horses
or chariots driven at speed?
Kreon is beaten!
Men from Kolonos

make powerful warriors!
The steel of every bridle
flashes, the mounted troop   <1170>
charges ahead at full gallop.
They worship Athena;
they worship Poseidon,
the ocean-embracing
son of the goddess Rhea.

Are they in action yet,
or do they hold back?
My heart gives me
hope that the girls,
harshly tested,   <1180>
brutally abused
at the hands of their uncle,
will soon see us, face to face.
Zeus will decide who wins.
He will end it today. I sense
the combat will go well.
Were I a dove right now, the storm's
thrust lifting my strong wings,
I might soar through a cloud,
the battle raging below me.   <1190>

Hear it, Zeus, who rules
all other gods, who sees
all that there is to see!
Let our country's defenders
strike the decisive blow
that will bring the prize home.
Help us, fearsome Athena!
Come, huntsman Apollo,
bring Artemis your sister!
Come all you trackers   <1200>
of the dappled fast-moving deer—
help this land and our people!

You won't find me a false prophet,
wandering friend. I'm looking now
at the girls and their escort coming home.

OEDIPUS   Where? Can you tell me? What are you saying?

               *(Enter Antigone and Ismene
               with Theseus and his Men.)*

ANTIGONE   *(From a distance.)*
             Father!—if only some god would show you
             this princely man who's brought us back to you!

OEDIPUS   Daughter? Is it you?

ANTIGONE   Yes! All these strong arms—
             the king and his loyal men—set us free.   <1210>

OEDIPUS   Come toward me, child. Returned to me,
             after I had lost hope. Come to my arms.

ANTIGONE   You ask for what I want to give.

OEDIPUS   Where are you, child?

ANTIGONE   We're both coming to you.

             (Oedipus embraces his daughters.)

OEDIPUS   My darling children!

ANTIGONE   You love us all.

OEDIPUS   You strengthen my old frame.

ANTIGONE   And share your grief.

OEDIPUS   I hold all my dear ones. If I die now
             I won't die totally wretched, so long
             as you two hold me like this. Cling so hard
             you graft yourselves to your father, so tight   <1220>
             I'll feel released at last from the wanderings
             that have left me bone-tired and miserable.
             Now tell me quickly what happened out there.
             A girl your size should keep it short.

ANTIGONE   The man who saved us is right here.
             It was all his doing, let him tell it.
             That's as brief as I can make it.

OEDIPUS   Don't be surprised, my friend, that I've spoken
             so long and so intently to my daughters.
             I was quite sure they were lost forever.   <1230>
             I owe the joy I'm feeling now
             to you. You freed them, no one else.

             May the gods grant all that I wish for you—
             both you and your city—for I've found you
             the most god-fearing, even-handed
             people on earth. And your tongues never lie.

I know your virtues. Let me honor them:
You—and no other—gave me what I have.

Please reach your right hand out to me, King,
so I may hold it and then kiss your face,   <1240>
if that's allowed.
              What am I asking for?
Ill-omened creature that I've been since birth—
why should I want you to touch someone
like me—steeped in every evil?

No, I can't let you do it, not even
if you wished it. Those who have lived through
misery the same as my own, only they
may touch me. Take my salute where you stand.
As for the future, treat me justly.
Just as you've done so far.   <1250>

THESEUS   I'm not surprised you've spoken at such length,
elated as you are at your daughters' return,
or that you wanted to speak first with them.
Nothing like that would ever annoy me.
I want my life to shine through my actions,
not through my words. The proof, old man, is this:
I've kept my promises to you—brought back
unharmed both your stolen daughters.
How did we win the skirmish? Why should I
bother with that? Your daughters will tell you.   <1260>

But something happened just as I returned.
Perhaps you could advise me about it.
A small matter, but a surprising one,
and even small things shouldn't be ignored.

OEDIPUS   Son of Aigeus, what is this small thing?
Please tell me. I don't know why you're asking.

THESEUS   They tell me a man—your kinsman, but not
one from your city—lies on his stomach,
a suppliant at Poseidon's altar,
where I sacrificed before I set out.   <1270>

OEDIPUS   What country is he from? What does he want?

THESEUS   They tell me he wishes to speak briefly
with you. Nothing very consequential.

OEDIPUS   Speak of what? No one asks a god's help lightly.

THESEUS	He prayed, I'm told, for a meeting with you— from which he'd be allowed to leave unharmed.
OEDIPUS	Who'd make an appeal like that to the god?
THESEUS	Do you recall having a kinsman in Argos— someone who might ask you for help?
OEDIPUS	Friend, don't say any more.

THESEUS   What's wrong with you?   <1280>

OEDIPUS   Don't question me.

THESEUS   Not ask you what? Say it!

OEDIPUS   From what you've said, I know this suppliant.

THESEUS   But why should he offend me? Who is he?

OEDIPUS   King, he's my son. I hate him. His voice would give me more pain than any other man's.

THESEUS   How so? Can't you listen, but do nothing you don't wish to? Is it harmful to listen?

OEDIPUS   His voice itself is loathsome to me, King. Don't compel me to do what you're asking.

THESEUS   You had better consider this: <1290>
aren't you compelled by his
suppliant status? Haven't you
a solemn duty to honor the god?

ANTIGONE   Father, please hear me, even though I'm young
to give advice. Respect the king's conscience—
let him honor his god the way he must!
And for your daughters' sake, let our brother
come here. No matter how he maligns you,
he can't force you to change your mind, can he?
Hear what he has to say. What's wrong with that?   <1300>

You are his father, and you know that even
if he blames you in the most ungodly
vicious way, to do him wrong can't be right.
Show him compassion! Other fathers
afflicted with bad children, and just as short-
tempered as you, have softened in response
to the calming influence of their loved ones.
Look at your own past, and remember how
your parents' misery became your own.
And when you consider how theirs happened   <1310>

I think you'll see that the surest outcome
of any evil you inflict—is more evil.

Please change your mind. It's not right for someone
pleading a just cause to plead it forever!
Or for a man who has been given help
to hesitate when asked to repay it.

OEDIPUS   Your arguments are winning me over,
daughter. Though what makes you happy
devastates me, I'll do what you ask.

(Turning to Theseus.)

But if you let that man come here,   <1320>
my friend, no one, at any time,
must be given power over my life.

THESEUS   I wouldn't want to hear you repeat that,
old man. I never boast, but believe me,
as long as the gods let me live, you're safe.

(Exit Theseus and his Men.)

OLD MEN   Anyone who craves
all the years he can have,
expecting to enjoy
a lifespan longer
than normal, makes,   <1330>
we promise you,
a foolish choice.

For the days that stretch out ahead
hold more sorrow than joy,
and the body whose limbs
once gave you pleasure
will soon give you none,
when you've lived past your prime.
And when the Caregiver comes,
he ends all lives the same way.   <1340>
Hades is suddenly real—
no lyre, no dancing, no marriage-song.
There is nothing but Death.

By any measure, it is best
never to have been born.
But once a man is born,
the next best thing, by far,
is for him to return,

as soon as he can,
to the place he came from.   <1350>
For once youth—with its mindless
indulgence—goes by, is there a single
punishing blow that won't find him?
Any misfortune that doesn't
attack his life? Envy, feuding,
revolt, battle and murder!
And finally, old age: despised,
decrepit, lonely, friendless old age
takes him in—there he keeps house
with the worst of all evils.   <1360>

(Looking toward Oedipus.)

He too has arrived at those years,
that ruin of a man—we're not alone.
He's like some headland facing north
lashed by the huge waves of winter.
He too is battered by the troubles
breaking over him, billows pounding in
from both the rising and the setting sun—
from the south, where it's noon all day long,
and from the black northern mountains.

ANTIGONE   I think a stranger's about to arrive.   <1370>
               Just one lone man, father. And he's in tears.

OEDIPUS   Who is he?

(Enter a distraught, weeping Polyneikes.)

ANTIGONE   The one we've been discussing:
               Polyneikes. He's here.

POLYNEIKES   What should I do? Feel sorry for myself?
               Or for the frail father I'm looking at?
               I find him banished to a foreign country—
               along with you two—living in rancid
               rags for so long they've bonded to his flesh
               like some disease. And his unruly hair   <1380>
               snarls in the wind over his blinded face.
               Just as miserable are the rations
               he carries to feed his aching belly.

(Polyneikes walks over to address Oedipus.)

               It shames me to have learned this so late.
               I'll admit it: in all that touches

your welfare I've been wholly
irresponsible. But you're hearing this
from my mouth, not from anyone else's.
Father, you know that the goddess Respect
joins every action that Zeus takes. May she   <1390>
inspire you! I can atone for my sins;
I can't possibly make them any worse.

(Polyneikes pauses for a response; Oedipus is silent.)

You're quiet, father. Why? Please speak to me.
Don't turn your back. You won't respond at all?
Will you deny me with silent contempt?
You'll give no explanation for your rage?
My sisters! His daughters! Please make him talk.
Break through his sullen, stony silence.
Stop him from disdaining me like this.
I have the god's protection, yet this man   <1400>
turns me away without a single word.

ANTIGONE   Then tell him what you came for! You coward!
If you speak freely you might give him pleasure.
Try glowing with anger or affection.
Maybe then this mute man will find a voice.

POLYNEIKES   That was harsh but just. I *will* speak
plainly. But first I must ask help—of the god
from whose altar the king of this country
pulled me up, so I could come make my case,
hear yours, and be granted safe conduct   <1410>
to go my way. I hope I can trust you—
father, sisters—to honor those assurances.

I want to tell you why I'm here, father.
I've been forced to flee my own country, exiled
after I claimed, as the elder son, my right
to inherit your throne and your power.
Eteokles, although my junior, expelled me.
He hadn't beaten me in court or tested
his strength against mine in battle, but he
somehow persuaded Thebes to back him.   <1420>

It's likely that the Fury who stalks you
strengthened his case. At least, that's what I'm told
by the omen-readers.
                        Soon after I arrived
in Argos I married King Adrastos'

daughter; that won me the support,
by a sworn oath, of the most battle-proven
warriors on the Peloponnesos, men
who would help me raise seven companies
of spearmen to fight Thebes, ready to die
for my cause—or drive out the guilty one.   <1430>
So bring it on!
              Why do I come here now?
I bring prayers, father, my own, and those
of my allies—seven columns, seven
poised spears surrounding Thebes on all sides.
Quick-thrusting Amphiaraos joins me,
unmatched in battle or in prophecy,
then Oineus's son, Tydeus,
from Aitolia; the third, Eteoklos,
comes from Argos; fourth is Hippomedon,
sent by his father, Talaos; the fifth one,   <1440>
Kapaneus, promises he'll use fire
to burn down Thebes; Parthenopaios
named after his mother, the aging virgin
Atalanta, whose late marriage produced him,
hurries to war from Arcadia.

And I, your son—or if I'm not really
your son, but the spawn of an evil fate,
at least I'm yours according to my name—
I lead Argos' brave army against Thebes.

All of us, father—for your children's sake,   <1450>
for the sake of your own life—beg you now
to give up your bitterness against me,
now that I'm ready to punish the brother
who banished me and robbed me of my country.

If what the oracles predict holds true
victory will go to the side you join.
Now, in the name of the fountains of home,
in the name of our tribal gods, I ask you
to listen and relent. I'm a beggar,
an exile, but so are you. The kindness   <1460>
of others supports us both, and we share
a common fate; while he, that arrogant
dictator back in our homeland, mocks us
equally. But if you support me now
I'll crush him soon and without much trouble.

When I've expelled him by force, I'll put you
back in your house, and myself back in power.

If you join me, I'll make good on that boast.
But if you don't help me, I'm a dead man.

LEADER   *(Sotto voce.)*

Respect the person who sent him to us,   <1470>
Oedipus. Say something expedient
to him—before you send him on his way.

OEDIPUS   No, my friends, you who oversee this grove:
if Theseus hadn't ordered him here,
believing me obliged to answer him,
he would never have heard me raise my voice.
But now, before he goes, he'll feel that blessing.
And he will hear from me some things
that won't make him happy:

(Suddenly turning on Polyneikes.)

There are no worse men than you!   <1480>
When you held the power your brother now holds
you made me an outcast with no city,
forced to wear rags that bring tears to your eyes—
now that you're facing the same ordeal.
I've put tears behind me. As long as I live
I'll bear the burden of knowing that you
would have killed me. You made me swallow filth,
you drove me out, and you made me a foul
tramp who begs his daily bread from strangers!
Had I not begotten caring daughters   <1490>
I'd be dead—for all the help you gave me.

These two girls keep me alive, they nurse me.
When the work's hard, they're men, not women.
You're not my sons, you're someone else's sons,
alien to me.
              Right now, Fate watches you,
but not as it soon will, when your soldiers
march on Thebes. You won't destroy Thebes; you'll die.
The blood you shed will defile you, just as
your blood defiles your brother as he dies.

I cursed you both from my heart long ago;   <1500>
I summon those same curses to help me
fight you now, to impress you with the need

to respect your parents, and not to treat
your father with contempt—a sightless man,
who begot the kind of men you became.
Your sisters never disgraced me!
                         My curses
will overpower your prayers and your thrones—
if Justice still sits there, alongside Zeus,
enforcing the laws of our ancestors.

As for you now, clear out! I spit on you!   \<1510\>
I'm not your father, you despicable
bastard! And don't forget to take with you
the curses I have called down on your head—
you'll never win this war on your homeland;
you won't survive to skulk back to the plains
of Argos. By your brother's hand you will
die—as you'll kill the man who threw you out.
That is my curse: and I ask the blackest
paternal darkness of the underworld
to become your new home in Tartaros;   \<1520\>
I summon the spirits native to this place;
I summon Ares the Destroyer, who has
inflamed your minds with murderous hatred!

Now that you've heard this, go tell Thebes, go
tell all your staunch allies, what a great favor
Oedipus has done for his own two sons.

LEADER   Polyneikes, this account of your life
gives me no pleasure. And now, you should go.

POLYNEIKES   So much for my journey and my wrecked hopes.
So much for my fellow soldiers. What a way   \<1530\>
to end our march from Argos! I'm finished!
There is no way I can tell my army
what happened here. Retreat? Out of the question.
I must face my destiny in silence.
My sisters, his daughters, since you've heard
my father's savage curse, promise me this:
if that curse does come true and you manage
to make your way home, don't dishonor me,
but bury me. Perform the rituals.
You've already won praise for the loyal   \<1540\>
care you've given this man, but you will earn
equal praise for the honor you show me.

ANTIGONE   Polyneikes, I've got to change your mind.

POLYNEIKES	About what, dear sister? Tell me, Antigone.
ANTIGONE	Turn your army around. Go back to Argos.
	Do it now. Don't destroy yourself and Thebes.
POLYNEIKES	That's something I can't do. How could I lead
	my troops out here again, once I'd shown fear?
ANTIGONE	Why would you renew your anger, brother?
	And what do you gain, razing your homeland? <1550>
POLYNEIKES	Because I was disgraced, banished,
	ridiculed, by my younger brother.
ANTIGONE	Don't you see, if you attack you'll fulfill
	your father's prophecies—that you will both
	kill each other?
POLYNEIKES	Isn't that what he wants?
	Why shouldn't I obey him?
ANTIGONE	Listen to your wretched sister: who will
	obey you, once they've heard his prophecies?
POLYNEIKES	Why should I tell them bad news? Skillful
	generals report good news and censor bad. <1560>
ANTIGONE	Oh my brother! You're absolutely determined?
POLYNEIKES	That's right. Please don't get in my way. My job
	is to take that road, no matter what deadly
	consequences father predicts for me—
	him and his Furies. But you two—I hope
	Zeus will protect your future, so you can
	carry out my wishes after I'm killed.
	Let me leave—say goodbye. For you'll never
	again see me alive.

(Polyneikes pulls away from her arms.)

ANTIGONE	This breaks my heart.
POLYNEIKES	Don't let it.
ANTIGONE	Who wouldn't feel grief for a brother <1570>
	when he's headed toward certain death?
POLYNEIKES	If that's my fate, then I must die.
ANTIGONE	Don't die. Please listen to me!
POLYNEIKES	You must stop this. My mind's made up.

ANTIGONE   And I am truly devastated.
              Now that I'm sure I'll lose you.

POLYNEIKES   No, Fate will determine how my life goes.
              I pray that you two never come to harm.
              All men know that you don't deserve it.

              (Exit Polyneikes.)

OLD MEN   We've just seen   <1580>
              the blind stranger
              start a new round
              of deadly violence—
              unless Fate working
              its will is the true cause.
              You'll never hear us declare
              that a god wills something in vain:
              for Time always keeps watch
              over the gods' decrees—
              ruining somebody's chances,   <1590>
              then rescuing somebody else
              the very next morning
              when his turn comes.

              (A crash of thunder.)

              That was thunder! O Zeus!

OEDIPUS   Children! Children!
              Is there someone nearby
              who could bring Theseus?
              There is no better man.

ANTIGONE   Father, why do we need Theseus here?

OEDIPUS   Because Zeus sends that thunder, and its great wings   <1600>
              will carry me to Hades. Find him now.

              (More and louder thunder.)

OLD MEN   Look, Zeus throws down
              a great unspeakable
              blast of fire!
              Terror races
              to the tips of my hair,
              my spirit cowers,
              the lightning strikes again—
              crackles down the sky—
              forcing what?—to be born.   <1610>

I am afraid. Lightning never
erupts to no purpose, it always
portends something horrendous.
O mighty sky! O Zeus!

OEDIPUS   Daughters, the death promised to your father
is at hand. Nothing can stop it now.

ANTIGONE   How do you know? What warnings have you had?

OEDIPUS   It's beyond doubt. Quickly now, someone go
find the king and bring him back to me.

(Another blast of thunder.)

OLD MEN   Yes! Yes! Hear it! That voice of raging thunder   <1620>
is yet again all around us!
Be gentle with us, god, gentle—
if you are about to darken
our motherland.
Forgive us, if we've sheltered
a man you despise.
Don't punish our compassion!
I ask that of you, Zeus!

OEDIPUS   Is he nearby? Will he find me alive,
children, when he comes? Will my mind be clear?   <1630>

ANTIGONE   Why do you worry that your mind's unsound?

OEDIPUS   I promised I'd repay Theseus
for his kindness. Now I must give him
everything he has earned.

LEADER   *(Calling offstage.)*
You there, my son, we need you! Come!
Break off the sacrifice to seagod Poseidon,
leave the crevice among the high rocks
and come back! The stranger is moved
to provide you, your city, your friends,
with the fruits of your kindness to him.   <1640>
Move quickly, King.

(Enter Theseus and his Men.)

THESEUS   What's all this noise,
this frantic summons—from both
my people and our guest?
Did Zeus's lightning upset you? Did
a hailstorm raise a sudden uproar?

A storm like that, when a god sends it,
inspires every kind of fear.

OEDIPUS   We're reassured, King, now that you've come.
A god's behind this good timing.   <1650>

THESEUS   What's happened, son of Laios?

OEDIPUS   My life is weighted to sink down.
I must not die without fulfilling
my guarantees to you and Athens.

THESEUS   What makes you think your death is imminent?

OEDIPUS   The gods themselves told me. Every sign
I was promised has now been given me.

THESEUS   Which sign made it entirely clear?

OEDIPUS   A great crash of thunder and bolts of lightning
flashing from the All-Powerful's hand.   <1660>

THESEUS   I believe you. You've made some prophecies,
not one of them false. What should I do now?

OEDIPUS   I will describe, son of Aigeus,
how the future of Athens will become
impervious to the ravages of time.
Soon, I myself, with no hand guiding me,
will lead you to the place where I must die.
Never reveal that place to anyone;
not how it's hidden, nor its whereabouts.
It will endure, an ever-present defense,   <1670>
more powerful than a rampart of shields,
or allies with spears racing to save you.

As for those mysteries speech would profane,
you will see what they are, once you are there,
alone. I will not reveal them now, not
to these people, not even to the children
I love. No, you must keep all those secrets.
When you're near death, tell them to your successor.
Let him teach his heir, and so on forever.

In this way, your own city will survive   <1680>
unscathed any attack launched by the Thebans.
Many cities, even well-governed cities,
slide smoothly into violence.
Though the gods act slowly, they see clearly

men who cease to believe and go mad.
Keep this from happening to you, son of Aigeus.

But you don't need such tutoring from me.
Now we must move toward that place,
for god's power drives me on.
Don't linger, follow where I lead.   <1690>
Daughters, in some uncanny way
I have become your guide, as you
once guided your father. Come with me, but
don't touch me with your hands, let me find
the sacred tomb with no help, and the ground
where it's my destiny to be buried.
This way. That's right. Through here. Down this path
my guide Hermes escorts me, he and the dark goddess.

*(Oedipus with uncanny ease leads his daughters
and Theseus toward the grove, his voice still heard
after he vanishes offstage. Theseus, Antigone, and
Ismene one by one follow Oedipus out of sight.)*

O light—dark to me now,
though once you were mine—I feel   <1700>
your warmth on my body one last time.
I'm going down, to hide my death
in Hades. Come, dearest stranger:
bless you, bless this land, bless your people.
And in your prosperous state,
remember me when I am dead,
the source of your boundless well-being.

OLD MEN   If she, the unseen goddess,
accepts my solemn prayer,
and if you, god of the night people,   <1710>
will hear me out, Aidoneus, Aidoneus!
I pray you let this stranger go
untortured and undamned
down to the dark fields of the dead,
down to the house of Styx.
Troubles beyond reason
besieged him; in return
a just god shall pull him clear.

Earth Goddesses! And you,
invincible apparition!   <1720>
Savage guard-dog! Rumor

has told us for ages that you
kennel at Hades' gate, snarling

from cavernous jaws at every
stranger who walks past.
Hear me, Death!
Son of Earth and Tartaros!
Let the hound clear a path
for this stranger who craves
the sunken fields of the dead.   <1730>
Grant him eternal rest.

(Enter Messenger.)

MESSENGER   Townsmen, I could shorten my news to this:
Oedipus is gone. But the full story
of what happened out there cannot be shortened,
nor did the things themselves happen quickly.

LEADER   Is he dead—that tormented man?

MESSENGER   You can be sure
this man has left our common life behind.

LEADER   How? Did the gods take him? Did he feel pain?

MESSENGER   How it happened will take your breath away.
How he left, you saw. None of his loved ones   <1740>
knew the way, but he knew where to lead us.
As soon as he neared the gateway where you climb
down those steep brass steps rooted in the earth,
he paused—within a maze of crossing paths—
where a bowl had been hollowed from a rock shelf.
There the immortal pact that Theseus
made with Peirithous is written in stone.

He stood between that basin and the rock
of Thoricos, easing himself to the ground
beside a hollow pear trunk and a stone tomb.   <1750>
He peeled off all his filthy clothes, then called
to his daughters, asking them to bring water
from the stream nearby, so he could bathe
and then pour out some libations.
The green hill of Demeter rose close by
in plain sight. They climbed it, and soon
carried out these duties for their father.
First they washed him and then they dressed him
in white clothes customary for the dying.

When he was content with what had been done,   <1760>
every last one of his orders obeyed,
Zeus of the Underworld thundered, and the girls
shuddered when they heard it. Then, clinging
to their father's knees, they cried out and kept
pounding their breasts and weeping and shouting.
When he heard them crying, he wrapped his arms
around both their bodies and told them,
"Children, this day will end your father's life.
All the acts I lived for have come to pass.
No longer will you need to care for me—   <1770>
a burden, I know, that has not been easy.
But let one word relieve you of this hardship:
For no man loves you more than I love you.
Now you must live out your lives without me."

Holding each other close, all of them sobbed,
and when they had finished their lamenting,
as the sounds died away, there was stillness.
Suddenly an enormous voice called him,
making everyone's hair rise in terror.
For the god called many times and his voice   <1780>
echoed from all sides: "You there, Oedipus!
You! Oedipus! Why do we hesitate?
You've waited far too long. Far too long!"

Now that he knew it was the god calling,
he asked King Theseus to stand by him.
And when the king approached, Oedipus said,
"Dear friend, will you promise, by giving your
right hand to my daughters, while they give you
their hands, that you will never willingly
forsake them, and that you will always act   <1790>
as their friend, providing what they will need?"

And like a prince, with no hesitation,
Theseus swore to the stranger that he would.
And after this promise, Oedipus at once
embraced his children with enfeebled hands,
and said, "Daughters, you must have the courage
to leave this place now. Don't look back
at things you must not see, and must not hear.
Leave quickly as you can. Let Theseus,
who is entitled to do so, remain   <1800>
to witness all that will happen here."

That's what he said, we all heard him, and followed

his daughters as they left, tears blurring
our own eyes. When we had walked on awhile,
we looked back and saw he was gone, and saw
our king, his hand screening his eyes, reacting
to the shock of a terrifying sight, something
he could not bear to look at, something still
happening. A moment later, we saw him
silently saluting the earth, then the sky   <1810>
where the Olympian gods live, his arms
opened in prayer.
                            But the exact nature
of the death Oedipus died, no man
but Theseus could tell you. Zeus didn't
incinerate him with a lightning blast,
no sudden squall blew inland from the sea.
So it was either a god spiriting
him away, or else the Earth's lower world—
her deep foundations—opening to him,
for he felt nothing but welcoming kindness.   <1820>

When this man vanished, there was no sorrow,
he suffered no sickness; his death, like no
other man's, was a cause for wonder.
If anyone listening doesn't believe me,
I have no interest in persuading him
that I am not some credulous fool.

LEADER   Where are the girls and their escort now?

MESSENGER   Not far away. The sounds of their grief
                growing louder tells you they're almost here.

ANTIGONE   *(Anguished cries.)*
                No reason now   <1830>
                for us two woeful sisters
                to hold back the full
                wretchedness that we feel—
                the doomed blood of our father
                flowed at birth into our blood.
                As long as our father lived
                we suffered its relentless agony.
                Even from his last moments,
                we take with us things seen and things
                suffered that defy understanding.   <1840>

LEADER   What did you see?

ANTIGONE   Friends, we can only guess.

LEADER   Then he's gone?

ANTIGONE   In the very way you'd wish—
            because it wasn't the war god or the waves,
            it was the endless marsh of death that drew
            him away, in a weird, sudden vanishing.
            And now, sister, there's a deathly darkness
            clouding our vision—for how can we stand
            our harsh life to come, drifting across some
            remote back country, or over breaking seas?   <1850>

ISMENE   I don't know. I'd rather murderous Hades
            forced me to share my aged father's death.
            I'm shaking. I can't face the life ahead.

LEADER   You two sisters,
            loving daughters,
            accept what the god brings.
            Do not inflame yourselves
            with so much grieving;
            you should not regret
            the path your life took.   <1860>

ANTIGONE   Yes, there was something
            to treasure in our pain.
            What gave me no comfort then
            did, in the end, console me.
            Yes it did—while I held him
            lovingly in my arms.
            Dear father, loved one, you
            will wear Earth's darkness
            forever, but even down there
            you won't be denied   <1870>
            my love and her love.

LEADER   Then what took place . . .

ANTIGONE   . . . was what he desired.

LEADER   How so?

ANTIGONE   To die on foreign earth
            was his wish; he will sleep
            in that dark grave forever;
            and the mourners he left
            behind are not dry-eyed.
            With my own eyes pouring
            I grieve for you, father;   <1880>
            I don't know how to stop,

my ache is so huge.
I know your wish was to die
in a distant country.
But now you have died
bereft of my care.

ISMENE   Poor desolate sister,
           what will come of us both,
           now that father is gone?

LEADER   Since the way he met death   <1890>
           was a blessing, children,
           stop grieving. Not one of us
           escapes misfortune.

ANTIGONE   Sister, we must go back there.

ISMENE   To do what?

ANTIGONE   I'm filled with . . .

ISMENE   With what?

ANTIGONE   . . . longing. To see the earthly resting place . . .

ISMENE   Whose?

ANTIGONE   *Our father's!*   <1900>

ISMENE   Such a thing can't possibly
           be right. Can't you see that?

ANTIGONE   Why are you judging me?

ISMENE   There's one more thing that you don't know . . .

ANTIGONE   What will you tell me next?

ISMENE   No one saw him die! There's no tomb!

ANTIGONE   Take me out there, and kill me too.

ISMENE   That would kill *me!* With no friends and no strength,
           where would I live out my deserted life?

LEADER   Children, you have nothing to fear.   <1910>

ANTIGONE   Then where can we go?

LEADER   We know of a refuge . . .

ANTIGONE   What do you mean?

LEADER   . . . where you'll be safe.

ANTIGONE   I think I know it . . .

LEADER   What are you thinking?

ANTIGONE   I don't see how we can go home.

LEADER   Then I don't think you should try.

ANTIGONE   Trouble pursues us.

LEADER   It has from the start.   <1920>

ANTIGONE   It was horrible. Now it's worse.

LEADER   Your life has been a huge sea of hardship.

ANTIGONE   So it has.

             (Enter Theseus with his Men.)

THESEUS   Stop weeping, children. When the Earth Powers
             have shown all of us so much grace,
             grief is uncalled for. Don't anger them.

ANTIGONE   Son of Aigeus, please help us.

THESEUS   What do you want me to do, children?

ANTIGONE   Let us see father's tomb with our own eyes.

THESEUS   That would violate divine law.   <1930>

ANTIGONE   What do you mean, my lord?

THESEUS   Daughters, his orders were to let no one
             approach that place; to let no one
             speak to the sacred tomb where he's sleeping.
             If I keep my word, this land
             will never be harmed. Horkos,
             the servant of Zeus
             who hears all oaths,
             heard mine. He misses nothing.

ANTIGONE   I'm content, if my father's wishes   <1940>
             are fulfilled. Now send us home
             to prevent, if we can, the slaughter
             that threatens our brothers.

THESEUS   I will do that. I'll give you all the help
             you may need: anything the dead man,
             now gone under the earth, would approve.

LEADER   Stop mourning now. Let it be. In all
             that's happened, there's nothing you can change.   <1948>

             (All leave.)

Modern-day rebels, whether their convictions are honed in the library, among the oppressed, or facing riot troops, claim kinship with Sophokles' Antigone, the most loving, acerbic, and intensely focused sister in dramatic literature. Acting on her beliefs, she takes on the tyrant Kreon; by dying for those beliefs, she leaves him in ruins and her cause triumphant. Both characters, in fact, have demonstrated a chameleon-like capacity to represent opposite sides of many and diverse political antagonisms. In the perennially renewed bout between the two, those of an older school might grant Kreon, the embattled commander, some wartime slack; Cedric Whitman, for instance, wrote in 1951 that "such a challenging piece of ungentle womanhood . . . has tended to throw some sympathy on Creon's side."[1] But Antigone's élan usually proves far more appealing. During the play's extraordinary run as a politicized drama in the twentieth century, Antigone has been cast as a member of the French resistance (Anouilh), an anarchist who disrupts a barbarous power structure (Brecht-Hölderlin), and the sister of an Argentinian "disappeared" who vents her fury to a street-smart chorus in a Buenos Aires café (Griselda Gambaro). In Athol Fugard's *The Island,* two black prisoners in apartheid-riven South Africa stage *Antigone* for their white jailers, an ultimate expression of defiance against tyranny. The possibilities are legion.[2]

There's a downside, however, to interpreting *Antigone* through its capacity for embodying political battles. Sophokles' Kreon has principles—heed advice, subordinate family interests for the civic good, punish traitors—widely held in his own and later eras; he fails because he betrays those principles. But when a director or adaptor arms Kreon with the ethos of a male chauvinist or a fascist dictator, for instance, and dresses him in pinstripes or jackboots, the repellent ideology discredits him the minute he strides on stage. There is an analogous danger in making Antigone a poster girl for martyrdom; it tends to deemphasize (or eliminate) her cruelties and inconsistencies, her obsession with family, her sexuality, and her ultimate desire to live. In short, imposing contemporary political orthodoxies on *Antigone* risks turning a blazing but nuanced play into propaganda. *Antigone* deserves better.

Untampered with, much in Sophokles' drama turns out to be other than it first seems. The surprises include paradoxes and plot turns that undermine clear-cut delineations between wrong and right, winning and losing, divine grace and divine malice. Politics and ideology are of limited use in interpreting *Antigone* because they are instruments of control. Uncontrollable realities dominate this drama—realities imag-

[1] Whitman, 85.
[2] Goldhill (88) lists the wider ideological terms of the conflict: "right against right, idea against idea, individual against society, family against state, feminine against masculine, divine law against secular order."

ined by the ancients to be god-driven and by moderns, more vaguely, as dangerous forces at work within and around us.

Greek dramatists in the fifth century did in fact reflect the impact of political issues on Athens and its adversaries, though they did so by shaping myth to echo an audience's present-day misery, a strategy that both aroused and distanced emotional response. In *Antigone*—the earliest of his plays devoted to Oedipus and the curse of the Labdakid clan, a story part of Greek lore since the time of Homer—Sophokles tackles a bitter and sometimes deadly public issue in fifth-century Athenian life: the burial of war casualties. But Sophokles never lets politics hijack his dramas, especially not this one. His *Antigone,* as it unfolds, becomes less about dictatorship and honoring the dead than about love's destructive powers. A central battleground in the play is, in fact, the Greek word for loved one, *philos,* in all its variations.

In its primary use *philos* is the term for a family member but also a lover; *philia* refers to affection and obligation that bind blood kin but also married couples. The word, however, reaches far beyond the "household" to embrace members of wider groups: political associates, social intimates, citizens of the *polis,* shipmates and fellow soldiers. Therefore *philos* inherently possesses a terrible potency and a potential for conflict; those joined in *philia,* whether intimately or politically, are honor-bound to support each other. Because Polyneikes is *philos* to Antigone and *ekkthros* (enemy) to Kreon, no compromise is possible for either. The deep-seated Greek cultural imperative to "harm enemies and help loved ones" confronts a situation its single-minded ferocity cannot resolve.

Antigone opens just before dawn in Thebes, a city some seventy miles north of Athens, on the day after the city's defenders repelled a massive assault by fighters from seven Argive cities. The Argive objective had been to rout Thebes' army, breach its outer walls, burn its buildings, and return the throne to Polyneikes, son of Oedipus. But Polyneikes and his younger brother Eteokles, Thebes' reigning king, killed each other during the failed assault.[3] The beaten Argive troops have fled overnight, and Kreon (Oedipus' brother-in-law and the slain brothers' uncle) has assumed power.

Attention turns to the bodies of the dead soldiers. Kreon orders Eteokles to be honored, mourned, and buried; he dishonors the traitor Polyneikes by denying him any burial rites at all. Anyone who violates his edict, he declares, will be stoned to death. But Antigone believes family obligation and divine law demand she bury Polyneikes despite the extreme danger. When her sister Ismene refuses to help, Antigone heads toward the battlefield alone.

[3] Eteokles is never named as the king whom Kreon succeeds, but it is implicit in 170–74/203–6. See *Kolonos* n. 1420 and *Antigone* n. 20.

A short time later one of the guards assigned by Kreon to watch over Polyneikes' corpse reports back that the body has been "dusted over" with earth, in keeping with ancient Greek ritual. But the criminal left no footprints, no trace, nothing. This uncanny lack of evidence prompts the Leader of the Theban Elders to suggest the likelihood that gods were involved. A furious Kreon rejects such a possibility and threatens to torture the Guard if he doesn't find the perpetrator. When the Guard returns to the battlefield where Polyneikes' body lies, a dust storm whirls around the body. As it clears off, he and his squadron see Antigone standing over her dead brother. The Guard brings her to be interrogated by Kreon, and she confesses to performing the forbidden rituals. Confident that only those who support Thebes may claim true *philia,* Kreon condemns her to die.

By the time *Antigone* was first produced, possibly in 442, Athens' frequent military expeditions, to maintain its empire, had cost many soldiers' lives and brought grief to their families. Wives, mothers, and daughters, by tradition the primary mourners, readied the bodies for burial, then for several days sang, screamed, poured sacred drink offerings to the dead—and directed their rage at the male citizens of the Athenian assembly who had voted for war. These prolonged and passionate expressions of grief remain to this day a primary function of Greek womanhood. As the number of war dead swelled, Athens' leaders devised a calculated policy to limit the women's freedom to mourn and demand revenge. The city channeled grief into patriotic emotion by lumping the dead quite literally together—grouping them by tribe into ten huge trunks on biers under a tent—and communally mourning them once a year with eloquent speeches by a male orator.[4] But the city excluded dead traitors from these impersonal rituals and forbade that their bodies be buried within Athens' frontiers.

Antigone's ancient prerogatives, like those of the bereaved women in Sophokles' Athens, have been usurped by the city. Kreon alone now judges who can be mourned and how. The mythical Theban clash over burial obligations between the two characters is thus emblematic of a much larger power struggle between Athens and its ancient extended family units. Athens' own history can be seen, in part, as a process through which the city successfully sought to bind its citizens more loy-

[4] Thucydides, 2.34: "In the same winter [431–430] the Athenians gave a funeral at the public cost to those who had fallen in this war. It was a custom of their ancestors, and the manner of it follows. Three days before the ceremony, the bones of the dead are laid out in a tent which has been erected; and their friends bring to the relatives such offerings as they please. In the funeral procession the cypress coffins are borne in carts, one for each tribe. . . . [T]he female relatives are there to wail at the burial. . . . After the bodies have been laid in the earth, a man chosen by the state, of approved wisdom and eminent reputation, pronounces over them an appropriate eulogy; after which all retire."

ally to it than to their own blood relatives.[5] Thus, the play's drama
springs from seemingly irreconcilable allegiances—Antigone's to kin,
Kreon's to state. Whose side, then, is Sophokles—an exemplary, lifelong Athenian citizen—on?

The question may suggest that *Antigone* is a play that declares the
moral value of each of its characters without equivocation—and that
the battle for the primacy of one sense of *philia* over another will determine a victor. But the battle is not one to be decided by human conflict
alone. The gods have a hand in this clash of wills—gods who distort vision and force mortals to suffer events that warp their understanding.
In a single choral ode (583–630/628–91) Sophokles sums up the ways in
which gods exercise their own wills to confuse and destroy human lives:
gods *batter and strike;* they *hack away strength* and the *roots of all hope;*
they *punish arrogance;* they *tempt and unbalance minds.* When gods attack a family, their curse never relents. It rises, the Elders sing,

> . . . like a deep
> sea swell, a darkness
> boiling from below, driven
> by the wild stormwinds
> of Thrace that churn up
> black sand from the sea floor— (586–91/635–40)

The gods will indeed churn up Antigone's and Kreon's lives and
force discoveries on them both; the gods will disrupt each character's
and our own understanding of *philia,* the loyalty and affection binding
friends and loved ones in one community, the city and its citizens in
another. Sophokles reminds us that human lives affected by Fate cannot be easily categorized. Winners and losers in this drama will register
neither the full depth of their defeat nor the agony that invades their
victory. But the audience sees both.

As a child of Oedipus, Antigone grew up awash in the curse of the
Labdakids—the "sorrows that struck" (593/643) her family, "wave on
wave of sorrows!" (595/646). Her parents' unnatural deaths[6] concentrated her imaginative life on Hades, on the curse that killed them and
threatens her and her siblings, and on the form or means through which
the curse will strike. Many of these anxieties come through plainly in
her opening rush of questions to her sister:

[5] Seaford, 191–234, 341–44.
[6] Jokasta, Antigone's mother, committed suicide after discovering that Oedipus was both her son and her husband. Ismene speaks of Oedipus in *Antigone*
as if he died in disgrace soon after he discovered he was an incestuous parricide, whereas in the *Kolonos* he dies a mysterious and wondrous death, transformed by the gods in one day from a homeless exile to a revered *heros.*

ANTIGONE   Ismene, dear one, born
            like me from that same womb,
            can you think of one evil,
            of all those Oedipus started,
            that Zeus hasn't used *our lives*
            to finish? There's *nothing*—no pain,
            no shame, no terror, no humiliation!—
            you and I haven't seen and shared. (1–6/1–8)

She then announces their latest shame and terror—Kreon's threat to
kill any who honor Polyneikes' corpse—and makes a vehement case
for burying Polyneikes. Ismene's horrified (albeit reasoned and sympathetic) refusal to participate would make sense to a sister less seized by
self-sacrificing conviction than Antigone: *Think,* Ismene says: *our parents' and brothers' deaths have left us defenseless. Kreon's threatened stoning
will make our deaths much worse than theirs. As women we lack the force
to stand up to men in power. Besides, the gods will understand why we can't
honor Polyneikes; we should fear breaking our city's laws more than dis-
obeying the gods.* Ismene knows Antigone too well to be surprised by
her stubbornness. Antigone is reckless—despite knowing that the gods
have doomed her, or perhaps because of that certainty. She loves battles
she can't win (92/108). As Antigone, recoiling from her sister, sets out
to perform Polyneikes' burial rituals, all Ismene can do is temper her
scathing judgment of Antigone's desperate mission with assurance of
her own (and their dead kin's) unconditional love:

> If you're determined, go ahead.
> And know this much: you are a fool
> to attempt this, but all the more dear
> to the family you love. (98–99/117–20)

Earlier in the scene Antigone made a seemingly hyperbolic promise that bears on her affection for Polyneikes, the nature of the inherited curse, her obsession with death, and perhaps on her planned marriage to Haimon, Kreon's son. If she's killed for honoring Polyneikes,
she tells Ismene:

> I who love him will lie down
> next to him who loves me—
> my criminal conduct blameless!—
> for I owe more to the dead, with whom
> I will spend a much longer time,
> than I will ever owe to the living. (73–76/87–92)

The intensity of this grave-invading, Laertes-like pledge cannot be
passed off as simply grief-stricken devotion to her dead brother. Her desire to join Polyneikes in his grave exposes a passion that Antigone im-

plicitly acknowledges as part of her "blameless criminal conduct." Her vow "to lie down" with Polyneikes carries a suggestion of incestuous desire: the words she uses—*keisomai*, "to lie down with," and *phile . . . philou meta*, "lover with beloved"—commonly refer to reciprocal desire and sexual union.[7] By giving Antigone's love for Polyneikes this brief jolt of sexual intensity Sophokles marks early in the play that her love for her brother is both tender and extreme. In her family-obsessed inner life—a necessity the gods have permanently imposed, and which the play has yet to reveal fully—Antigone conflates sex with incest and marriage with death.

Kreon's obsession with loyalty to Thebes runs directly counter to Antigone's fixation on family. True "friends," he tells his Theban supporters, are only those with whom one serves, sailing the ship of state, keeping her upright (188–90/221–23). In his formal address to the Elders, Kreon stakes his claim to power and expounds the principles he will use to exercise it:

> You cannot measure a man's character,
> policies, or his common sense—until
> you see him at work enforcing old laws
> and making new ones. To me, there's nothing
> worse than a man, while he's running a city,
> who fails to act on sound advice—but fears
> something so much his mouth clamps shut. (175–81/207–13)

> Believe me, Zeus, for you miss nothing,
> I'll always speak out when I see Thebes choosing
> destruction rather than deliverance. (184–86/216–18)

At first, Kreon presents himself as a formidable adversary for his imminent encounters with Antigone. His vow to Zeus, the ultimate source of knowledge and power, assumes divine sanction of his policies. And there's no doubt that his case for honoring Eteokles and denying burial to Polyneikes is well founded in Greek law:

> Such are the principles I will follow
> to preserve Thebes' greatness. Akin to these
> are my explicit orders concerning
> Oedipus' sons: Eteokles, who died
> fighting for our city, and who excelled
> in combat, will be given the rituals
> and burial proper to the noble dead.

[7] The verb Antigone uses in line 523/567–68, *sumphilein*, "to join in love," implies through its intensifying prefix a deep personal emotion that we might be tempted to read back into her lines at 74/87–88.

> But his brother—I mean Polyneikes, who
> returned from exile utterly determined
> to burn down his own city, incinerate
> the gods we worship, revel in kinsmen's blood,
> enslave everyone left alive—
> as for him, it is now a crime for Thebans
> to bury him or mourn him. (191–204/224–37)

But Kreon's words, despite their statesmanlike ring, reveal potential insecurities. They proclaim apparently reasonable principles but project latent character flaws.[8] His habit of personalizing every assertion with first-person pronouns predicts his soon pervasive self-infatuation.[9] Here, he applies a lofty maxim with bloodthirsty zeal: No enemy of his country can ever be his "friend" or *philos,* therefore he will hideously punish his dead nephew Polyneikes by proxy: "Dogs and birds / will savage and outrage his corpse— / an ugly and a visible disgrace. / That is my thinking" (205–6/237–40). Such "thinking" seems imperiled by sadism. Has Kreon forgotten that Zeus misses nothing?

An edgy (and wonderfully insolent) Guard appears next and cowers before Kreon with the news that the ruler's edict has been violated:

> . . . No marks from a pickaxe,
> no dirt thrown up by a shovel. The ground's
> all hard and dry, unbroken—no wheel ruts.
> Whoever did this left no trace. (249–52/282–85)

>   . . . The dead man
> had dropped out of sight. He wasn't entombed,
> but dusted over, as though someone had tried
> to stave off defilement. There was no sign
> dogs or wild animals had chewed the corpse. (255–58/287–91)

The crime seems not to have been committed by a human criminal, but the oblivious Kreon makes the classic mistake of threatening to punish the "messenger." He accuses the Guard of taking a bribe from traitors who plot rebellion. When the Leader proposes that "this business was inspired by the gods" (278/310), Kreon lashes out at him in anger. Although the suggestion of divine intervention is still ambiguous at this point in the drama, a more astute ruler could have read the gods' message correctly—Bury Polyneikes!—and rescinded his edict. What if the gods have conspired to bring out Kreon's worst?

---

[8] Kreon's principles begin to sound bizarre when he assures his advisors that he'll speak out if Thebes is about to destroy itself and then goes on to link Thebes' greatness to mutilating a dead soldier.
[9] For instance at 173/205, 178/210, 184/214, 188/217, 207/240. See Winnington-Ingram, 123.

In the midst of calamity at the end of the play, Kreon will attribute both his blunders and his brutal conduct to a god's malice: "Sometime back, a god struck / my head an immense blow" (1273–74/1410–11). Kreon blames the blow, and the gods who struck it, for his multiple and lethal errors of judgment. One such error is his assumption that the gods share his opinion of his nephew:

> How could anyone possibly believe
> *the gods* protect this corpse? Did *they* cover
> his nakedness to reward him for loyal
> service—this man who came here to burn
> their colonnaded temples and treasuries,
> to wipe out their country and tear up its laws?
> Do you think that the gods honor rebels? (282–88/313–19)

Kreon's mind-set in this scene typifies the human attitude the gods of Greek myth were fond of punishing. Gods test the character and intelligence of those whom they wish to destroy. But these tests frequently resemble "sting operations" in which situations or circumstances are constructed to play upon a character's weakness and tempt him to make a fatal choice. Kreon's contempt for people and his presumption toward gods—coarsened by his lack of insight—lay the groundwork for the destruction of his family and his lifelong misery.

When Kreon first interrogates the captured Antigone, she makes the distinction between his edict, imposed on her by "a mere man" (452/490), and the "gods' unwritten and infallible laws" (454/492). She speaks eloquently and passionately about honoring her family by obeying divine law, and of defying Kreon and dying young. Doesn't a person like herself, "besieged by trouble, escape by dying?" (461–62/502). If Kreon thinks her foolhardy, she says, *"Look at the fool charging me with folly"* (470/508). Antigone's insult is the last straw. Kreon's disdain for family and for the gods, as expressed in these lines, will come back to haunt him:

> I don't care if she is my sister's child,
> a blood relative, closer than all those
> who worship Zeus in my household,
> she—and her sister—still must die. (486–89/524–27)

After Kreon orders his men to bring Ismene from the house the verbal duel between king and culprit continues, but the battleground narrows. Should Polyneikes be treated as a *philos* in the familial sense of the term, or have his treacherous acts as Thebes' (and Eteokles') hated enemy defined and condemned him? Kreon's power will prevail over Antigone's passionate opposition, but Kreon does more than shout her down. He uses Socratic techniques familiar to readers of Plato (or fans of courtroom drama) to force her into defending her position precisely where it's most vulnerable. He does this by compelling her to look at Polyneikes' treachery from her brother Eteokles' point of view. Antigone is rapidly backed into a corner. Why is she defending a despicable traitor in a way that dishonors her "patriotic" good brother?

ANTIGONE	Since when is it shameful to honor a brother?
KREON	You had another brother who died fighting him?
ANTIGONE	Yes, born to the same mother and father.
KREON	Then why do you honor Polyneikes when the act desecrates Eteokles?
ANTIGONE	Eteokles wouldn't agree with you.
KREON	Oh, but he would—because you've honored treachery as though it were patriotism.
ANTIGONE	It was his *brother* who died, not his *slave!*
KREON	That brother died ravaging our country! Eteokles fell fighting to protect it.
ANTIGONE	Hades will still expect his rituals!
KREON	The brave deserve better than the vile.
ANTIGONE	Who knows what matters to the dead?
KREON	Not even death reconciles enemies.
ANTIGONE	I made no enemies by being born! I made my lifelong friends at birth. (511–23/552–68)

Antigone argues against Kreon's powerful logic by first insisting that Hades demands burial rituals be carried out for all dead kin. But when Kreon counters with a "truth" acknowledged by the ancient Greeks—that the dead never cease to hate[10]—she suddenly personalizes her argument. She states, in effect, that hers is the only opinion that matters; she committed to loving her brothers forever at birth. Later, the Leader will give a name to this attitude: *autognotos* (self-willed). "It was your own hot-headed / willfulness that destroyed you," he tells her (875/960–61). Antigone is indeed willful, her argument both illogical and irrefutable. Kreon cannot repeal her autonomous fiat, but he can silence her permanently; he does not continue the debate. And Antigone, obviously driven by deep affection (whether or not it embraces erotic feeling), retains the moral advantage, having exposed Kreon as pursuing "enmity beyond the grave"[11]

When Antigone declares that shared birth parents, and nothing else, established her *philoi* for life, Kreon responds: "Then go down to them! Love your dead brothers!" (524/569). The taunt coincides with Antigone's expressed wish to rejoin her family, a wish Kreon is eager to indulge. He may or may not be accusing Antigone of incestuous at-

---

[10] Homer, *Odyssey*, 11, the "Book of the Dead," shows Aias still furious at Odysseus.
[11] Winnington-Ingram, 135.

traction to her brothers, but the intensity of her emotion clearly disgusts him. And it reminds us that she and her siblings were all born of incestuous sexual intercourse. Kreon knows this, too. We can imagine the difficulty, for a man who can't relate to "normal" familial bonds, in dealing with a person who feels no shame for, and is in fact proud of, loving siblings born from incest.

During his confrontation with Oedipus' daughters, Kreon commits a gross misreading of his son Haimon's attachment to his fiancée Antigone: "He will find other fields to plow." (569/615). This curt vulgarity prefigures the shift in dramatic attention from father to son. But before Haimon arrives, the Leader asks precisely the right question: Does he come here enraged at his father for condemning his bride? If the answer is "yes," which seems likely, Haimon must conceal his feelings to remedy a desperate situation.

Haimon approaches his father with caution and deference, aware that if he attacks or offends him Antigone will die. Throughout this increasingly rancorous scene, one of the most absorbing in the play, Haimon strains to keep discourse on a respectful and political level, while Kreon goads Haimon to admit and renounce his love for and allegiance to Antigone. In this Kreon succeeds, with results from which neither will recover.

As Kreon lectures his son on filial obligation, he relies on patriarchal clichés: loyal sons must harm a father's enemies and help his friends; citizens must obey their leaders even when they are wrong; insubordination is the worst of crimes. But the anxiety underlying these platitudes boils to the surface when he warns Haimon against Antigone in terms that sound like grounds for breaking an engagement, not for execution: *frigidity, scorn in the bedroom, poisonous love.* He tries to undermine his son's affection for a woman he considers a traitor and concludes his advice with a gratuitous non sequitur:

> Discipline is what saves the lives of all
> good people who stay out of trouble.
> And to make sure we enforce discipline—
> never let a woman overwhelm a king.
> Better to be driven from power, if it
> comes to that, by a man. Then nobody
> can say you were beaten by some female. (676–80/749–55)

Kreon expects Haimon to share his own aversion to women, Antigone in particular. His paranoia is fully warranted; she will in fact drive him from power.

Haimon begins his counter-appeal with the utmost tact and subtlety; he's loyal, so far, though not the totally submissive son Kreon demands. He tries to save Antigone by strategically presenting new in-

formation and ideas that will make it easier for his father to rescind the
death sentence. He knows the Theban street supports Antigone's attempt to honor her dead brother: "Thebes aches for this girl" (693/768).
"Hasn't she earned, they ask, golden honor?" (699/775). Haimon then
suggests that Kreon has made a horrible but correctible error; his skillful analogies derive from different value systems that promote flexibil-
ity. *Intellectual resourcefulness:* "Attitudes are like clothes; you can change
them" (705/781). *Open-mindedness:* "It's never shameful for even a wise
man / to keep on learning new things all his life" (711/786–87). *The
Wisdom of Nature:* "Think of trees / caught in a raging winter torrent:
those / that bend will survive . . ." (712–13/788–80). *Seamanship:* "A
captain who . . . never [eases] off in a blow / [will] capsize . . ." (715–
16/792–94). Rather than take his son's impressive advice seriously—exactly the kind of advice he swore to heed in his "inaugural" speech to
the Elders—Kreon takes offense.

   In the crossfire of accusations that follows, Haimon exposes his
father's tyranny and lack of wisdom:

KREON   Look at yourself! A woman overpowers you.
HAIMON   But no disgraceful impulse ever will.
KREON   Your every word supports that woman.
HAIMON   And you, and me, and the gods of this earth.
KREON   You will not marry her while she's *on* this earth.
HAIMON   Then she will die, and dead, kill someone else.
                                   (746–51/824–29)

   Haimon's passionate diversion of his father's accusation does not
deny, and therefore implicitly admits, that Antigone has indeed overwhelmed him. His arguments also envision a peaceful harmony among
philoi of all groupings—and between the laws of men and those of
gods—that Kreon cannot abide. With typical self-regarding obtuse-
ness Kreon hears Haimon's suicide warning as a threat on his own life,[12]
and responds by threatening to kill Antigone before his son's eyes. Haimon explodes with wrath and leaves the scene, unable to control his
fury any longer. Kreon, just barely chastened by the Leader's incredu-
lous question—*"Then you intend to execute them both?"* (770/849)—
decides to spare Ismene's life but orders his soldiers to lead Antigone on
a deserted road, away from the city, and to imprison her in a hollow
cave; if she commits suicide, as he hopes, neither he nor Thebes will be
defiled by her murder.

[12] Haimon's threat is both reckless and ambiguous: "Then she will die, and
dead, kill someone else" (751/829). Indeed, he's beginning to sound like his father in this line. See Goldhill's assessment (101) of Haimon's increasingly stubborn Kreon-like behavior in the last lines of the scene (747–65/825–38).

The brief, incandescent choral ode that comes next warns of Love's power, the force that "wrench[es] . . . men's minds . . . off course" (791–92/872–73). Kreon's insensitivity to sexual love has unleashed the intensity of Haimon's love for Antigone; that passion will drive Haimon to kill himself. His death, and his mother's to follow, will drain the happiness from his father's life. Kreon's focus on civic *philia* made him underestimate not only Hades and the death gods, but the gods of life as well: Aphrodite the implacable and her son Eros, who causes even good men's lives to crash.

Though Eros is clearly a major force in the play,[13] Antigone's expression of erotic feeling is muted; she outwardly evinces little or none. But she does have sexual feelings, however complicated they are by her obsessions with death and incest, and she will reveal them in a remarkable way.

Antigone never once acknowledges that she is meant to marry Haimon, nor does she even mention his name. But she does tell her sister she pursues quite a different commitment: "Long ago / I dedicated [my life] to the dead" (559–60/604–5). These hardly sound like the words of a young woman happily anticipating marriage and motherhood,[14] but they help explain the extraordinary fusion of motives and ceremonies that takes place in her affecting and surprising final scene. Deprived of the earthly marriage that is the expected destination for young Greek girls, she imagines a marriage implicit in her devotion to her dead parents and their afterlife in the underworld. She presents herself as a bride, but one wedded to Death himself.[15]

A lovely long *kommos,* or antiphonal song of mourning, immediately follows her final entrance. Sophokles uses its melody and imagery to express the sadness in her heart. When the Leader suggests that Antigone will enter Hades of her own free will—his exchanges with her are in lyric verse as well—she answers by identifying with a mythological character who was cruelly punished by a god for her presumption.

> I once heard that a Phrygian stranger,
> Niobe, the daughter of Tantalos,
> died a hideous death on Mt. Sipylos.
> Living rock, like relentless ivy,
> crushed her. Now, people say, she slowly
> erodes; rain and snow

[13] Winnington-Ingram (92–116) has explored its decisive impact on the characters' actions and its powerful presence in several choral odes.
[14] The name Antigone means "anti-generation," a word and concept that sum up the aversion to life and childbearing implied by some, but not all, of her speech and actions.
[15] The actress should appear in the traditional Greek purple wedding gown. See *Antigone* notes, p. 259.

never leave her, they constantly
pour like tears from her eyes,
drenching the clefts of her body.
My death will be like hers,
when the god at last lets me sleep. (823–33/903–13)

Niobe is one of the unluckiest mothers myth has to offer. After
she boasted that she was more fertile, and therefore a better mother,
than the goddess Leto (who had given birth to only two children), Leto
persuaded her formidable pair, Apollo and Artemis, to kill each and
every one of Niobe's many offspring. Like Niobe, Antigone has lost her
children, in her own case unconceived and unborn children. Her tears,
like Niobe's, will be unending. But while the "living rock" that crushes
Niobe symbolizes the end of her fertility, Antigone's "heaped up rock-
bound prison" locks her permanently in virginity. She identifies with
Niobe as a naked girl, forever drenched in rain.

The Leader gently chastises Antigone for comparing herself to
Niobe, "a goddess," he says, "with gods for parents" (834–35/914–15). In
most versions of the myth, however, Niobe is a mortal whose grief was
caused by her brazen attempt at surpassing a goddess. But Sophokles,
like his fellow tragedians, altered received myths in his plays, and here
his purpose might have been twofold: By likening herself to a god,
Antigone reminds the Leader that although the underworld gods approve her attempt to bury Polyneikes, her mortal parents' lives (and her
own) were undeniably wrecked, as were Niobe's and her children's lives,
by a divine force.

When the Leader consoles Antigone by saying that whatever mistakes she's made, she's also paying for the sins of her father, she responds:

You've touched my worst grief,
the fate of my father, which I
keep turning over in my mind.
We all were doomed, the whole
grand house of Labdakos,
by my mother's horrendous,
incestuous, coupling with her son.
From what kind of parents was I born? (857–67/943–50)

Her parents' incest has forced her to think how that defilement
might affect her own sexual existence. Her outburst, "From what kind
of parents was I born?" is a muted version of Oedipus' thunderous
denunciation of marriage in *Oedipus the King* (1403–8/1591–96). Antigone naturally fears that her parents' incestuous marriage will have an
evil impact, in some unforeseen way, on any marriage she consummates. When she assigns sole responsibility for the curse on her family
to her mother's "horrendous coupling" with her father—women in an-

cient Greek culture were commonly blamed for incestuous sexual relationships no matter if men or gods initiated them—she might be re-
membering incestuous desire that was stirred in her. She pauses on the
grimly comforting thought that dying before marriage will avoid any
damage inherited incest could inflict on her choice of mate or on her
children's lives: "I'm going to them now, / I'm dying unmarried" (867–
68/951–52). Then she remembers Polyneikes' marriage—deadly both
because it enabled the war on his native city that killed him and because
its consequences will kill her:

> And brother Polyneikes,
> wasn't yours too a deadly
> marriage? And when you
> were slaughtered, so was I. (869–71/953–56)

Antigone's extreme love for Polyneikes has played its part in arranging
the marriage to Hades she now awaits.[16]

At the end of Antigone's lament Kreon prods his guards to take
Antigone and seal her in her cave. Before they can lead her away she
launches into a strangely legalistic and controversial explanation of
why she is willing to die for Polyneikes, her blood brother, whereas she
would not die for a husband or a child. Because she suddenly abandons
her former convictions, the authenticity of this passage (904–20/996–
1013) has long been contested.[17] The passage does seem at considerable
odds with Antigone's repeated insistence that all dead kin must receive
Hades' rituals from their families. But the lines are far more likely to
have been written by Sophokles than by anyone else; a century later
Aristotle trusted and quoted from them.[18] As Lloyd-Jones and Wilson

[16] See Sophokles' treatment of the Antigone/Polyneikes relationship in the
Kolonos (1181–1203/1294–1316, 1280–84/1402–5, 1414–46/1543–79). Her famil-
iarity, her sincere caring, suggests that her intense affection for him in *Antigone*
is of long standing and never relinquished.

[17] Goethe simply (and subjectively) thought that Antigone's restated position
included conditions unworthy of her. The scholars who challenge the lines'
authenticity argue that they introduce incoherence into Antigone's character
and thus into the play. Scholars who judge them authentic usually base their
case on their very early origins and the fact that Aristotle accepted the lines.
The most impressive subjective defense of the lines belongs to Knox (1964,
104ff.), who finds in them a further instance of her unstable and intense love
for Polyneikes: "In the almost hysterical hyperbole of her claim that she would
not have run such a risk for that husband and those children she will now never
live to see, she is telling Polynices that no other love, not even that she might
have had for the child of her own body, could surpass her love for him." For a
still highly relevant discussion of the lines see Jebb 1888, 258–63. Also see
Antigone n. 996–1013.

[18] *Rhetoric,* 3.16.9.

write, "the arguments leveled against [the suspect lines] have been purely subjective."[19]

If the lines are Sophokles' own (I include 994–95 here for context) we need to assess their impact, for they tell us something awkward and unforeseen, but highly significant about Antigone:

> Now, because I honored your corpse,
> Polyneikes, *this* is how I'm repaid!
> I honored you as wise men would think right.
> But I wouldn't have taken that task on
> had I been a mother who lost her child,
> or if my husband were rotting out there.
> For them I would never defy my city.
> You want to know what law lets me say this?
> If my husband were dead, I could remarry.
> A new husband could give me a new child.
> But with my father and mother in Hades,
> a new brother could never bloom for me.
> *That* is the law that made me die for you,
> Polyneikes. But Kreon says I'm wrong,
> terribly wrong. And now I'm his captive,
> he pulls me by the wrist to no bride's bed;
> I won't hear bridal songs or feel the joy
> of married love, and I will have no share
> in raising children. No, I will go grieving,
> friendless, and alive to a hollow tomb. (904–20/994–1013)

What Antigone implies here is a shock. It seems to betray the uncompromising loyalties that have made her so powerful a character in modern politicized productions. The woman who declared her love of kin absolute *would not have disobeyed Kreon to bury a dead husband, or a dead child.* And she would never have tried to bury Polyneikes *if she could have replaced him with another brother,* one whose body she could have honored in death. Much earlier she asserted the primacy of family over country in her battle with Kreon: "I made no enemies by being born! I made my lifelong friends at birth!" (523/567–68).[20] This declaration anticipates Antigone's justification here for choosing Polyneikes over a hypothetical husband or child; neither of these *acquired* loved ones *(philoi)* could she have gained at birth.

[19] Lloyd-Jones and Wilson, 138.
[20] Lloyd-Jones and Wilson (126) give the rationale for this interpretation of 523: "One has φιλοι, *[philoi]* but not εκθροι, *[ekthroi]* by virtue of one's φυσισ *[physis],* so that the sentimental effusions this line has provoked are unwarranted." Lloyd-Jones (1994, 50) translates the line: "I have no enemies by birth, but I have friends by birth." An example of the effusions they have in mind might be "It's my nature to share love, not hatred."

While this abrupt revision departs from her once inflexible principles, it does seem fully consistent with her mounting regret for what she's about to lose—marriage, lovemaking, a bride's joy, children, the comfort of friends, her fellow citizens' regard—because it offers a glimpse of her inner turmoil. She would rather live, she would rather obey the city, if the laws of kinship and burial rights allowed her to do so. Her vivid appreciation of all she will lose in death leaves no doubt that she does care about life, her own life. Not to express such remorse and loss would make her much less real and human. Because they are hypothetical, her regrets have no practical effect on her situation. Her focus on a possible husband and child, however, might have been a sign from Sophokles that Antigone allies herself with Athenian women who willingly relinquished their husbands and sons to so many wars, so long as they could reclaim their bodies and mourn them in death.[21]

Antigone now seems to make one final, extremely dramatic gesture.[22] She reaches up to the veil hiding her face—the first layer of cloth protecting a bride's virginity—and uncovers her whole head, saying:

> Look at me, princely citizens of Thebes:
> I'm the last daughter of the kings who ruled you.
> Look at what's done to me, and by whom
> it's done, to punish me for keeping faith. (940–43/1032–35)

Antigone enacts the climactic moment of a Greek wedding, in which the bride rises and reveals her naked face to the penetrating gaze of the men in attendance. At this moment in a bride's earthly wedding, her groom would seize her by the hand and lead her to a waiting mule cart that would carry her to his family home and the immediate loss of her virginity. Antigone will not go to a new family, or lose her virginity; she will return to her natal family residing in Hades and consummate a truly anti-marriage, but one that she defiantly celebrates.

Before she leaves the stage Antigone faces Kreon and the Elders to deliver her final judgment on them all and, by implication, on the gods who have allowed Kreon to kill her:

[21] See Tyrrell and Bennett, 111–118, whose interpretation I accept and follow in detail. In this excerpt from Perikles' famous funeral oration (in Thucydides, 2.44.3) the great general spoke directly to parents who had lost sons in the war. "Yet you who are still of an age to beget children must bear up in the hope of having others in their stead; not only will they help you forget those whom you have lost, but will be to the state at once a reinforcement and a security; for never can a fair or just policy be expected of the citizen who does not, like his fellows, bring to the decision the interests and apprehensions of a father."

[22] She invites the Elders to look at her. The request could be mere self-dramatization (since the Elders have surely been looking at her), but if she has just lifted a bridal veil to reveal her head, the lines become highly dramatic and poignant.

> If the gods are happy I'm sentenced to die
> I hope one day I'll discover
> what divine law I have broken.
> But if my judges are at fault, I want *them*
> to suffer the pain they inflict on me now. (925–28/1018–1022)

A Greek's prayer could be a curse, and this one surely is. Kreon will soon be left alone to grieve—just as Antigone was, just as if he were a woman—to sing the dirge for his son and his wife.

The ancient, blind prophet Tiresias, a figure with direct access to the ever-dangerous divinities, is appropriately the last to confront Kreon. His intervention is unusual because it is secular, not, strictly speaking, that of a prophet delivering a god-sanctioned prediction or divine advice. Tiresias has saved Kreon from disaster before, but during this emergency, when the prophet attempts to communicate with the gods, they ignore him. Tiresias interprets their refusal to mean that they are too enraged at Kreon to send any helpful omens. The lack of divine instruction compels Tiresias to speak his own mind to Kreon. What he tells him is religiously informed common sense, and Kreon fumes to hear it. The prophet's blunt denunciation of Kreon's folly activates the king's suspicion of bribable prophets. "My conscience can't be bought," Kreon self-righteously postures. But Tiresias' authority, his unblemished record for being right, will prevail:

> Then tell your conscience this: You will not live
> for many circuits of the chariot sun
> before you trade a child from your loins
> for all the corpses whose deaths you have caused.
> You have thrown children from the sunlight
> down to the shades of Hades, ruthlessly
> housing a living person in a tomb,
> while you detain here, among us, something
> that belongs to the gods who live below
> our world—the naked unwept corpse you've robbed
> of the solemn grieving we owe our dead.
> None of this should have been any concern
> of yours—or of the Olympian gods—
> but you have involved them in your outrage!
> Therefore, avengers wait to ambush you—
> the Furies sent by Hades and its gods
> will punish you for the crimes I have named. (1064–76/1176–92)

The rhetorical weight of Tiresias' prediction gains further power from its comprehensive indictment. Besides causing the deaths of two young people, Kreon has dishonored and savaged a corpse, cheated the corpse's kin of their right to mourn, and robbed the gods of the respect owed them. By the time Tiresias' message sinks in, nothing Kreon can say or do will save him and his family from his own irretrievable errors. He should indeed fear the vengeful gods he has scorned.

When the Messenger reports the confrontation of father and son in Antigone's "bridal tomb," every shocking detail radiates significance. As the Eros ode made clear, Haimon's mind—like his father's—has been wrenched off course by the love god. The ode makes explicit that Justice, whose unwritten laws Antigone earlier proclaimed, and Eros, who sits beside her, have equal force:

> . . . allure flashing
> from the keen eyes of the bride
> always wins, for Desire wields
> all the power of ancient law:
> Aphrodite the implacable
> plays cruel games with our lives. (795–99/875–80)

The unwritten law of love drives those it seizes mad. The flashing eyes of Haimon's "bride," the source of his vulnerability, now look dimly out at him from the land of death. The Messenger describes Haimon turning away from Antigone to stare at his father:

> His son then glared straight at him
> with savage eyes, spat in his face, spoke not
> one word in answer, but drew his two-edged sword.
> His father leapt back, Haimon missed his thrust.
> Then this raging youth—with no warning—turned
> on himself, tensed his body to the sword,
> and drove half its length deep into his side.
> Still conscious, he clung to her with limp arms,
> gasping for breath, spurts of his blood pulsing
> onto her white cheek.
> Then he lay there, his dead
> body embracing hers, married at last,
> poor man—not up here, but somewhere
> in Hades—proving that of all mankind's
> evils, thoughtless violence is the worst. (1231–43/1364–77)

Minutes earlier Haimon had spoken calmly and eloquently to his father in favor of taking thought before acting, and in favor of going (quite literally, like a tree in a river) with the flow. Now possessed by murderous hatred he becomes the person he just warned his father against. His devastation at Antigone's death, his father's shame in causing it, and his own shame in failing to prevent or avenge it, make his life intolerable. The Messenger ends his account with self-evident, but in this case useless, words of wisdom: *Destructive impulses will pass, but not if you act on them instantly.* The wanton cruelty of Aphrodite's influence is confirmed anew.

The death scene's imagery is affecting enough, but its quotations from gestures and rituals of ancient Greek weddings add to its significance. Haimon lifts up the stiffened, hanging Antigone by her waist. Hers is the posture in which a bride was lifted by her groom into the waiting cart after the wedding. The dying Haimon's blood spurting onto the bride's cheeks consummates this marriage in Hades just as the bleeding of a new bride after sexual intercourse would consummate a marriage on earth.

As Kreon speaks to his household, now barren of children and the hopes of more to come, we hear a voice purged of its former arrogance and disabling self-regard:

> You all see it—the man
> who murdered, and the son
> who's dead. What I did
> was blind and wrong!
> You died so young, my son,
> your death happened so fast!
> Your life was cut short
> not through your mad acts,
> but through mine. (1263–69/1397–405)
>
> Why hasn't someone
> driven a two-edged
> sword through my heart?
> I'm a wretched coward,
> awash with terror. (1308–11/1461–65)
>
> There's no one I can blame,
> no other mortal.
> I am the only one. (1317–19/1472–74)

As the Leader tells him, the revelation comes far too late. Kreon alone caused the deaths of his *philoi*; Kreon alone remains alive to mourn them. Eurydike kills herself, cursing Kreon for causing the "deaths of her sons" (1305/1468).[23] He condemns himself yet again and wonders at the insatiable hunger Hades has for the dead.

The keening end to *Antigone* resembles that of the other Greek dramatists but differs in one important respect from Sophokles' own surviving works. The suffering of his protagonist Kreon is fully de-

---

[23] Eurydike uses the word *paidoktonos,* lit. "child-killer." In one mythic account of the war between Thebes and Argos, Kreon sacrifices their eldest son, Megareus, to ensure a Theban victory.

served. The man who denied Antigone the right to act on her love of family withers into utter misery as his son and wife choose death rather than continued life with him. Kreon "offends and is punished, he is proud and is brought low, he is infatuated and brings disaster on himself."[24] The joy sung early in the morning by the Elders, giving thanks for Thebes' survival of a raging assault on its walls, has been replaced by cries of mourning—mourning for the fragile happiness of a family whose leader, failing to honor his own loved ones, took shameless revenge on a defenseless corpse and an innocent girl. Kreon's joy dies with his family. But any surge of sympathy we might feel is chastened by the fact that Kreon never voices the slightest regret for killing Antigone; in this scene of general remorse he never mentions her name.

Without shifting blame for the catastrophe away from Kreon, Sophokles has altered our understanding of all the major characters and the reality they inhabit. Antigone has grieved for the womanhood and motherhood she once rejected; though she upheld an honorable and divine custom, she has actively collaborated with the remorseless curse that has now wiped out the Labdakids. Haimon has succumbed to the kind of impulsive action he warned his father against. His self-discipline is no match for the daimonic tidal wave that surges through him. Kreon emerges from his homicidal self-obsession to the forced discovery that his own happiness was wholly invested in the lives of his wife and son. Of the gods who have so deeply penetrated the minds of the characters and the actions they take, what can be said? Are they more terrifying if they impose their will on mortals, as the Greeks feared—or if, as the malign powers we sometimes imagine embedded in the human psyche, they wait inside us for the chance to punish their hosts?

An attempt to answer such a question takes us a long way from any pat analysis of *Antigone* as a play about a tyrannical suppression of civilized values. *Antigone* leaves both Kreon and the royal house of Thebes mortally wounded. Its king is a "living corpse" who knows something of what hit him, but nothing at all of what was (and is) missing from his character, his policies, and his common sense. To judge from the Chorus' authoritative tone, the city will soon be in the hands of its Old Men. Tragedy, as Sophokles practiced it in *Antigone,* proposes that destructive energies are inseparable from the morally admirable and life-generating consciences with whom they cohabit.

[24] Winnington-Ingram, 147.

Antigone

SCENE

Dawn in front of Kreon's palace in Thebes, the day after the battle in which the Theban defenders repelled an attack on the city by an Argive coalition that included the rebel Polyneikes, elder son of Oedipus. Polyneikes and his younger brother Eteokles, who has remained loyal to Thebes, have killed each other simultaneously in face-to-face combat at one of Thebes' seven gates. Kreon has suddenly seized the throne. In dim, streaky light Antigone runs from offstage into a side door calling Ismene's name. Within a short time Antigone and Ismene enter through the central doors.

ANTIGONE	Ismene, dear one, born like me from that same womb, can you think of one evil, of all those Oedipus started, that Zeus hasn't used *our lives* to finish? There's *nothing*—no pain, no shame, no terror, no humiliation!— you and I haven't seen and shared.
	Now there's this new order our commander-in-chief <10> imposes on the whole city— do you know about it? Have you heard? You don't know, do you? It threatens our loved ones the same as our enemies!
ISMENE	No word of our family has reached *me*, Antigone, welcome or painful, not since we sisters lost our brothers in one day, when their hands struck the double blow that killed them both. <20> And since the Argive army fled last night I've heard nothing that could improve our luck— or make it any worse.
ANTIGONE	That's what I thought. That's why I've brought you out past the gates— where no one but you can hear what I say.
ISMENE	What's wrong? It's plain you're shaken by grim news.
ANTIGONE	It's Kreon. The way he's treated our brothers. Hasn't he buried one with honor? But he's shamed the other. Disgraced him! Eteokles, they say, was laid to rest <30> according to law and custom. The dead will respect him in Hades. But Polyneikes' sorry body can't be touched.
	The city is forbidden to mourn him or bury him—no tomb, no tears—just a sweet rich find for the birds to feast on. That's the clear order our good general gives you and me—yes, I said me! They say he's coming here to proclaim it in person to those who haven't heard it. <40>

This is not something he takes lightly.
Violate any provision—the sentence is
you're stoned to death in your own city.
Now you know.
                        And soon you'll prove
how nobly born you really are.
Or did our family breed a coward?

ISMENE   If that's the bind we're in, you poor thing,
what good can *I* do by yanking the knot
tighter—*or* by trying to pry it loose?

ANTIGONE   Make up your mind. Will you join me?   <50>
Share the burden?

ISMENE   At what risk? What are you asking?

ANTIGONE   *(Raising up her hands.)*
Will you help these hands lift his body?

ISMENE   You want to bury him? Break the law?

ANTIGONE   I'm going to bury my brother—your brother!—
with or without your help. I won't betray him.

ISMENE   You scare me, sister. Kreon's forbidden this.

ANTIGONE   He's got *no right* to keep me from what's mine!

ISMENE   He's mine too!
                        Just think what our father's
destruction meant for us both.
Because of those horrible deeds—   <60>
all self-inflicted, all self-detected—
he died hated and notorious,
his eyes battered into blindness
by his own hands. And then
his wife and mother—two roles
for one woman—disposed
of her life with a noose
of twisted rope. And now
our poor brothers die the same day
in a mutual act of kin murder!   <70>
Think how much worse
our own deaths will be—abandoned
as we are—if we defy the king's
proclamation and his power.
Remember, we are women. We're not
able to fight men. They're stronger!

We must accept these things—and worse to come.
I want the Spirits of the Dead
to understand this: I'm not free.
I must obey whoever's in charge.   <80>
It's crazy to attempt the impossible!

ANTIGONE   Then I'll stop asking you! And if you change
your mind, I won't accept your help.
Go be the person you've chosen to be.
I'll bury Polyneikes myself. I'll do
what's honorable, and then I'll die.
I who love him will lie down
next to him who loves me—
my criminal conduct blameless!—
for I owe more to the dead, with whom   <90>
I will spend a much longer time,
than I will ever owe to the living.
Go ahead, please yourself—defy
laws the gods expect us to honor.

ISMENE   I'm not insulting them! But how can I
defy the city? I don't have the strength.

ANTIGONE   Then make that your excuse. I'll heal
with earth the body of the brother I love.

ISMENE   I feel so sorry for you. And afraid.

ANTIGONE   Don't waste your fear. Straighten out your own life.   <100>

ISMENE   At least tell nobody what you're planning!
Say nothing about it. And neither will I.

ANTIGONE   No! Go on, tell them all!
I will hate you much more for your silence—
if you don't shout it everywhere.

ISMENE   You're burning to do what should stop you cold.

ANTIGONE   One thing I do know: I'll please those who matter.

ISMENE   *As if* you could! You love fights you can't win.

ANTIGONE   When my strength is exhausted, I'll quit.

ISMENE   Hopeless passion is wrong from the start.   <110>

ANTIGONE   Say that again and I'll despise you.
So will the dead—and they'll hate you
far longer. But go! Let me and my
recklessness deal with this alone.

No matter what I suffer
I won't die dishonored.

*(Exit Antigone toward open country; Ismene
calls out her next lines as her sister leaves, then she
enters the palace through the great central doors.)*

ISMENE   If you're determined, go ahead.
            And know this much: you are a fool
            to attempt this, but all the more dear
            to the family you love.   <120>

(Chorus of Theban Elders enters singing.)

ELDERS   Morning sunlight, loveliest ever
            to shine on seven-gated Thebes!
            Day's golden eye, risen at last
            over Dirke's glittering waters!
            You stampede the Argive!
            Invading in full battle gear,
            his white shield flashing, he's wrenched
            by your sharp piercing bit
            into headlong retreat!
            This attacker who championed   <130>
            quarrelsome Polyneikes
            skimmed through our farmland—
            a white-feathered Eagle
            screeching, horse-hair
            flaring from the helmets
            of well-armed troops.

            He had circled our houses, threatening
            all seven gates, his spearpoints
            out for blood, but he was thrown back
            before his jaws could swell   <140>
            with our gore, before the Firegod's
            incendiary pinetar
            engulfed the towers ringing our walls.
            He cannot withstand the harsh blare
            of battle that roars up
            around him—and the Dragon
            wrestles him down.

            How Zeus hates a proud tongue!
            And when this river of men
            surged forward, with arrogance   <150>
            loud as its flash of gold,

he struck—with his own lightning—
that firebrand shouting in triumph
from the battlements!
Free-falling from the mad
fury of his charge, torch
still in his hand,
he crashed to earth, the man
who'd turned on us the raving
blast of his loathsome words.   <160>
But threats stuck in his throat:
To each enemy soldier
Ares the brute wargod,
our surging wheelhorse,
assigned a separate doom,
shattering every attack.

Now seven captains facing seven gates,
our captains matching theirs,
throw down their arms as trophies
for Zeus—all but the doomed pair   <170>
born to one father, one mother—
who drive their twin spears home:
Their deaths mirror each other.

Victory is now ours!
Her name is pure glory,
her joy resounds
through Thebes' own joy—Thebes
swarming with chariots!
Let us now banish
this war from our minds   <180>
and visit each god's temple,
singing all night long! May
Bakkhos, the god whose dancing
rocks Thebes, be there to lead us!

(Enter Kreon.)

LEADER   Enter our new king,
              Kreon, the son of Menoikeus,
              who came to power
              abruptly, when the gods changed our luck.
              What plans does he turn over
              in his mind—what will he ponder   <190>
              with the Council of Elders
              summoned in his new role?

KREON   Men, we have just survived some rough weather.
Monstrous waves have battered our city,
but now the gods have steadied the waters.
I sent my servants to gather you here
because, of all my people, I know
your veneration for Laios' royal
power has never wavered. When Oedipus
ruled our city, and then was struck down, you   <200>
stood by his children. Now his two sons fall
together, killed in one lethal exchange.

Because each struck the other's deathblow, each
was defiled by his own brother's blood.
I've taken power, and as the nearest kin
to the men killed, assumed the throne.

You cannot measure a man's character,
policies, or his common sense—until
you see him at work enforcing old laws
and making new ones. To me, there's nothing   <210>
worse than a man, while he's running a city,
who fails to act on sound advice—but fears
something so much his mouth clamps shut.
Nor have I any use for a man whose friend
means more to him than his country.
Believe me, Zeus, for you miss nothing,
I'll always speak out when I see Thebes choosing
destruction rather than deliverance.
I'll never think our country's enemy
can be my friend. Keep this in mind: <220>
Our *country* is the ship that must keep us safe.
It's only on board her, among the men
who sail her upright, that we make true friends.

Such are the principles I will follow
to preserve Thebes' greatness. Akin to these
are my explicit orders concerning
Oedipus' sons: Eteokles, who died
fighting for our city, and who excelled
in combat, will be given the rituals
and burial proper to the noble dead.   <230>

But his brother—I mean Polyneikes, who
returned from exile utterly determined
to burn down his own city, incinerate
the gods we worship, revel in kinsmen's blood,
enslave everyone left alive—

as for him, it is now a crime for Thebans
to bury him or mourn him. Dogs and birds
will savage and outrage his corpse—
an ugly and a visible disgrace.
That is my thinking. And I will never   <240>
tolerate giving a bad man more respect
than a good one. Only those faithful to Thebes
will I honor—in this life and after death.

LEADER   That is your pleasure, Kreon: Punish Thebes'
              betrayers and reward her defenders.
              You have all the authority you need
              to discipline the living and the dead.

KREON   Are you willing to help enforce this law?

LEADER   Ask someone younger to shoulder that burden.

KREON   But I've already posted men at the corpse.   <250>

LEADER   Then what instructions do you have for me?

KREON   Don't join the cause of those who break this law.

LEADER   Who but a fool would want to die?

KREON   Exactly. He'd be killed. But easy money
              frequently kills those it deludes.

              (Enter Guard. He tends to mime the actions he describes.)

GUARD   I didn't run here at such a breakneck
              pace, King, that I'm winded. Pausing to think
              stopped me, wheeled me around, headed me back
              more than once. My mind kept yelling at me:
              "Reckless fool—why go where you'll be punished?"   <260>
              Then: "Lazy clod! Dawdling, are you? What if
              Kreon hears this news from somebody else?—
              you'll pay for it."
                                I made myself dizzy,
              hurrying slowly, stretching out a short road.
              I finally realized I had to come.
              If I'm talking annihilation here,
              I'll still say it, since I'm of the opinion
              nothing but my own fate can cause me harm.

KREON   What's making you so agitated?

GUARD   I've got to explain my role in this matter.   <270>
              I didn't do it, I didn't see who did.
              So it wouldn't be right to punish me.

KREON   You're obsessed with protecting yourself.
         That's a nice fortified wall you've thrown up
         around your news—which must be odd indeed.

GUARD   You bet. And bad news must be broken slowly.

KREON   Why not just tell it? Then you can vanish.

GUARD   But I *am* telling you! That corpse—someone's
         buried it and run off. They sprinkled thirsty
         dust on it. Then did all the rituals.   <280>

KREON   What are you saying? What man would dare do this?

GUARD   I've no idea. No marks from a pickaxe,
         no dirt thrown up by a shovel. The ground's
         all hard and dry, unbroken—no wheel ruts.
         Whoever did this left no trace.
         When the man on dawn-watch showed it to us,
         we all got a nasty surprise. The dead man
         had dropped out of sight. He wasn't entombed,
         but dusted over, as though someone had tried
         to stave off defilement. There was no sign   <290>
         dogs or wild animals had chewed the corpse.
         Then we all started yelling rough words, threats,
         blaming each other, every guard ready
         to throw punches—nobody to stop us.
         Every man under suspicion—but none
         of us convicted. We all denied it—
         swearing to god we'd handle red-hot iron
         or walk through fire to back up our oaths.

         After interrogation got us nowhere,
         one man spoke up and made us hang our heads   <300>
         toward the ground in terror. We couldn't do
         what he said—or avoid trouble if we did.
         He advised us to tell you what happened,
         not try to hide it. That seemed our best move.
         So we drew lots to choose the messenger.
         I lost—I'm no happier to be here
         than you are to see me. Don't I know that.
         Nobody loves the man who brings bad news.

LEADER   King, something has been bothering me: Suppose
         this business was inspired by the gods?   <310>

KREON   Stop! Before your words fill me with rage.
         Now, besides sounding old, you sound senile.
         How could anyone possibly believe

the gods protect this corpse? Did *they* cover
his nakedness to reward him for loyal
service—this man who came here to burn
their colonnaded temples and treasuries,
to wipe out their country and tear up its laws?
Do you think that the gods honor rebels?
They don't. But for a good while now   <320>
men who despise me have been muttering
under their breaths—my edict bruised their necks.
They were rebelling against a just yoke—
unlike you good citizens who support me.
I'm sure these malcontents bribed my sentries
to do what they did.
                    Mankind's most deadly
invention is money—it plunders cities,
encourages men to abandon their homes,
tempts honest people to do shameful things.
It instructs them in criminal practice,   <330>
drives them to act on every godless impulse.
By doing this for silver, these men have
guaranteed that, sooner or later,
they'll pay the price.
                    But you who worship Zeus—
since Zeus enforces his own will through mine—
be sure of this, it is my solemn oath:
If you don't find the man who carried out
this burial and drag him before me,
a quick trip to Hades won't be your fate.
You will all be strung up—and you'll hang   <340>
for a while, your insolence on display.
From then on, you may calculate exactly
how much profit to expect from your crimes.
More men are destroyed by ill-gotten wealth
than such "wealth" ever saved from destruction.

GUARD   May I speak further? Or shall I just leave?

KREON   Don't you realize that your words pain me?

GUARD   Do your ears ache, or does the pain go deeper?

KREON   Why does the source of my pain interest you?

GUARD   I just sting your ears. The man   <350>
             who did this stabs your gut.

KREON   You've run off at the mouth since you were born.

GUARD   Maybe so. But I had no part in this crime.

KREON   I think you did. Sold your life for some silver.

GUARD   It's a sad thing when a judge gets it wrong.

KREON   You'll soon be on the wrong end of a judgment
yourself.
               If you don't find the guilty one,
you'll find your greed buys you nothing but grief.

GUARD   I hope he's caught, but Fate will decide that.
And you'll never see me coming back here.   <360>
Now that I have been spared—when everything
seemed so desperate—all I can think about
is how much gratitude I owe the gods.

(Exit Guard to open country; Kreon enters his palace.)

ELDERS   Wonders abound, but none
more astounding than man!
He crosses to the far side
of white seas, blown
by winter gales, sailing
below huge waves;
he wears Earth down—   <370>
our primal, eternal,
inexhaustible god—
his stallion-sired mules
plowing her soil
back and forth
year after year.

All breeds of carefree
bird, savage beast
and deep-sea creature,
ingenious man   <380>
snares in his woven nets;
he drives the mountain herds
from wild lairs down to his folds;
he coaxes rough-maned horses
to thrust their necks through his yoke;
he tames the tireless mountain bull.

He has taught himself speech,
wind-quick thought,
and all the talents
that govern a city;   <390>
how to take shelter

from cold skies or pelting rain;
never baffled,
always resourceful,
he accepts every challenge;
but from Hades alone
has he found no way out—
though from hopeless disease
he has found a defense.

Exceeding all expectation,   <400>
his robust power to create
sometimes brings evil,
at other times, excellence.
When he follows the laws
Earth teaches him—
and Justice, which he's sworn
the gods he will enforce—
he soars with his city.
But reckless and corrupt,
a man will be driven   <410>
from his nation disgraced.

Let no man guilty of such things
share my hearth or invade my thoughts.

(Enter Guard, from countryside, leading Antigone.)

LEADER   I'm stunned—what's this? A warning from the gods?
I know this girl. She is Antigone.
Don't we all recognize her?
Unlucky Oedipus was her father,
now her own luck runs out.
What's happening? You—under guard?
Are you a prisoner? Did you break   <420>
the king's law? Commit some thoughtless act?

GUARD   There's your perpetrator. We caught her
burying the corpse. Where's Kreon?

(Enter Kreon.)

LEADER   Here he comes. Just in time.

KREON   What makes my arrival so timely?

GUARD   Sir, never promise something won't happen;
second thoughts can make your first one a lie.
I vowed I'd never come back here,
after you tongue-lashed me with those threats.

Then came a pleasure like no other,   <430>
because it's a total surprise, something
we hope for but can't believe will happen.
So I came back—though I swore I wouldn't—
to bring you the girl we caught sprinkling dust
on the dead body. No need to throw dice—
this time the good fortune was all mine.
Now she's all yours. Question and convict her—
do as you see fit. But I have the right
to go free of trouble once and for all.

KREON   Your prisoner—where was she when captured?   <440>

GUARD   Covering up the dead body. There you have it.

KREON   Do you know what you just said? No mistake?

GUARD   I saw her bury the man you said no one
         could bury. How can I say it plainer?

KREON   How did you see her? Was she caught in the act?

GUARD   Here's what happened. We went back there
         after those ugly threats of yours, to brush
         the dirt off the body and strip it down
         to its rotting flesh. Afterwards, we hunkered
         upwind under some hills to spare us any stench   <450>
         the body might have sent our way. Each man
         kept alert, and kept his neighbor alert,
         by raking him with outbursts of abuse
         if he seemed to neglect his watch.
         We kept at it until the round sun had climbed
         the heavens and baked us in the noon heat.
         Then, rising from the earth, a whirlwind
         whipped up the dust, and terror filled the sky,
         choking the grasslands, tearing leaves off trees,
         churning up grit all around us.
                              Our eyes squeezed shut,   <460>
         we waited out this god-sent pestilence.
         After a bit the dust cleared, and we saw her
         cry out in anguish, a piercing scream
         like a bird homing to find her nest robbed.
         When she saw the body stripped naked,
         she wailed one more time, then yelled a string
         of curses at those who'd done it. She scooped up
         powdery dust and, from a graceful bronze
         urn, poured out three cool swallows for the dead.
         Soon as we saw this, we moved in to stop her.   <470>

She wasn't a bit shocked, when we charged her
with the earlier crime, and now this one—
didn't deny a thing. That pleased,
but also troubled me. Escaping blame
oneself is always a relief; still, it hurts
to cause your own people grief. But all that
matters much less to me than my own safety.

KREON   *(To Antigone.)*
             You! Don't stand there nodding your head.
             Out with it! Admit this or deny it.

ANTIGONE   I swear I did. And I don't deny it.   <480>

KREON   *(To Guard.)*
             You are excused from this grim business.
             You're now free to go anywhere you please.

             (Exit Guard. To Antigone:)

             Explain something to me without elaborating.
             Were you aware of my decree forbidding this?

ANTIGONE   Of course I knew. We all knew.

KREON   And still you dared to violate the law?

ANTIGONE   I did. It wasn't *Zeus* who issued me
             this order. And Justice—who lives below—
             was not involved. They'd never condone it!
             I deny that your edicts—since *you,* a mere man,   <490>
             imposed them—have the force to trample on
             the gods' unwritten and infallible laws.
             Their laws are not ephemeral, they weren't
             made yesterday, and they will last forever.
             No man knows how far back in time they go.
             I'd never let any man's arrogance
             bully me into breaking the gods' laws.
             I'll die someday—how could I not know that?
             I knew it without your proclamation.
             If I do die young, that's an advantage,   <500>
             for doesn't a person like me, who lives
             besieged by trouble, escape by dying?
             My own death isn't going to bother me,
             but I would be devastated to see
             my mother's son die and rot unburied.
             I've no regrets for what I've done. And if you
             consider my acts foolhardy, I say:
             Look at the fool charging me with folly.

LEADER   It's apparent this girl's nature is savage
          like her father's. She hasn't got the sense   <510>
          to back off when she gets into trouble.

KREON   Stubborn spirits are the first to crack.
          It's always the iron tool hardened by fire
          that snaps and shatters. And headstrong horses
          can be tamed by a small iron bit.
          There's no excuse for a slave
          to preen when her master's home.
          This girl learned insolence long before
          she broke this law. What's more, she keeps on
          insulting us, and then gloats about it.   <520>
          There is no doubt that if she emerges
          victorious, and is never punished,
          I am no man, *she* will be the man here.

          I don't care if she is my sister's child,
          a blood relative, closer than all those
          who worship Zeus in my household,
          she—and her sister—still must die.
          I charge her sister too with conspiring
          to bury Polyneikes. Bring her out.
          I observed her inside just now,   <530>
          screaming, hysterical, deranged.
          Someone who intends to commit a crime
          can lose control of a guilty conscience.
          Her furtive treason gives itself away.

          (Two of Kreon's Men enter the palace. Kreon turns to Antigone.)

          But I also hate it when someone caught
          red-handed tries to glorify her crime.

ANTIGONE Take me and kill me—is that your whole plan?

KREON   That's it. When that's done I'll be satisfied.

ANTIGONE Then what stops you? Are you waiting for me
          to accept what you've said? I never will.   <540>
          And nothing I say will ever please you.
          Yet, since you did mention glory, how
          could I do anything more glorious
          than build my own brother a tomb?
          These men here would approve my actions—
          if fear didn't seal their lips.
                              Tyranny

	is fortunate in many ways: it can, for instance, say and do anything it wants.	
KREON	These Thebans don't see it your way.	
ANTIGONE	But they do. To please you they bite their tongues.	\<550\>
KREON	Aren't you ashamed not to follow their lead?	
ANTIGONE	Since when is it shameful to honor a brother?	
KREON	You had another brother who died fighting him?	
ANTIGONE	Yes, born to the same mother and father.	
KREON	Then why do you honor Polyneikes when the act desecrates Eteokles?	
ANTIGONE	Eteokles wouldn't agree with you.	
KREON	Oh, but he would—because you've honored treason as though it were patriotism.	
ANTIGONE	It was his *brother* who died, not his *slave!*	\<560\>
KREON	That brother died ravaging our country! Eteokles fell fighting to protect it.	
ANTIGONE	Hades will still expect his rituals!	
KREON	The brave deserve better than the vile.	
ANTIGONE	Who knows what matters to the dead?	
KREON	Not even death reconciles enemies.	
ANTIGONE	I made no enemies by being born! I made my lifelong friends at birth.	
KREON	Then go down to them! Love your dead brothers! While I'm alive, no woman governs me.	\<570\>

(Enter Ismene, led in by Kreon's Men.)

LEADER	Ismene's coming from the palace. She cries the loving tears of a sister; her eyes fill up, her flushed face darkens; tears pour down her cheeks.
KREON	Now you—a viper who slithered through my house, quietly drinking my blood! I never knew I nurtured *two* insurrections, both attacking my throne.

	Go ahead,	
	confess your role in this burial	
	party. Or do you claim ignorance?	<580>

ISMENE
I confess it—if she'll let me.
I accept my full share of the blame.

ANTIGONE
Justice won't let you make that claim, sister!
You refused to help me. You took no part.

ISMENE
You're leaving on a grim voyage. I'm not
ashamed to suffer with you the whole way.

ANTIGONE
The dead in Hades know who buried him.
I don't want love that just shows up in words.

ISMENE
You'll disgrace me, sister! Don't keep me
from honoring our dead! Let me come with you!   <590>

ANTIGONE
Don't try to share my death! Don't try to claim
you helped me bury him! My death's enough.

ISMENE
With you dead, why would I want to live?

ANTIGONE
Ask Kreon that! You sprang to his defense.

ISMENE
Why do you wound me? It does you no good.

ANTIGONE
I'm sorry if my scorn for him hurts you.

ISMENE
I can still help you. Tell me what to do.

ANTIGONE
Go on living. I'd rather you survived.

ISMENE
Then you want to exclude me from your fate?

ANTIGONE
You made the choice to live. I chose to die.   <600>

ISMENE
And I've told you how much I hate that choice.

ANTIGONE
Some think you're right, others think I am.

ISMENE
Then aren't we both equally wrong?

ANTIGONE
Gather your strength. Your life goes on. Long ago
I dedicated mine to the dead.

KREON
One woman only now shows her madness—
the other's been out of her mind since birth.

ISMENE
King, when you are shattered by grief
your native wit vanishes. It just goes.

KREON
You surely lost your wits when you teamed up   <610>
with a criminal engaged in a crime.

ISMENE	What would my life be like without her?
KREON	You're living that life now. Hers is over.
ISMENE	Then you're willing to kill your own son's bride?
KREON	Oh yes. He will find other fields to plow.
ISMENE	No other woman would suit him so well.
KREON	I want no pernicious wives for my son.
ISMENE	Dearest Haimon! How your father hates you!
KREON	Enough! No more talk about this marriage.
ISMENE	You're going to rob your son of his bride? <620>
KREON	Hades will cancel their marriage for me.
ISMENE	Then you've made up your mind she will die?
KREON	Both *my* mind and *your* mind. No more delay, men, take them in. Make sure they behave like women. Don't let either slip away. Even the brave will try to run when they see death closing in.

(Kreon's Men take Antigone and Ismene inside.)

ELDERS Lucky are those
whose lives
never taste evil!   <630>
For once the gods
attack a family,
their curse never relents.
It sickens life after life,
rising like a deep
sea swell, a darkness
boiling from below, driven
by the wild stormwinds
of Thrace that churn up
black sand from the sea floor—   <640>
the battered headlands
moan as the storm pounds in.

I see sorrows that struck
the dead Labdakids long ago
break over their children,
wave on wave of sorrows!
Each generation fails

to protect its own youth—
because a god always hacks
at their roots, draining   <650>
strength that could set them free.
Now the hope that brightened
over the last rootstock
alive in the house
of Oedipus, in its turn
is struck down—
by the blood-drenched dust
the death-gods demand,
by reckless talk,
by Furies in the mind.   <660>

O Zeus,
what human arrogance
can rival your power?
Neither Sleep,
who beguiles us all,
nor the tireless, god-driven months
overcome it.
                    O Monarch
whom time cannot age—
you live in the magical
sunrays of Olympos!   <670>
One law of yours rules
our own and future time,
just as it ruled the past:
Nothing momentous man
achieves will go unpunished.

For Hope is a wanderer
who profits multitudes
but tempts just as many
with light-headed longings—
and a man's failure   <680>
dawns on him only
when blazing coals
scald his feet.

The man was wise
who said these words:
"Evil seems noble—
early and late—to minds
unbalanced by the gods,
but only for a moment

will such men   <690>
hold off catastrophe."

(Enter Haimon.)

LEADER   There's Haimon,
          the youngest of your sons.
          Does he come here enraged
          that you have sentenced Antigone,
          the bride he's been promised,
          or in shock that his hopes
          for marriage have been crushed?

KREON   We'll soon have an answer
          better than any prophet's.   <700>
          My son, now that you've heard
          my formal condemnation
          of your bride, have you come here
          to attack your father?
          Or will I be dear to you still,
          no matter what I do?

HAIMON   I'm yours, father. I respect your wisdom.
          Show me the straight path, and I'll take it.
          I couldn't value any marriage more
          than the excellent guidance you give me.   <710>

KREON   Son, that's exactly how you need to think:
          Follow your father's orders in all things.
          It's the reason men pray for loyal sons
          to be born and raised in their houses—
          so they can harm their father's enemies
          and show his friends respect to match his own.
          If a man produces worthless children,
          what has he spawned? His grief, his rivals' glee.

          Don't throw away your judgment, son,
          for the pleasure this woman offers.   <720>
          You'll feel her turn ice cold in your arms—
          you'll feel her scorn in the bedroom. No wound
          cuts deeper than poisonous love. So spit
          this girl out like the enemy she is.
          Let her find a mate in Hades.
          I caught her in open defiance—
          she alone in the whole city—and I will take
          her life, just as I promised. I will not
          show myself as a liar to my people.
          It is useless for her to harp on the Zeus   <730>

of family life: If I indulge my own
family in rebelliousness,
I must indulge it everywhere.

A man who keeps his own house in order
will be perceived as righteous by his city.
But if anyone steps out of line, breaks
our laws, thinks he can dictate to his king,
he shouldn't expect any praise from me.
Citizens must obey men in office
appointed by the city, both in minor matters   <740>
and in the great questions of what is just—
even when they think an action unjust.
Obedient men lead ably and serve well.
Caught in a squall of spears, they hold their ground.
They make brave soldiers you can trust.
Insubordination is our worst crime.
It wrecks cities and empties homes. It breaks
and routs even allies who fight beside us.
Discipline is what saves the lives of all
good people who stay out of trouble.   <750>
And to make sure we enforce discipline—
never let a woman overwhelm a king.
Better to be driven from power, if it
comes to that, by a man. Then nobody
can say you were beaten by some female.

LEADER   Unless the years have sapped my wits, King,
              what you have just said was wisely said.

HAIMON   Father, the gods instill reason in men.
              It's the most valuable thing we possess.
              I don't have the skill—nor do I want it—   <760>
              to contradict all the things you have said.
              Though someone else's perspective might help.
              Look, it's not in your nature to notice
              what people say—what they're condemning.
              That harsh look on your face makes men afraid—
              no one tells you what you'd rather not hear.
              But I hear, unobserved, what people think.
              Listen. Thebes aches for this girl. *No person
              ever*, they're saying, *less deserved to die—
              no one's ever been so unjustly killed*   <770>
              for actions as magnificent as hers.
              When her own brother died in that bloodbath
              she kept him from lying out there unburied,

fair game for flesh-eating dogs and vultures.
Hasn't she earned, they ask, *golden honor?*
Those are the words they whisper in the shadows.

There's nothing I prize more, father,
than your welfare.
                              What makes a son prouder
than a father's thriving reputation?
Don't fathers feel the same about their sons?   <780>

Attitudes are like clothes; you can change them.
Don't think that what you say is always right.
Whoever thinks that he alone is wise,
that he's got a superior tongue and brain,
open him up and you'll find him a blank.
It's never shameful for even a wise man
to keep on learning new things all his life.
Be flexible, not rigid. Think of trees
caught in a raging winter torrent: those
that bend will survive with all their limbs   <790>
intact; those that resist are swept away.
Or take a captain who cleats his mainsheet
down hard, never easing off in a blow;
he'll capsize his ship and go right on sailing,
his rowing benches where his keel should be.
Step back from your anger, let yourself change.

If I, as a younger man, can offer
a thought, it's this: Yes, it would be better
if men were born with perfect understanding.
But things don't work that way. The best response   <800>
to worthy advice is to learn from it.

LEADER   King, if he has said anything to ease
              this crisis, you had better learn from it.
              Haimon, you do the same. You both spoke well.

KREON   So men my age should learn from one of yours?

HAIMON   If I happen to be right, yes! Don't look
              at my youth, look at what I've accomplished.

KREON   What? Backing rebels makes you proud?

HAIMON   I'm not about to condone wrongdoing.

KREON   Hasn't *she* been attacked by that disease?   <810>

HAIMON   Your fellow citizens would deny it.

KREON   Shall Thebans dictate how I should govern?

HAIMON   Listen to yourself: You talk like a boy.

KREON   Should I yield to them—or rule Thebes myself?

HAIMON   It's not a *city* if one man owns it.

KREON   Don't we say men in power *own* their cities?

HAIMON   You'd make a first-rate king of a wasteland.

KREON   It seems this *boy* fights on the woman's side.

HAIMON   Only if you're the woman. You're my concern.

KREON   Then why do you make open war on me?   <820>

HAIMON   What I attack is your abuse of power.

KREON   Is protecting my interest an abuse?

HAIMON   What is it you protect by scorning the gods?

KREON   Look at yourself! A woman overpowers you.

HAIMON   But no disgraceful impulse ever will.

KREON   Your every word supports that woman.

HAIMON   And you, and me, and the gods of this earth.

KREON   You will not marry her while she's *on* this earth.

HAIMON   Then she will die, and dead, kill someone else.

KREON   You are brazen enough to threaten me?   <830>

HAIMON   What threatens you is hearing what I think.

KREON   Your mindless attack on me threatens *you.*

HAIMON   I'd question *your* mind if you weren't my father.

KREON   Stop your snide deference! You are her slave.

HAIMON   You're talking at me, but you don't hear me.

KREON   Really? By Olympos above, I hear you.
             And I can assure you, you're going to
             suffer the consequences of your attacks.

             (Kreon speaks to his Men.)

             Bring out the odious creature. Let her
             die at once in his presence. Let him watch,   <840>
             this bridegroom, as she's killed beside him.

(Two Men enter palace.)

HAIMON   Watch her die next to me? You think I'd do that?
Your eyes won't see my face, ever again.
Go on raving to friends who can stand you.

(Exit Haimon.)

LEADER   King, the young man's fury hurls him out.
Rage makes a man his age utterly reckless.

KREON   Let him imagine he's superhuman.
He'll never save the lives of those two girls.

LEADER   Then you intend to execute them both?

KREON   Not the one with clean hands.   <850>
I think you're right about her.

LEADER   The one you're going to kill—how will you do it?

KREON   I will lead her along a deserted road,
and hide her, alive, in a hollow cave.
I'll leave her just enough food to evade
defilement—so the city won't be infected.
She can pray there to Hades, the one god
whom she respects. Maybe he will spare her!
Though she's more likely to learn, in her last hours,
that she's thrown her life away on the dead.   <860>

*(Kreon remains on stage during the next choral ode, presumably
retiring into the background.)*

ELDERS   Love, you win all
your battles!—raising
havoc with our herds,
dwelling all night
on a girl's soft cheeks,
cruising the oceans,
invading homes
deep in the wilds!
No god can outlast you,
no mortal outrun you.   <870>
And those you seize go mad.

You wrench even good men's minds
so far off course they crash in ruins.
Now you ignite hatred in men
of the same blood—but allure flashing
from the keen eyes of the bride

always wins, for Desire wields
all the power of ancient law:
Aphrodite the implacable
plays cruel games with our lives.   <880>

*(Enter Antigone, dressed in purple as a bride,
guarded by Kreon's Men.)*

LEADER   This sight also drives *me*
            outside the law. I can't stop
            my own tears flowing when I see
            Antigone on her way
            to the bridal chamber,
            where we all lie down in death.

ANTIGONE   Citizens of our fatherland, you see me
            begin my last journey. I take one last look
            at sunlight that I'll never see again.
            Hades, who chills each one of us to sleep,   <890>
            will guide me down to Acheron's shore.
            I'll go hearing no wedding hymn
            to carry me to my bridal chamber, or songs
            girls sing when flowers crown a bride's hair;
            I'm going to marry the River of Pain.

LEADER   Don't praise and glory go with you
            to the deep caverns of the dead?
            You haven't been wasted by disease;
            you've helped no sword earn its keep.
            No, you have chosen of your own free will   <900>
            to enter Hades while you're still alive.
            No one else has ever done that.

ANTIGONE   I once heard that a Phrygian stranger,
            Niobe, the daughter of Tantalos,
            died a hideous death on Mt. Sipylos.
            Living rock, like relentless ivy,
            crushed her. Now, people say, she slowly
            erodes; rain and snow
            never leave her, they constantly
            pour like tears from her eyes,   <910>
            drenching the clefts of her body.
            My death will be like hers,
            when the god at last lets me sleep.

LEADER   You forget, child, she was a goddess,
            with gods for parents, not a mortal

begotten by mortals like ourselves.
It's no small honor for a mere woman
to suffer so godlike a fate—in both
how she has lived, and the way she will die.

ANTIGONE   Now I'm being laughed at!   <920>
In the name of our fathers' gods,
wait till I'm gone, don't mock me
while I stand here in plain sight—
all you rich citizens of this town!

At least I can trust you,
headwaters of the river
Dirke, and you, holy
plains around Thebes, home
of our great chariot-fleet,
to bear me witness: Watch them   <930>
march me off to my strange tomb,
my heaped-up rock-bound prison,
without a friend to mourn me
or any law to protect me—

me, a miserable woman
with no home here on earth
and none down with the dead,
not quite alive, not yet a corpse.

LEADER   You took the ultimate risk when you smashed
yourself against the throne of Justice.   <940>
But the stiff price you're paying, daughter,
is one you inherit from your father.

ANTIGONE   You've touched my worst grief,
the fate of my father, which I
keep turning over in my mind.
We all were doomed, the whole
grand house of Labdakos,
by my mother's horrendous,
incestuous, coupling with her son.
From what kind of parents was I born?   <950>

I'm going to them now,
I'm dying unmarried.

And brother Polyneikes,
wasn't yours too a deadly
marriage? And when you
were slaughtered, so was I.

LEADER   Your pious conduct might deserve some praise,
              but no assault on power will ever
              be tolerated by him who wields it.
              It was your own hot-headed   <960>
              willfulness that destroyed you.

ANTIGONE   No friends, no mourners, no wedding songs
              go with me, they push me down a road
              that runs through sadness;
              they have prepared it for me, alone.
              Soon I will lose sight of the sun's holy eye,
              wretched, with no one to love me,
              no one to grieve.

              (Kreon moves forward, speaking first to Antigone, then to his Men.)

KREON   You realize, don't you, that singing
              and wailing would go on forever   <970>
              if they did the dying any good?

              Hurry up now, take her away.
              And when you've finished
              enclosing her, just as I've ordered,
              inside the cave's vault,
              leave her there—absolutely
              isolated—to decide whether
              she wants to die at once, or go
              on living in that black hole.
              So we'll be pure as far as she's concerned.   <980>
              In either case, today will be the last
              she'll ever spend above the ground.

ANTIGONE   My tomb, my bridal bedroom, my home
              dug from rock, where they'll keep me forever—
              I'll join my family there, so many of us dead,
              already welcomed by Persephone.
              I'll be the last to arrive, and the worst off,
              going down with most of my life unlived.
              I hope my coming will please my father,
              comfort my mother, and bring joy   <990>
              to you, brother, because I washed your dead
              bodies, dressed you with my hands, and poured
              blessèd offerings of drink on your graves.
              Now, because I honored your corpse,
              Polyneikes, *this* is how I'm repaid!
              I honored you as wise men would think right.
              But I wouldn't have taken that task on

had I been a mother who lost her child,
or if my husband were rotting out there.
For them, I would never defy my city.   <1000>
You want to know what law lets me say this?
If my husband were dead, I could remarry.
A new husband could give me a new child.
But with my father and mother in Hades,
a new brother could never bloom for me.
That is the law that made me die for you,
Polyneikes. But Kreon says I'm wrong,
terribly wrong. And now I'm his captive,
he pulls me by the wrist to no bride's bed;
I won't hear bridal songs, or feel the joy   <1010>
of married love, and I will have no share
in raising children. No, I will go grieving,
friendless, and alive to a hollow tomb.
Tell me, gods, which of *your* laws did I break?

I'm too far gone to expect your help.
But whose strength can I count on, when acts
of blessing are considered blasphemy?
If the gods are happy I'm sentenced to die
I hope one day I'll discover
what divine law I have broken.   <1020>
But if my judges are at fault, I want *them*
to suffer the pain they inflict on me now.

LEADER   She's still driven by raw gusts
            raging through her mind.

KREON   I have no patience with such outbursts.
            And none for men who drag their feet.

ANTIGONE   I think you're saying that my death is near.

KREON   It will be carried out. Don't think otherwise.

ANTIGONE   I leave you, Thebes, city of my fathers.
            I leave you, ancient gods. This very moment,   <1030>
            I'm being led away. They cannot wait!
            Look at me, princely citizens of Thebes:
            I'm the last daughter of the kings who ruled you.
            Look at what's done to me, and by whom
            it's done, to punish me for keeping faith.

            (Kreon's Men lead Antigone offstage.)

ELDERS   Like you, lovely Danae
            endured her loss

of heavenly sunlight
in a brass-bound cell—
a prison secret as a tomb.   <1040>
Night and day she was watched.
Like yours, my daughter,
her family was a great one.
The seed of Zeus, which fell
on her as golden rain,
she treasured in her womb.
Fate is strange and powerful;
wealth cannot protect us,
nor can war, high city towers,
or storm-beaten black ships.   <1050>

Impounded too, was Lycurgos,
short-tempered son of Dryas,
King of Edonia: To pay
him back for insulting
defiance, Dionysos shut
him up in a rocky cell;
there his surging madness ebbed.
He learned too late how mad
he was to taunt this god
with derisive laughter: <1060>
When he tried to suppress
Bakkhanalian torches
and women fired by their god,
he angered the Muses
who love the oboe's song.

By waters off the Black Rocks,
a current joins two seas;
the Bosphoros' channel
follows the Thracian
coast of Salmydessos.   <1070>
Ares from his nearby city
saw this wild assault—
the savage wife of Phineus
attacking his two sons:
Her stab-wounds darkened
their vengeance-craving eyes,
burst with a pointed shuttle
gripped in her blood-drenched hands.

Broken spirits, they howled
in their pain—these sons   <1080>

of a woman unhappy
in her marriage, this daughter
descended from the ancient
Erektheids. Nursed in caves
among her father's stormwinds,
this daughter of the gods,
this child of Boreas,
rode swift horses over the mountains—
yet Fate broke her brutally, my child.

(Enter Tiresias and the Lad who guides him.)

TIRESIAS   Theban lords, we walk here side by side,   \<1090\>
one pair of eyes looking out for us both.
Blind men must travel with somebody's help.

KREON   What news do you bring, old man Tiresias?

TIRESIAS   I'll tell you. Then you must trust this prophet.

KREON   I've never questioned the advice you've given.

TIRESIAS   And it helped you keep Thebes on a straight course?

KREON   I know your value. I learned it first-hand.

TIRESIAS   Take care.
You're standing on the razor's edge of fate.

KREON   What do you mean? That makes me shudder.   \<1100\>

TIRESIAS   You'll comprehend when you hear the warnings
issued by my art. When I took my seat
at my accustomed post of augury,
birds from everywhere fluttering nearby,
I heard a strange sound coming from their midst.
They screeched with such mindless ferocity,
any meaning their song possessed was drowned out.
I knew the birds were tearing at each other
with lethal talons; the hovering beats
of thrashing wings could have meant nothing else.   \<1110\>
Alarmed, I lit a sacrificial fire,
but the god failed to keep his flames alive.
Then from charred thighbones came a rancid slime,
smoking and sputtering, oozing out
into the ashes; the gall-bladder burst open;
liquefying thighs slid free from the strips
of fat enfolding them.
                              But my attempt
at prophecy failed; the signs I had sought

never appeared—this I learned from my lad.
He's my guide, just as I'm the guide for others.   <1120>

Kreon, your mind has sickened Thebes.
Our city's altars, and our city's braziers,
have been defiled, all of them, by dogs
and birds, with flesh torn from the wretched
corpse of Oedipus' fallen son.
Because of this, the gods will not accept
our prayers or the offerings of burnt meat
that come from our hands. No bird now sings
a clear omen—their keen cries have been garbled
by the taste of a slain man's thickened blood.   <1130>
Think about these facts, son.
                              All men go wrong;
but when a man blunders, he won't be stripped
of his wits and his strength if he corrects
the error he's committed and then ends
his stubborn ways. Stubbornness, you well know,
will provoke charges of stupidity.

Respect the dead. Don't spear the fallen.
How much courage does it take
to kill a dead man?
                    Let me
help you. My counsel is sound and well meant.   <1140>
No advice is sweeter than that from a wise
source who has only your interests at heart.

KREON   Old man, like archers at target practice,
             you all aim arrows at me. And now you
             stoop to using prophecy against me.
             For a long time I have been merchandise
             sold far and wide by you omen-mongers.
             Go, make your money, strike your deals, import
             silver from Sardis, gold from India,
             if it suits you. But you won't hide that corpse   <1150>
             under the earth! Never—even if Zeus'
             own eagles fly scraps of flesh to his throne.

             Defilement isn't something I fear—it won't
             persuade me to order this burial.
             I don't accept that men can defile gods.
             But even the cleverest of mortals,
             venerable Tiresias, will be brought
             down hard, if, hoping to turn a profit,
             they clothe ugly ideas in handsome words.

TIRESIAS   Does any man grasp . . . does he realize . . .   <1160>

KREON   Realize . . . what? What point are you making?

TIRESIAS   . . . that no possession is worth more than good sense?

KREON   Just as its absence is our worst disease.

TIRESIAS   But hasn't that disease infected you?

KREON   I won't trade insults with you, prophet.

TIRESIAS   You do when you call my prophecies false.

KREON   Your profession has always loved money.

TIRESIAS   And tyrants have a penchant for corruption.

KREON   You know you're abusing a king in power?

TIRESIAS   You hold power because I helped you save Thebes.   <1170>

KREON   You're a shrewd prophet. But you love to cause harm.

TIRESIAS   You'll force me to say what's clenched in my heart.

KREON   Say it. Unless you've been paid to say it.

TIRESIAS   I don't think it will pay you to hear it.

KREON   Get one thing straight: My conscience can't be bought.

TIRESIAS   Then tell your conscience this: You will not live
            for many circuits of the chariot sun
            before you trade a child born from your loins
            for all the corpses whose deaths you have caused.
            You have thrown children from the sunlight   <1180>
            down to the shades of Hades, ruthlessly
            housing a living person in a tomb,
            while you detain here, among us, something
            that belongs to the gods who live below
            our world—the naked unwept corpse you've robbed
            of the solemn grieving we owe our dead.
            None of this should have been any concern
            of yours—or of the Olympian gods—
            but you have involved them in your outrage!
            Therefore, avengers wait to ambush you—   <1190>
            the Furies sent by Hades and its gods
            will punish you for the crimes I have named.

            Do you think someone hired me to tell you this?

            It won't be long before wailing breaks out
            from the women and men in your own house.

And hatred against you will surge in all
the countries whose sons, in mangled pieces,
received their rites of burial
from dogs, wild beasts, or flapping birds
who have carried the stench of defilement   <1200>
to the homelands and the hearths of the dead.

Since you've provoked me, these are the arrows
I have shot in anger, like a bowman,
straight at your heart—arrows you cannot dodge,
and whose pain you will feel.
                              Lad, take me home—
let this man turn his anger on younger
people. That might teach him to hold his tongue,
and to think more wisely than he does now.

(Exit Tiresias led by the Lad.)

LEADER   This old man leaves stark prophecies behind.
            Never once, while my hair has gone from black   <1210>
            to white, has this prophet told Thebes a lie.

KREON   I'm well aware of that! It unnerves me.
            Surrender would be devastating,
            but if I stand firm, I could be destroyed.

LEADER   What you need is some very clear advice,
            son of Menoikeus.

KREON   What must I do?
            If you have such advice, give it to me.

LEADER   Free the girl from her underground prison.
            Build a tomb for the corpse you have let rot.

KREON   That's your advice? I should surrender?   <1220>

LEADER   Yes, King. Do it now. For the gods
            act quickly to abort human folly.

KREON   I can hardly say this. But I'll give up
            convictions I hold passionately—
            and do what you ask. We can't fight
            the raw power of destiny.

LEADER   Then go!
            Yourself. Delegate this to no one.

KREON   I'll go just as I am. Move out, men. Now!
            All of you, bring axes and run toward
            that rising ground. You can see it from here.   <1230>

Because I'm the one who has changed, I who
locked her away will go there to free her.
My heart is telling me we must obey
established law until the day we die.

(Exit Kreon and his Men toward open country.)

ELDERS   God with myriad names—
lustrous child
of Kadmos' daughter,
son of thundering Zeus—
you govern fabled Italy;
you preside at Eleusis,   <1240>
secluded Valley of Demeter
that welcomes all pilgrims.
O Bakkhos! Thebes
is your homeland,
mother-city of maenads
on the quietly flowing
Ismenos, where the dragon's
teeth were sown.

Now you stand on the ridges rising
up the twin peaks of Parnassos.   <1250>
There through the wavering
smoke-haze your torches flare;
there walk your devotees,
the nymphs of Korykia,
beside Kastalia's fountains.
Thick-woven ivy on Nysa's sloping hills,
grape-clusters ripe on verdant shorelines
propel you here, while voices
of more than human power
sing "Evohoi!"—your name divine   <1260>
when the streets of Thebes
are your final destination.

By honoring Thebes
beyond all cities,
you honor your mother
whom the lightning killed.
Now a plague
ravages our city. Come home
on healing footsteps—down
the slopes of Parnassos,   <1270>
or over the howling channel.
Stars breathing their gentle fire

shine joy on you as they rise,
O master of nocturnal voices!
Take shape before our eyes, Bakkhos,
son of Zeus our king, let the Thyiads
come with you, let them climb
the mad heights of frenzy
as you, Iakkhos, the bountiful,
watch them   <1280>
dance through the night.

(Enter Messenger.)

MESSENGER   Neighbors, who live not far from the grand
old houses of Amphion and Kadmos,
you can't trust anything in a person's life—
praiseworthy or shameful—never to change.
Fate lifts up—and fate cuts down—both the lucky
and the unlucky, day in and day out.
No prophet can tell us what happens next.
Kreon always seemed someone to envy,
to me at least. He saved from attack   <1290>
the homeland where we sons of Kadmos live;
this won him absolute power. He was
the brilliant father of patrician children.
Now it has all slipped away. For when things
that give pleasure and meaning to our lives
desert a man, he's not a human being
any more—he becomes a breathing corpse.
Amass wealth if you can, show off your house;
display the panache of a great monarch.
But if joy disappears from your life   <1300>
I wouldn't give the shadow cast by smoke
for all you possess. Only happiness matters.

LEADER   Should our masters expect more grief? What's happened?

MESSENGER   Death. And the killer is alive.

LEADER   Name the murderer. Name the dead. Tell us.

MESSENGER   Haimon is dead. The hand that killed him was his own . . .

LEADER   . . . father's? Or do you mean he killed himself?

MESSENGER   He killed himself. Raging at his killer father.

LEADER   Tiresias, you spoke the truth.

MESSENGER   You know the facts, now you must cope with them.   <1310>

(Enter Eurydike.)

LEADER   I see Eurydike, soon to be crushed,
              approaching from inside the house.
              She may have heard what's happened to her son.

EURYDIKE   I heard all of you speaking as I came out—
              on my way to offer prayers to Athena.
              I happened to unlatch the gate,
              to open it, when words of our disaster
              carried to my ears. I fainted, terrified
              and dumbstruck, in the arms of my servants.
              Please tell me your news. Tell me all of it.   <1320>
              I'm someone who has lived through misfortune.

MESSENGER   O my dear Queen, I will spare you nothing.
              I'll tell you truthfully what I've just seen.
              Why should I say something to soothe you
              that will later prove me a liar?
              Straight talk is always best.
              I traveled with your husband to the far
              edge of the plain where Polyneikes' corpse,
              mangled by wild dogs, lay still uncared-for.

              We prayed for mercy to the Goddess   <1330>
              of Roadways, and to Pluto, asking them
              to restrain their anger. We washed his remains
              with purified water. Using boughs stripped
              from nearby bushes, we burned what was left,
              then mounded a tomb from his native earth.

              After that we turned toward the girl's deadly
              wedding cavern—with its bed of cold stone.
              Still far off, we heard an enormous wail
              coming from somewhere near the unhallowed
              portico—so we turned back to tell Kreon.   <1340>
              As the king arrived, these incoherent
              despairing shouts echoed all around him.
              First he groaned, then he yelled out in raw pain,

              "Am I a prophet? Will my worst fears come true?
              Am I walking down the bitterest street
              of my life? That's my son's voice greeting me!

              "Move quickly, men, run through that narrow gap
              where the stones have been pulled loose from the wall,
              go where the cavern opens out. Tell me

the truth—is that Haimon's voice I'm hearing,   <1350>
or have the gods played some trick on my ears?"

Following orders from our despondent
master, we stared in. At the tomb's far end
there she was, hanging by the neck, a noose
of finely woven linen holding her aloft.
He fell against her, arms hugging her waist,
grieving for the bride he'd lost to Hades,
for his father's acts, for his own doomed love.

When Kreon saw all this he stepped inside,
groaned horribly, and called out to his son: <1360>
"My desperate child! What have you done? What
did you think you were doing? When did the gods
destroy your reason? Come out of there, son.
I beg you."
          His son then glared straight at him
with savage eyes, spat in his face, spoke not
one word in answer, but drew his two-edged sword.
His father leapt back, Haimon missed his thrust.
Then this raging youth—with no warning—turned
on himself, tensed his body to the sword,
and drove half its length deep into his side.   <1370>
Still conscious, he clung to her with limp arms,
gasping for breath, spurts of his blood pulsing
onto her white cheek.
                    Then he lay there, his dead
body embracing hers, married at last,
poor man—not up here, but somewhere
in Hades—proving that of all mankind's
evils, thoughtless violence is the worst.

(Exit Eurydike.)

LEADER   What do you make of that? She turns and leaves
             without saying one word, brave or bitter.

MESSENGER   I don't like it. I hope that having heard   <1380>
             the sorry way her son died, she won't grieve
             for him in public. Maybe she's gone
             to ask her maids to mourn him in the house.
             This woman never loses her composure.

LEADER   I'm not so sure. To me this strange silence
             seems ominous as an outburst of grief.

MESSENGER   I'll go in and find out.
              She could have disguised the real
              intent of her impassioned heart.
              But I agree: Her silence is alarming.   <1390>

              (Exit Messenger into the palace; Kreon
              enters carrying the body of Haimon wrapped in
              cloth; his Men follow, bringing a bier on which
              Kreon will lay his son in due course.)

LEADER   Here comes our king, burdened
              with a message all too clear:
              This wasn't caused by anyone's vengeance—
              may I say it?—but by his own father's blunders.

KREON   Oh, what errors of the mind I have made!
              Deadly, bull-headed blunders.
              You all see it—the man
              who murdered, and the son
              who's dead. What I did
              was blind and wrong!   <1400>
              You died so young, my son,
              your death happened so fast!
              Your life was cut short
              not through your mad acts,
              but through mine.

LEADER   You saw the right course of action
              but took it far too late.

KREON   I've learned that lesson now—
              in all its bitterness.
              Sometime back, a god struck   <1410>
              my head an immense blow,
              it drove me
              to act in brutal ways,
              ways that stamped out
              all my happiness.
              What burdens and what pain
              men suffer and endure.

              (Enter Messenger from palace.)

MESSENGER   Master, your hands are full of sorrow,
              you bear its full weight.
              But other sorrows are in store—   <1420>
              you'll face them soon, inside your house.

KREON   Can any new
               calamity make
               what's happened worse?

MESSENGER   Your wife is dead—so much
               a loving mother to your son,
               poor woman, that she died
               of wounds just now inflicted.

KREON   Oh Hades, you are hard
               to appease! We flood   <1430>
               your harbor, you want more.
               Why are you trying
               to destroy me?

               (Turning to Messenger.)

               What have you to tell me
               this time?—you who bring
               nothing but deadly news.
               I was hardly alive, and now, my young friend,
               you've come back to kill me again.
               Son, what are you telling me?
               What is this newest message   <1440>

               (The palace doors open; Eurydike's corpse is revealed; Kreon sighs.)

               that buries me? My wife is dead.
               Slaughter after slaughter.

LEADER   Now you see it. Your house no longer hides it.

KREON   I see one more violent death. With what
               else can fate punish me? I have
               just held my dead son in my arms—
               now I see another dear body.
               Oh unhappy mother, oh my son.

MESSENGER   There, at the altar, she pierced
               herself with a sharp blade.   <1450>
               Her eyes went quietly dark
               and she closed them.
               She had first mourned aloud
               the empty marriage bed
               of her dead son Megareus.
               Then with her last breath
               she cursed you, Kreon,
               killer of your own son.

KREON   Ahhh! That sends fear
             surging through me.   <1460>
             Why hasn't someone
             driven a two-edged
             sword through my heart?
             I'm a wretched coward,
             awash with terror.

MESSENGER   The woman whose corpse you see
             condemns you for the deaths of her sons.

KREON   Tell me how she did it.

MESSENGER   She drove the blade below her liver,
             so she could suffer the same wound   <1470>
             that killed Haimon, for whom she mourns.

KREON   There's no one I can blame,
             no other mortal.
             I am the only one.

             *(Kreon looks at and touches the body of Haimon as
             his Men assemble to escort him offstage.)*

             I killed you, that's the reality.
             Men, take me inside,
             I'm less than nothing now.

LEADER   You are doing what's right,
             if any right can be found
             among all these misfortunes.   <1480>
             It's best to say little
             in the face of evil.

KREON   Let it come, let it happen now—
             let my own kindest fate
             make this my final day on earth.
             That would be kindness itself.
             Let it happen, let it come.
             Never let me see
             tomorrow's dawn.

LEADER   That's in the future. We   <1490>
             must deal with the present.
             The future will be shaped
             by those who control it.

KREON   My deepest desires are in that prayer.

LEADER   Stop your prayers.
            No human being
            evades calamity
            once it has struck.

            (Kreon puts his hand on Haimon's corpse.)

KREON   Take me from this place.   <1500>
            A foolish, impulsive man
            who killed you, my son, mindlessly,
            killed you as well, my wife.
            I'm truly cursed! I don't know
            where to rest my eyes,
            or on whose shoulders
            I can lean my weight.
            My hands warp
            all they touch;

            *(Kreon, still touching Haimon's corpse, looks
            toward Eurydike's, then lifts his hand
            and moves off toward the palace.)*

            and over there,
            fate's avalanche   <1510>
            pounds my head.

LEADER   Good sense is crucial
            to human happiness.
            Never fail to respect the gods,
            for the huge claims of proud men
            are always hugely punished—
            by blows that, as the proud grow old,
            pound wisdom through their minds.   <1518>

            (All leave.)

Notes to the Plays

1–7   *My children . . . Healing God?*   These first lines in the Greek are compressed—dense with mythic, dramatic, and ironic significance. Oedipus emerges from the palace to confront a sea of green branches—the olive boughs his agitated Theban subjects have brought to him in supplication (see n. 4). He plays on that image—"fresh green life / old Kadmos nurtures and protects"—to acknowledge the citizens' ancestry: they are the latest crop, the newest descendants of Kadmos, Thebes' legendary founder and its first king, who seeded the ground with dragon's teeth from which sprang fully armed soldiers. That Oedipus invokes Kadmos as the still-fathering source of Thebes' newest generation registers the power enduring paternal bloodlines held for fifth-century Greeks. By referring to the delegation as *trophê*—an abstract noun used here to mean "those cared for" or "those protected" by Kadmos—Oedipus seems briefly to shift responsibility for their welfare away from himself. But the compassion he extends to them in his first words—by calling them his "children," as though he were related by blood—turns out to be more than a metaphoric gesture when Oedipus discovers that Kadmos is his ancestor as well.

4   *beseeching, with your wool-strung boughs*   Suppliants left branches of laurel or olive, with tufts of wool tied on to them, at the altars of gods to whom they appealed for help. But here the use of suppliant boughs to seek help from a mortal man is highly unusual. Oedipus' initial puzzlement as to why he is being petitioned with ritual emblems of supplication also suggests his reluctance to get involved, perhaps his sense of inadequacy. This momentary doubt vanishes as he feels his subjects' need and as his strength and competence recover. He has indeed, we soon learn, been totally aware of Thebes' widespread devastation.

7   *prayers . . . Healing God*   Lit. "paeans." A paean was a hymn to Apollo as a healer of disease, one of the god's many roles. Although the oracle that predicted the plague was given by Apollo—and Homer's *Iliad* tells us he could send a plague as well as cure one—nothing in the text implicates him as the cause of plague now inflicting Thebes.

26–27   *river shrine . . . embers . . . prophecy*   Lit. "prophetic embers of Ismenos." A temple on the shores of the Ismenos, one of the two Theban rivers, was dedicated to Apollo. Embers in the temple smoldered under a sacrificed animal whose burnt remains could be read to interpret the will of a god, in this case Apollo's.

31   *Plague*   The plague that had struck Thebes was general, destroying crops, animals, and people. The fiery heat characteristic of the fever is referred to again at 227–28. (See n. 224–39.) The resemblance between the plague in this play and the Athenian plague of 430 as described by Thucydides has led some scholars to date it shortly after 429. See especially Bernard Knox, "The Date of the *Oedipus Tyrannus* of Sophocles," in *American Journal of Philology* 77, no. 2 (1956).

34   *A burning god*   The Greeks assumed a god to be responsible for a general and devastating plague. At 224 the Chorus names Ares, symbol of violence or destructiveness, as the responsible divinity.

37   *Hades*   The god who presides over the underworld.

38–41   *We haven't come . . . confronting gods*   The Priest explains why he, a man who himself has access to the gods, comes to Oedipus, a political leader, for help in this crisis; Oedipus has proven his ability to act effectively in situations requiring direct contact with a divinity.

42–44   *freed us . . . rasping Singer*   The "rasping Singer" is the Sphinx, pictured by Greek artists of Sophokles' time with a lion's body, a woman's head and breasts, and wings. She arrived in Thebes shortly after Laios' departure and destroyed young Thebans ("the tax we paid with our lives") by posing a riddle that resulted in the death of those who answered incorrectly. (In some versions of the myth the victims were thrown from a cliff, in others they were strangled, perhaps in some sexual embrace; the word "Sphinx" is related to the Greek verb meaning "to strangle.") Oedipus triumphed by solving the riddle and killing the Sphinx, thus liberating Thebes from a reign of terror. One version of the riddle follows; it appears in myth in slightly different formulations: "There exists on land a thing with two feet and four feet, with a single voice, that has three feet as well. It changes shape alone among the things that move on land or in the air or down through the sea. Yet during periods when it is supported by the largest number of feet, then is the speed in its limbs the feeblest of all" (Gould 1970, 19). By answering "Man" Oedipus demonstrated his lifelong attribute, intellectual resourcefulness in harrowing circumstances. Sophokles refrains from presenting the riddle itself, perhaps because its folk-tale cleverness seemed too insufficient a proof of real intelligence.

51   *god's whisper*   An oracle; an interpretation of a divine signal.

62   *a bird from god*   Birdlife was a major medium of communication between gods and mortals. Prophets and seers divined messages from birds' songs and flight patterns. Oedipus himself is ironically seen here as a favorable birdlike omen. See *Antigone* n. 463–64.

62   *good luck*   The first of many invocations of the Greek concept of *Tyche,* which can mean "luck," "chance," or "fate." I generally translate "luck" when the speaker is gratified, "chance" when the outcome seems uncertain or unfortunate, and "fate" when a divinity seems involved.

69   *I know what need*   Oedipus' grasp of the situation might seem contradictory to his initial professed ignorance of the suppliants' appeal. In his first speech he was simply searching for new developments and urging his people to voice fears and needs. Here he reveals his continued concern and reports specific actions he has taken.

69   *this sickness*   Oedipus refers both to the literal "sickness" of the suppliants, all victims in some respect of the plague, and to his own metaphoric sickness— his mental suffering for his fellow Thebans. But the Greek audience understood that the "sickness" which affects Oedipus, of which he is unaware, is not metaphoric at all but a literal pollution of his entire being. Sophokles will continue to reveal how characters' metaphoric speech turns out to be unexpectedly and horrifyingly literal.

81   *Phoibos*   Apollo

85   *He takes too long*   The Pythoness at Delphi delivered answers to questioners only once a month, and the shortest possible elapsed time for a trip from Thebes to Delphi and back would be about four or five days.

90   *Lord Apollo*   This exclamation could be as much an impromptu prayer as an oath. The stage might contain a statue of Apollo to whom Oedipus turns or nods as he speaks these lines.

91–92   *Luck so bright . . . see it*   I follow the interpretation of these lines given by Lowell Edmunds in "Sophocles' *Oedipus Tyrannus*," in *Harvard Studies in Classical Philology* 80–81 (1976): 41–44, who disputes the traditional interpretation, "May his radiant look prove the herald of good news." Arguing that Sophokles uses an idiom dependent on a suppressed preposition, Edmunds believes *eu* should be understood before *ommati* and the lines literally be translated, "May he come bright with saving fortune as he is bright to view."

94   *laurel crown*   A laurel crown customarily signified that a pilgrimage to a shrine or an oracle had been a success.

96   *Menoikeos*   One of the "Sown Men" who grew up instantly and fully armed in Thebes when Kadmos seeded the earth with dragon's teeth. Pronounced Me nee' kius.

98–99   *Good news . . . strokes of luck*   A deliberately obscure answer. Kreon here resists revealing, until directed by Oedipus, the shocking nature of the oracle he has received. The lines also suggest Kreon's annoying use of a Sophist's quibbling idiom.

102–3   *in front . . . go inside*   Kreon gives Oedipus the option of keeping Thebes in the dark about the oracle's disturbing accusations.

107   *very clear*   Kreon remarks on the lack of evasion or surface difficulty in this new oracle. Oracles (frequently delivered in lines of hexameter verse) were sometimes cryptic and demanded interpretation. The oracles to Oedipus are among the rare ones in Greek myth that mean exactly what they literally say.

113   *banishing . . . killing*   Apollo offers Thebes two choices for purging itself of Laios' murderer: death or exile. This choice comes up again when Oedipus charges Kreon with the crime and when Oedipus and Kreon debate Oedipus' ultimate fate.

113–14   *blood—kin murder*   The presence in a city of a person who had shed the blood of someone in his own family was absolutely horrifying and unacceptable to a Greek. Even in the late fifth century lawyers made dramatic use of this horror when prosecuting murderers.

120   *own hands*   The first of many references to hands, especially hands that shed blood. In Greek law the hands of a person who committed a crime retained the pollution inherent in that crime, regardless of motive or intent. Here Oedipus' avenging hands are paired rhetorically with the hands that murdered Laios. The two pairs of hands will be shown to be only one pair, Oedipus' own.

129–30   *journey . . . close to god*   The Greek word so translated is *theoros*, lit. a spectator of (or witness to) a divine rite or event. We know from Euripides' *Phoenician Women*, 36–37, that Laios was on his way to Delphi to ask the Pythoness whether or not the son he had exposed was really dead. But by not specifically naming Laios' destination, Sophokles permits Oedipus to postpone facing the possibility that Laios and he were traveling on the same road at the same time.

141   *bandit*   Though Kreon clearly used the plural in 138, Oedipus speaks of a single bandit with chilling, unconscious accuracy. But because his sentence is a hypothetical question, it is logically proper.

144–45   *new troubles*   Kreon portrays a rapid sequence of events: Laios' departure; news of his death; attack by the Sphinx; arrival of Oedipus; death of the Sphinx. The elapsed time might have been only a few days, or at most a week or two.

147   *blocked*   The Greek word so translated, *empodon,* refers to stumbling, tripping, or impeding the legs.

150   *at our feet*   Kreon continues the foot imagery, which may carry a reference to Oedipus' own swollen feet.

160   *exacting vengeance*   Oedipus strangely imagines himself the victim of a second crime by Laios' original murderer. That this should be an act of "vengeance" is hard to explain given the state of Oedipus' knowledge, but it will indeed be an act of vengeance when the same hands that killed Laios blind Oedipus.

164   *people of Kadmos*   Theban citizens. When they arrive, the Chorus will represent the "people of Kadmos."

173   *Voice from Zeus*   Though Apollo was the resident deity who issued his prophecies through the Pythoness at Delphi, the Chorus here attributes the commands to Zeus, the ultimate source of knowledge and power.

179   *Delos*   The island at the center of the Cyclades, sacred birthplace of Apollo, was said to be the navel of the sea, as Delphi was the navel of the earth. Gods communicated with mortals through both connections.

181   *new threat . . . old doom*   The Chorus distinguishes between a curse that has been known for some years and one that has newly emerged. The Voice of Zeus will invoke an old curse against the murderer of Laios.

186–91   *Athena, Artemis, Apollo*   The Chorus, not knowing which god will be the truly relevant one, prays to three divinities to focus their powers on rescuing Thebes.

208   *death god*   Hades

224–39   *Ares . . . who kills us*   The war god Ares is not associated with the plague in myth, but Sophokles probably alludes to the plague's spread in Athens during the Spartan attacks of 430–425. The image of Ares as a murderer "without armor now" reflects the fifth-century Greeks' lack of knowledge about infectious diseases. Throngs of rural Greeks, assuming Athens a safe haven from the Spartans, flocked to the city; there the overcrowded conditions facilitated the plague's swift and deadly spread. In Aeschylus' *Suppliants,* 659 ff. and 678 ff., Ares personifies the plague or destruction itself.

229–30   *vast sea-room of Amphitritê*   Lit. "great hall of Amphitritê." Amphitritê was a sea nymph whose home was the Atlantic Ocean; hence her name became synonymous with that body of water.

232 *jagged harbors* Lit. "welcomeless anchorage."

233 *seas off Thrace* The Black Sea. The Thracians, who lived on its shores, were warlike; Ares was their primary god.

233–35 *If night . . . finish it.* The meaning is obscure, but Gould suggests "if the night lets anything survive, the day moves in to finish it."

240 *lord of the morning light* Lit. "Lycean Lord." Lycean was one of Apollo's epithets, and could suggest either "light" or "wolf." The Chorus surely calls on him here in his protective, light-bringing aspect.

246 *morning hills* Lit. "Lycian hills," in southwestern Asia Minor, where Artemis was worshipped, with her brother Apollo, as a fire deity. Sophokles puns on the similarity between Lycean and Lycian to stress the light-bearing character of the sibling gods.

250 *Bakkhos* An alternate name for Dionysos, the god of wine and other forms of intoxication and ecstasy. He was a native Theban, the son of Zeus and Semele, Kadmos' daughter.

251 *maenads* Lit. "Madwomen." Revelers loyal to Dionysos.

262 *I'm a stranger* According to Athenian law a blood relative of a slain person should act to interdict his murderer. Unknowingly, Oedipus is in fact such a relative, though here he acts as a representative of the state speaking for the next of kin, who is presumed to be absent.

265 *mesh some clue* The word translated "clue" is *symbolon,* a fragment of some larger object, typically a potsherd. When matched to fit its other half, it established the identity of a messenger or long-lost parent or relative. See *Oed King* introduction, p. 28.

268 *come late* Oedipus arrived in Thebes after the report of Laios' death had reached the city.

272 *Labdakos* An earlier king of Thebes.

286–89 *roof. . . speak . . . pray . . . sacrifice . . . pour* The prohibitions in Oedipus' decree reveal the extreme aversion felt by a Greek of Sophokles' time to any contact with a person whose hands had committed a defiling act. See *Kolonos* n. 1029.

316–17 *Laios had no luck . . . children* An example of words whose second meaning will be grasped when the true facts of Oedipus' life are known. Oedipus means to say that Laios was childless, but the words also suggest that any child Laios fathered was the *source* of his ill fortune.

318 *came down on his head* This idiom through which Oedipus explains Laios' death is uncannily appropriate to the way in which Laios actually died: from a blow to the head, struck by Oedipus himself.

324 *all our kings* My gloss added to explain Oedipus' list.

335 *None of us is the killer* The blunt denial is understandable, because Oedipus has addressed the Chorus as if it potentially harbored Laios' killer.

343   *Tiresias*   The blind Theban prophet, who figures in many of the most famous myths of his native city. His association with the god Apollo, and his access to the god's knowledge, are crucial here, because Apollo is the source of the oracles that predicted Oedipus' incest and patricide.

348   *Kreon's urging*   An important point. Later, when Tiresias accuses Oedipus of causing the pollution, Oedipus remembers that it was Kreon who advised consulting the seer. Kreon's involvement thus lends plausibility to Oedipus' countercharges.

352   *travelers*   The Leader substitutes a word that is nearer the truth than Kreon's "bandits." Oedipus does not react to the difference.

354   *who did it*   Here I accept an anonymous emendation cited by Burton in Jebb 1883, 50. The manuscripts literally say "the one who saw it no one sees." But the emendation fits the context of the next three speeches, which concern not the eyewitness, but the killer, the one who did it.

390–91 *lawful . . . guidance*   Greek cities were morally, if not legally, entitled to benefit from the wisdom of an acknowledged prophet. Here, at first, Oedipus' remonstrance is gentle. See Jebb 1883, 54.

393–94 *What you've said . . . happen to me*   Tiresias refers here most probably to the part of Oedipus' speech that curses Laios' murderer. Less probably, he might be referring to the plea with which Oedipus greets him. The manuscripts contain a possible variant of these lines, which Gould translates, "I see your understanding comes to you inopportunely. So that won't happen to me. . . ." This variant makes sense in the larger context of Oedipus' discovery of his true past. I have, however, translated the line to make the most sense in the immediate context.

399   *You know and won't help?*   Tiresias' scornful refusal to respond seems not only inexplicable to Oedipus but unacceptable. Tiresias must be made to tell what the city needs to know for its survival. Oedipus' fury is fully justified as necessary to force the truth from him.

406   *rage*   A cunning double meaning. Tiresias speaks of "rage" (*orgei,* a feminine noun in Greek) as something Oedipus "co-habits" or "dwells" with and of which he is ignorant. Oedipus thinks he is being accused of possessing a violent nature. But because this "rage" is also spoken of as a sexual partner, Tiresias' words could mean as well that Oedipus is ignorant of the identity of his own wife. Sophokles has the Messenger describe the last frantic actions of Jokasta, after she knows Oedipus is her son, as *orge,* or raging (1406). The characterization of Oedipus' whole family by rage is prominent in Aeschylus and even earlier writers.

425–26 *charge . . . flushed out*   The metaphor is from hunting and suggests, first, that the accusation is like an animal driven from its cover and, second, that Tiresias himself has become an animal fleeing Oedipus' wrath.

440–41 *living . . . intimacy*   This phrase normally means "to live under the same roof," but it also frequently means "to have sexual intercourse with."

442   *nearest and most loving kin*   The most frequent reference of this phrase (*philatoi*) is to one's blood kin; less often it refers to those whom one loves, re-

gardless of blood relationship. Tiresias' lines seem to Oedipus an astonishing insult because their true import, that his wife is his closest blood relative, is unthinkable. See introduction to *Antigone,* passim.

451   *You can't harm me*   This phrase could also mean "I shall not harm you." My translation is governed by acceptance of Brunck's emendation in the next speech (as cited in Jebb 1883, 61).

453   *I'm not the one who will bring you down*   All but one of the manuscripts give, "It's not my fate to be struck down by you." If this version is sound, the rest of Tiresias' speech makes little sense. If, however, Brunck's emendation of a fourteenth-century manuscript is correct, as most modern editors believe, Apollo's involvement in Oedipus' downfall follows quite logically.

455   *Or was it Kreon?*   In seeking an explanation for what he sees as false and treasonous accusations by Tiresias, Oedipus connects Kreon's recommendation to call in Tiresias with the fact that banishing Oedipus would leave Kreon in position to assume the throne. This sudden accusation against Kreon suggests not only Oedipus' quick mind but the suspiciousness and ruthless initiative required of a *tyrannos.* (See n. 1006–7.) Gould has drawn a useful distinction between Tiresias and Oedipus under duress. While Oedipus sharpens his ability to make inferences, Tiresias can only clarify and elaborate on Oedipus' guilt with an intuitive vision. The prophet is unreasonable but correct, Oedipus plausible but wrong.

465   *bogus beggar-priest*   The Greeks used the word *magus* to refer to what they considered an unreliable and corruptible breed of fortunetellers from Persia.

476   *the know-nothing*   Oedipus himself stresses the difference between his ability to solve problems intellectually and Tiresias' failure to solve them using the arts of prophecy. Oedipus smugly boasts of his "ignorance" but is in fact truly and desperately ignorant of the hidden facts that will ruin him.

506   *terror-stricken feet*   The phrase may mean that the curse pursuing Oedipus is itself "terrible footed." But the sound of the word for "terrible footed," *deinopous,* echoes Oedipus' name (lit. "Swollenfoot") so as to suggest that Oedipus' scarred feet, which were pinned together when he was exposed at birth, are in some way terrible or terrified.

511   *Kithairon*   The mountain on which Oedipus, as an infant, was left to die. See *Oed King* introduction, p. 21.

517   *bring you down to what you are*   This sentence is obscure in Greek. Jebb suggests that it means Oedipus will be leveled, i.e., "equal" to his true self by being revealed as Laios' son, and "equal" to his own children, all of whom have the same mother, Jokasta.

520   *warning spoken through my mouth*   This seeming circumlocution conveys the fact that Tiresias is not the source his prophecies, but the transmitter of Apollo's messages. The word *stoma,* or "mouth," also means the message spoken by the mouth.

531   *Who was my father?*   Lit. "the one who gave me birth." The word is masculine, indicating that Oedipus asks who his male parent is.

557   *father's seed and his seed*   Lit. "seed fellow to his father." The word *homosporos* names one who impregnates the same woman as his father, but it also carries the suggestion of blood relationship to the father.

571   *Fates*   The *keres,* who execute the will of Zeus and Apollo.

574   *Parnassos*   The mountain home of the Muses, visible from Thebes.

582   *Earth . . . mouth*   Lit. "from earth's mid-navel." The navel was a white stone at Delphi, at the spot where oracles or "dooms" such as mentioned here were spoken. The navel, or *omphalos,* was an avenue of communication to the wisdom of the earth. See n. 179.

585   *man who reads birds*   Tiresias.

589–97   *doubt . . . no proof*   The Chorus faces a hard choice. Either they must abandon their trust in divine oracles or they must accuse Oedipus of the death of Laios. They decide that before joining with Tiresias they must have some proof (lit. a "touchstone," *basanos,* which streaks black when rubbed with true gold), to remove their doubt. Because no metaphoric touchstone exists—no feud or crime that set the Korinthian royal house against the Theban House of Kadmos—they withhold their accusation.

608–9   *charges proved against him*   Here again the word "touchstone" is used, this time as a verb.

637   *master's murderer*   Oedipus' language is perhaps purposely ambiguous. He proleptically accuses Kreon of murdering him, but the phrase could accuse Kreon of Laios' murder also.

664   *Laios?*   Kreon has not yet heard Tiresias' charges, hence his surprise.

671   *hunt down the killer*   Oedipus may be hinting that the investigation of Laios' murder was less than thorough.

688   *rationally*   Kreon's pedantic reasonableness contrasts sharply with Oedipus' impatient quickness. His laborious catalog of the disadvantages of kingship may be heartfelt, but its pompous rhetorical expression generates suspicion in Oedipus.

696   *To be king*   These protestations should be compared with Kreon's later implicit acceptance of the kingship at 1730–32.

707   *Nor would I join someone*   This oblique reference is probably to Tiresias. Kreon accepts the possibility that Tiresias is treasonous in his accusations; he clearly does not believe such accusations against Oedipus to be valid.

732   *your death*   Oedipus chooses the harsher penalty of the two that the Delphi oracle proposed to cure Thebes at 113. But Oedipus may have in mind simply the normal punishment for treason.

733   *Then start by defining "betrayal"*   The text, in the judgment of many scholars, may be corrupt at this point. Editors have attempted to preserve continuous sense by reassigning the lines to other speakers and by positing a line to bridge the gap in logic after Gr. 625 (734). Gould, however, argues plausibly that

Kreon's proclivity for verbal analysis and Socratic love of general laws may explain his apparent non sequitur, which attempts to deflect Oedipus from violence into philosophical debate. I accept Gould's defense of the manuscripts and translate the text as received.

755   *or have me killed*   Kreon reverts to the choice of banishment or death proposed by the oracle he himself brought from Delphi. He also may have assumed Oedipus' recent threat of death to be hyperbole.

757   *False prophecy*   Lit. "evil arts." This implies that Kreon has employed Tiresias to make false charges disguised as prophecy to destroy Oedipus. Such treacherous use of prophecy was a part of fifth-century Greek political life.

758   *I ask the gods*   Kreon makes a formal declaration of innocence that invokes the gods; his innocence is instantly respected as valid by all but Oedipus.

763–812   *Give in . . . luck*   These lines are a *kommos,* a sung expression of grief or strong emotion in which the Leader joins one or more of the main characters. To judge by the root meaning of *kommos* (which is "beat"), this portion must have had a more strongly accented rhythm than the rest of the dialogue. Here the emotion might stem from the realization, by all present, of increasingly grave circumstances.

775   *No! We ask neither*   Though the Chorus reveres Oedipus for the success and prosperity of his kingship, it does not follow the harsh alternatives his quick mind suggests: Oedipus sees that if Kreon's conspiracy is not stamped out, it will lead ultimately to his own destruction. The Chorus gropes for a less severe outcome and gradually refrains from identifying with Oedipus as the events of his life are revealed to them.

776   *the Sun*   The Sun frequently appears as the source of final appeal in tragedy, as it will later at 1617 when Kreon orders Oedipus out of its "life-giving flame."

782   *let him go*   That Oedipus yields, however grudgingly, shows that his stubbornness and self-confidence are not immune to persuasion, nor is he insensitive to the wishes of those close to him.

818   *He says I murdered Laios*   Kreon did not say this, of course. Because Oedipus so passionately believes in the truth of his inference—that Kreon is responsible for Tiresias' charges—he puts Tiresias' words in Kreon's mouth.

827   *I don't say Apollo himself sent it*   This qualification both absolves Apollo from false prophecy and expresses skepticism concerning oracles, skepticism that must have been shared widely in a world where oracles were constantly put to dubious political use. The Chorus has the strongest commitment to the divine authority of oracles. Oedipus' belief is conditioned by experience and changes with events.

829–30   *destined to die at the hands of*   In Jokasta's version, the oracle to Laios was unqualified and not meant as a punishment. Gould notes that by omitting the aspect of punishment present in earlier versions of the myth, Sophokles establishes the pure and unexplained malice of Apollo's destruction of Oedipus.

832   *three roads meet*   This is the detail that disturbs Oedipus, and the one he reverts to as soon as Jokasta ends her speech. The actor playing Oedipus must make a gesture of recognition to account for Jokasta's question at 846. Sophokles might have meant such a pointed reaction to explain why Oedipus was distracted from picking up another fact with direct bearing on his identity: Jokasta's child's feet had been "pierced and pinned" together, as Oedipus' own had been, to produce the swollen scars that gave him his name. However, the weight to be given Oedipus' crippled feet may not be as conclusive as some commentators think. If exposure of children was common, Oedipus might not be expected to connect himself instantly and absolutely with Laios' son, even if he had heard Jokasta's words.

841–43   *god wants . . . showing what he's done*   Lit. "Of what things the god hunts the use, he reveals easily himself." Allusions to hunting appear also at 267, 425, and 671. The words here conjure the image of god seizing his prey and then displaying it.

846   *What fear made you turn*   Jokasta could refer either to a movement by Oedipus at 844–45 or earlier, at 832.

851–52   *Phokis . . . Daulis*   Towns near Delphi.

854   *before you came to power*   For the sequence of events leading to Oedipus' assumption of power in Thebes, see *Oed King* introduction, pp. 21–22.

858   *Was he a young man*   Oedipus poses as the first alternative the one he must hope is true: that Laios was not an older man of an age to be his father. In her response Jokasta not only dashes this hope but suggests a physical resemblance between Laios and Oedipus.

862   *that savage curse*   Oedipus declared this interdiction against Laios' murderer at 290–303.

869   *a herald*   The presence of a herald might have indicated to Oedipus that the party contained a prince or ruler.

876   *touched . . . begged*   A touch on the arm, like clasping a person's knees, was a formal supplication, an appeal to piety in hope of achieving a favorable response.

883   *I've said too much*   What Oedipus means here is uncertain. Most likely, as Gould suggests, he regrets the curse pronounced against himself—the curse to which he has already referred at 861.

890   *know the risks*   Lit. "while I cross through this chance (*tyche*)."

891–92   *Polybos . . . Merope*   Are we to understand that Oedipus has never before named his parents or his origins to Jokasta? Although such extreme reticence is possible, it is much more likely that Sophokles uses here an epic convention whereby a hero begins a piece of consequential autobiography by formally naming his homeland and immediate ancestors.

893–94   *Chance . . . blow*   An excellent instance of Sophokles' practice of having Oedipus label as chance or luck an event that, seen in retrospect, becomes part of the pattern of his ruin created by Apollo.

904   *the rumor still rankled, it hounded me*   The Greek word *hupheppe* could mean either that the rumor "crept abroad" or that "the memory recurred." I have tried to translate the phrase so as to include both possibilities.

905   *with no word to my parents*   Had Oedipus informed his parents of the mission to Delphi, they presumably would have intervened. By seeking assurance of his birth beyond his parents' word, Oedipus placed himself in the hands of the god Apollo. It was both a conventional and a rational act, because Delphi could serve as a locator of lost kin, and because Oedipus had no reason to suspect the god held any enmity toward him.

907   *the god would not honor me*   What was the question Oedipus put to the Pythoness? "Who are my true parents?" or "Is Polybos my true father?" For the oracle not to answer such a question, directly or indirectly, seems to Oedipus a violation of the normal treatment a pilgrim could expect from the god (lit. "Phoibos," or Apollo) at Delphi.

909–10   *his words flashed . . . horrible, wretched things*   The phrase is so vivid some scholars have questioned its authenticity. It does fit both Oedipus' present mental condition, in which he sees himself as a target for strange malice, and the verbs of leaping and striking that Sophokles uses for actions attributable to Apollo. The oracle given Oedipus is not an answer to his question, but an attack on Oedipus—not a clarification, but a condemnation that impacts Oedipus with a shock or flash. His reaction, to flee Korinth and his parents, is entirely comprehensible and in no way morally flawed. An oracle might be fulfilled in a metaphorical or oblique manner; in real life some oracles were never fulfilled, a frequent event in the experience of Sophokles' audience. In tragedy, however, the audience would expect all oracles to be completed. Many readers think that Oedipus ought eventually to have considered the oracle's broader implications. (Could the oracle be telling me that Polybos is not my father? Had I better avoid killing anyone old enough to be my father or marrying a woman old enough to be my mother?) But Sophokles gave his audience no opportunity in the play's swift action to consider such questions; the speed with which he shows us the oracle's completion fits with the consistent image of the god leaping or striking at Oedipus.

926   *man out front*   Presumably the herald.

929–36   *I smash . . . kill them all*   Oedipus uses the historical present tense in these lines. Although the events happened some twenty years earlier, they are vivid and immediate in his mind (Segal 2001, 90).

933–34   *staff this hand holds*   The hand was the instrument that retained the defilement of its acts. The actor might have raised his hand at this point, as he might have at other times when his hand is named. In Athenian law, acts committed by an agent's own hand, even if involuntarily, resulted in pollution, but masterminding or delegating the act escaped such stigma.

936   *kill them all*   Said in pride perhaps, but not in boastfulness. Laios' men would have attacked him; only by killing or disabling all would he have survived. In fact, Oedipus killed only four; the fifth (the herald) escaped, or perhaps recovered from a wound after being left for dead.

937   *stranger and Laios . . . were the same blood*   In Greek the word for stranger, *xenos,* could apply to Oedipus himself.

938   *triumph*   The Greek word so translated is *athlios,* a superlative form of *athlon,* a contest or combat.

949   *utter filth*   The Greek word so translated is *anagnos,* meaning "guilty," "unclean," or "unholy," and is usually translated "polluted," which I avoid to escape confusion with modern uses of that word.

955   *brought me up and gave me birth*   By reversing the natural order—birth followed by nurture—Sophokles reminds us that Polybos "gave birth" to Oedipus only by bringing him up and falsely claiming him as his own son.

965   *eyewitness*   Lit. "person who was there."

976   *braving the road alone*   The Greek word here is somewhat mysterious and might be translated literally as "with solitary belt." The word appears nowhere else in surviving Greek. It may mean simply "dressed as a traveler."

978   *evidence will drag me down*   Lit. "the balance tips toward me." The metaphor is from scales for weighing, a typical one in judicial contexts. See *Kolonos* n. 1652.

986   *poor doomed child*   Lit. "unhappy person" *(dystanos).* Here Jokasta is thinking of the short, doomed life of her baby and uses the most common word for "unfortunate one." In her final speeches to Oedipus (at 1214 and 1217) she will use the same word to sum up his life.

989   *look right, then left*   Lit. "shoot frightened glances right and left" (Gould 1970, 106). Ancient Greeks, who habitually took actions and made decisions based on signs and omens from the divinities, interpreted the sudden presence of a person or bird as hopeful (if it appeared on the right) and dangerous (if it appeared on the left). Jokasta has abandoned such precautions.

996   *sky-walking laws*   Lit. "sky-footed." The laws to which the Chorus refers here are those whose origins go as far back as human consciousness does, laws inseparable from our instinctive behavior. The laws forbidding incest and kin murder would be those most on the Chorus' mind.

1006–7 *A violent will fathers the tyrant*   Lit. "*hubris* plants the seed of the *tyrannos.*" *Hubris,* a general word for violence, outrage, and moral insubordination, sums up the actions of a person who exercises pure will without constraint, and thus applies most exactly to a Greek *tyrannos.* The name *tyrannos* was given to powerful rulers from the late seventh to the early fifth centuries who "emerged from the aristocratic oligarchy as sole rulers of their city-states, responsible only to themselves. . . . They were necessarily energetic, intelligent, confident, ambitious, and aggressive; they also had to be ruthless and suspicious of plots to overthrow their sometimes precarious position" (Segal 2001, 6). The term did not acquire our pejorative meaning of "tyrant" until Plato in the fourth century. Throughout the play Sophokles uses *tyrannos* in the more neutral sense of a *basileus,* or king, except at 1007, where the modern sense of the tyrant is surely intended. See n. 455.

1039–41   *Delphi, Olympia, Abai*   All are holy shrines and destinations of religious pilgrimages. See n. 179.

1049   *the gods lose force*   Lit. "the things pertaining to divinity slowly depart."

1080   *isthmus*   The Isthmus of Korinth connects the Peloponnesus to the Greek mainland.

1104   *scour Pythian smoke*   Lit. "scrutinize the Pythian hearth." The Pythoness delivered the prophecies from within a basement cell inside the temple of Apollo in Delphi, located on the slopes of Mt. Parnassos. The smoky vapors that rose from the temple floor were reputed to put her in a trance. Recent geological studies of the soil around Delphi suggest that the fumes from its underlying rock structure contained ethylene—a sweet-smelling gas, once used as an anesthetic, which produces a pleasant euphoria. (See William J. Broad, "For Delphic Oracle, Fumes and Visions," *New York Times,* 19 March 2002, late ed.: F1.)

1131   *shines a great light*   Lit. "great eye." The Greeks believed eyes projected powerful rays toward the people and the objects they looked at. Other uses of this metaphor in Greek literature suggest that a "great eye" was a sign of wonderful good hope or good luck.

1155   *unforgivable harm*   Lit. "Lest you receive a religious pollution from those who planted you."

1214   *You poor child!*   Jokasta calls Oedipus *dystanos,* the same word she called her child who was exposed and presumed dead. (See n. 986.) She now knows that child is Oedipus, and will call him *dystanos* once more at 1217. In his next speech Oedipus will disclaim all human mothering and claim Luck *(Tyche)* for his parent (1226); he sees only the good in his situation at the moment.

1248   *Pan*   A god holy to rural people, Pan was a patron of shepherds and herdsmen, as well as a fertility god amorous to both sexes. The mountain he roves is Kithairon, the mountain on which Oedipus' parents instructed the shepherd to let him die.

1253–56   *Hermes . . . Kyllene . . . Helikon*   Like Pan, Hermes was a god well known to country people for playing childish tricks. Zeus made him his messenger and gave him the wide-brimmed hat, winged sandals, and *kerykeion (caduceus* in Latin, or herald's staff) with which he is often shown. Because of his association with roads Hermes is known as the patron of wayfarers—traders, travelers, and thieves. The Chorus' mention of him might allude to the crossroads, the place at which Oedipus killed Laios. Kyllene, a haunt of both Pan and Hermes, is a mountain in Arcadia in the central Peloponnesus, the largest peninsula south of Attica, connected to the mainland only by the Isthmus of Korinth. The Muses inhabited a sanctuary on Helikon, a mountain south of Thebes.

1288   *Arkturos*   A star near the Big Dipper which, when it appeared in September, signaled the end of summer in Greece.

1326   *Kill her own child?*   The Greek words so translated, *tlemon tekousa* (lit. "poor woman, she who gave birth") "shows how difficult it is to translate Sophocles' density and richness of meaning" (Segal 2001, 103). Here Sophokles implies that Jokasta found herself doing something utterly horrible for a mother to do: killing her own child.

1350   *Your fate teaches*   Lit. "with your example (or "paradigm," *paradigmos)* before us."

1351–52   *the story god spoke*   Lit. "with your *daimon* before us." See the introduction for a discussion of *daimon.*

1358   *who sang the god's dark oracles*   Lit. "singer of oracles." Presumably a reference to the Sphinx's riddles, but the word "oracle" usually refers to divinely sanctioned responses such as those given by Delphi. Sophokles may here be connecting the Sphinx to the other instances of divine intervention in Oedipus' life.

1371   *tumbling*   The Greek word so translated, *pesein,* lit. means to "fall on," or "attack," and can refer in one usage to a baby falling between the legs of a woman squatted or seated in childbirth. E. A. Havelock (in Gould 1970, 138) suggests another meaning for the verb—to mount sexually, in which case there is an overtone of violence. A variation of the same verb, *empiptein,* used at 1431, I translate as "burst into" to describe Oedipus' entry into Jokasta's bedroom after she's committed suicide.

1391   *Danube . . . Rion*   The river Danube was called the Ister in the ancient world. The Rion, the modern name of the Phasis, is a river near the Russian/Iranian border, on the edge of what was then the known world.

1394   *not involuntary evil, it was willed*   The Servant refers to Jokasta's suicide and Oedipus' self-blinding; he contrasts these conscious and willed actions with the ones Jokasta and Oedipus made without understanding their true consequences, such as their own marriage. Although Oedipus knew what he was doing when he blinded himself, the action was just as fated as the patricide and incest; Tiresias had predicted Oedipus' blindness earlier. When the Servant says that voluntary evils are more painful, he cannot mean that they are more blameworthy or more serious but that they are done in horror and desperation—in contrast to the earlier evils, such as the marriage, committed in optimism and confidence.

1415   *doubled lives*   The reference is to Oedipus' "double" *(diplos)* relationship to Jokasta, as her son and husband. The word appears again at 1429 with a comparable allusion, as Oedipus enters the "double doors" of their bedroom. Another significant image of doubled action appears in the piercing of Oedipus ankles and the striking out of his own eyes.

1419   *burst in*   The Greek word so translated is *eisepaiein,* an unusual compound (from *eis,* "into" and *paiein,* "to strike") that might have been a colloquial word for intercourse recognizable by the audience (Gould 1970, 47). It is used here to compare Oedipus' violent action to a sexual attack, and thus to link it both to incest and to parricide.

1424–25   *furrowed twice-mothering earth . . . children sprang*   The Messenger reports that Oedipus identifies Jokasta with an *aroura,* or furrowed field, as the source or origin of both Oedipus himself and the children he conceived with her. The image of the earth as mother figures significantly in the *Kolonos.* (See 1818–20 and *Kolonos* introduction, pp. 99–100.)

1431 *burst into*   Again the word *empiptein* (see n. 1371), used to refer to Oedipus violation of Jokasta's "harbor" and her "furrow."

1512–14 *Apollo . . . made evil, consummate evil, out of my life*   Lit. "It was Apollo, friends, Apollo who brought to completion these my evils *(pathea)."* A *pathos* (sing.) is here, as often in Greek literature, an unmerited suffering sent by a god.

1516 *these eyes*   Sophokles uses a pronoun *(nin)* for eyes, not a noun, which is the same for any gender, plural, dual, or singular. The ambiguity is surely deliberate but cannot be translated. Its inclusiveness, however, implies that *all* the blows that made his life evil, though struck by Oedipus himself, were caused by Apollo.

1724 *you will have your wish*   Some scholars believe that Kreon is agreeing to Oedipus' plea to be exiled. But it is more likely that the words are noncommittal in the usual way of politicians.

1733–46 *Thebans . . . god's victim*   Some scholars question the authenticity of these lines, partly because of the difficulty in making sense of several of them, and partly because of their suspicious resemblance to the ending of Euripides' *Phoenician Women.* Modern audiences object to them mainly because they seem less than climactic. This objection is illegitimate. Greek dramatists did not place strong emphasis on concluding lines the way modern dramatists do, but often used them to facilitate the departure of the Chorus.

1746 *never having been god's victim*   Lit. "having been made to undergo no anguish." The final word of the play, *pathon,* "having been made to undergo," is the same noun used at 1471 in a phrase I translate as "pure, helpless anguish." Oedipus also used *pathos* at 1513 when he explained that Apollo was the god who reduced him to misery. The word is often used as a technical phrase for the suffering of the *heros* in hero cults. The Latin translation is *passio,* which gives us in its Christian context the "passion" of Christ. The word appears in the concluding lines of two of Aeschylus' plays, *The Libation Bearers* and *Prometheus Bound,* as well as in the last sentence of Sophokles' *Electra.* It does not figure in the conclusion of any of Euripides' surviving plays.

Oedipus at Kolonos

2 *Have we come to a town?*   It's clear from the exchange at 28–29 that Oedipus and Antigone know they're approaching Athens. Oedipus wants to know both what place *(koros)* or piece of open ground they're near and what town *(polis).* The word *polis* normally means city, but here it more likely refers to a smaller inhabited entity. The eventual answer to Oedipus' last question is: Kolonos.

11 *on public land, or in a grove*   Oedipus is so tired that he doesn't care whether he and Antigone rest in a public space or risk trespass, which they will shortly do, into a sacred grove (or precinct) from which unauthorized folk are excluded.

23   *nightingales*   Nightingales symbolize death. This is the first allusion to the "holy place" where Oedipus will die.

25   *Be my lookout.*   Antigone maintains a sentinel's alertness throughout the play, spotting in turn the Stranger, the Old Men, Ismene, Kreon, and Polyneikes just before each enters.

37   *Stranger*   The word *xenos,* translated usually throughout the text as "stranger," can also mean, and is sometimes translated as, "host" or "guest" depending on the context. The character called the Stranger in the surviving texts would most probably be a local farmer.

44–50 *fearsome goddesses . . . harsher names*   The fearsome goddesses (lit. *emphoboi theai*) are the Eumenides, chthonian (or earth) powers associated with death and the underworld (as opposed to Olympian, the heavenly or sky gods). Originally known as the Erinys, or Furies, they avenge wrongs done to family members—disrespect for elders, for instance, but especially kin murder. They were worshipped under a variety of names. Thebans, including Oedipus in this play, address them as "Ladies." In Athens their cult name was "Solemn Ones" *(Semnai).* Those who called them Kindly Ones did so to deflect their ire. In 50 (lit. "other places have different names") I translate the euphemistic "different" as "harsher" to highlight the Stranger's subtext, which is that these goddesses are dangerous. See n. 92.

51   *suppliant*   Oedipus claims his formal status as a suppliant, one who makes a specific request of a higher authority, usually a god or his representative, or a ruler. Suppliants generally expected and were granted divine protection, though there were horrific exceptions, particularly during times of war or civil strife, in which suppliants were granted safety and then slaughtered.

54   *here is where I meet my fate*   Oedipus' words in Greek are compact and mysterious. They may also be translated: "It's the sign of my destiny." The Greek word *synthema,* if translated literally as "sign," means a particular agreed-upon token, signal, or code word (Jebb). Oedipus could be saying that the name "Eumenides" is the sign foretold to him by Apollo's priestess at Delphi. Or he could mean that his intended prayer or the grove itself is the sign. In any case, Apollo had promised that when Oedipus arrived at the grove of the Eumenides he would find rest at last. When Oedipus suddenly hears the name of the presiding goddesses, "the Kindly Ones," he turns brusquely decisive. He's arrived on promised ground and will not be moved.

62–64 *This entire grove . . . shrine here.*   Sacred groves in ancient Greece could harbor more than one divinity. This grove's major god is Poseidon, whose affinity with horses and the sea made him important to the Athenians, since navy and cavalry were crucial to their military prowess. The grove also contains shrines to Prometheus, and to the Eumenides, the grove's resident deities described in n. 44–50.

65   *brass-footed threshold*   In Sophokles' era a well-known grove was located in Kolonos about a mile north of the Acropolis on the main route into Athens. Somewhere near the grove was a steeply descending rift or cavern in the rock, perhaps reinforced with brass to forms "steps." Jebb calls them "the *stay of*

Athens: a phrase in which the idea of a physical basis is joined to that of a religious safeguard" (1886, n. 57). The ancient audience would have understood the grove's rich mythical and historical associations and connected them to the area "on stage." See nn. 1746–47 and 1748–50.

68   *We've all taken his name*   Inhabitants commonly added their hometowns to their given names; e.g., Sophokles of Kolonos; Ion of Chios.

76   *Theseus*   Theseus was a legendary hero who arrived in Athens as a formidable teenager after killing many human and bestial adversaries on the way from his birthplace in Troezen. He was unaware that the reigning king of Athens was actually his father, Aigeus (though in some versions of the myth Poseidon had actually sired him). Theseus' great political accomplishment was the unification of Attica under Athenian leadership.

81   *my words . . . of their own*   Oedipus claims here only the immediate cogency of his speech, but his confident assertion suggests the prophetic power his words will acquire and project during the course of the play.

84   *down on your luck*   Lit. *daimon,* a personal deity who directs the events of an individual's life. At this point the Stranger doesn't realize the full implication of the *daimon* on Oedipus' life. See intro. *Oed King* passim.

92   *eyes we dread*   Lit. *deinopes* or "dread-eyed." The Kindly Ones were dreaded for their power to "see everything," especially all kinds of malfeasance. That power enabled them to spot and punish intra-familial abuse.

95   *Apollo*   Apollo, one of the Twelve Olympian gods, was a symbol of light and sometimes associated with Helios, god of the sun. Apollo's primary epithet, *Phoibos,* means "shining." He also oversaw the sites, the practice, and the profession of prophecy. As revealed in *Oed King,* Apollo's priestess, the Pythoness at Delphi, prophesied Oedipus' fate: that Oedipus would kill his father and marry his mother.

107–8   *sober man . . . spurn wine*   Most Greek divinities received wine as an offering; the Eumenides were an exception. While Oedipus' sobriety might result from the recent austere circumstances of his life, it also alludes to the frightening countenance he shares with the goddesses. See n. 155.

127–87   *Look for him . . . keep quiet*   These lines comprise the *parodos* or Entry Song of the chorus, or Old Men, and like the choral odes to follow, were sung and accompanied by an oboe-like instrument, the *aulos.* This Entry Song is unusual in its utilitarian purpose; instead of reporting an event, it enacts an event: the search for and discovery of the grove's invader. The Old Men operate here and later as "security guards" who protect the sacred grove and the community of Kolonos. Oedipus addresses them as "Guardians."

147–51   *We've heard . . . hiding place*   The Leader and the Old Men, by interchangeably referring to themselves throughout the play as "I" or "we," reinforce their collective nature.

155   *The sight of you . . . appalls us.*   Lit. "dreadful (*deinos*) to see, dreadful to hear." Oedipus used the word *deinos* to refer to the Eumenides at 92.

234   *The horror I was born to*   Oedipus' life. He refers to the fate assigned him before birth by Apollo, a fate he began living as soon as he was born.

242–44   *Laios' son . . . house of Labdakos*   Laios was Oedipus's father, the man he killed
without knowing his true identity; Labdakos, an earlier king of Thebes, was
Laios' father.

259–60   *burden our city . . . deadly contagion*   Lit. "place a heavy obligation on the
city." The obligation here is a *miasma,* or pollution. Ancient Greeks believed
that those who murdered blood kin carried with them a contagion that would
inflict damage on those in contact with the murderer. At the beginning of *Oed
King* Thebes suffers from such a contagion, which causes deadly disease, crop
failure, and rampant miscarriage.

287–88   *Athens . . . haven for persecuted strangers*   Athens' reputation as a haven for ex-
iles in distress was prominent in myth and the dramas derived from myth.
Athens sheltered Orestes when pursued by the Furies, both the children of
Herakles, who were persecuted by King Eurystheus, and the crazed Herakles
himself after he had murdered his wife and children. Athens maintained that
reputation in Sophokles' era by welcoming and granting legal status to immi-
grants as *metics,* allowing them to work and take part in some civic activities.

303–4   *those who tried to murder me*   Oedipus here refers to Jokasta and Laios, his
true parents. When they heard an oracle's prophecy that doomed their son to
kill his father and marry his mother, they pinned the infant's ankles together
and left him to die. See *Oed King* 1173–79.

335   *busy with foot traffic*   The main road north from Athens passed through
Kolonos. The implication is that Oedipus' disclosure of his identity to the Old
Men would soon be bruited among the travelers heading toward Athens, and
that Theseus would hear it from them as he moved north.

362   *two wretched lives!*   Literally "twice-wretched." Ismene reacts to the grim
appearance of her father and sister. But "twice-wretched" also refers to the
doubling of roles, in which his two sisters are also Oedipus' children, and thus
adds psychic wretchedness to their physical and social misery.

371   *Those two boys imitate the Egyptians*   The Greeks' cultural norm for the divi-
sion of labor between the sexes was totally reversed in the lives of their Egyptian peers. Oedipus' sneering judgment of his sons reveals the tendency of
Greeks to consider foreigners as barbarians, morally and intellectually inferior
to themselves. Sophokles was possibly influenced here by the section of Hero-
dotus' *Histories* (2.35) that documented Egyptian customs and manners.

386   *the latest oracles to your father*   After Oedipus' banishment Ismene became her
father's informant—as Antigone, in a similarly helpful role became his companion and sentinel. Ismene brought Oedipus both Theban news and oracles
involving him. Since she was in effect a spy, she was living dangerously. Ismene
also volunteers to perform the purification ritual required of Oedipus by the
"dread goddesses," during which she's kidnapped.

398   *They were keen, at first, to let Kreon rule*   The decision to allow Kreon to succeed Oedipus was prudential—both brothers realized the curse on their

family might harm Thebes again, as it had during Oedipus' reign. But they changed their minds and contested the kingship, thus activating the curse. They had agreed to alternating terms. First Polyneikes ruled Thebes, but then Eteokles, who succeeded him, refused to step down, apparently with the approval of the Theban population. See n. 930.

405   *that hot-head*   Eteokles inherited Oedipus' impetuousness without his father's intelligence and judgment.

410   *Argos*   An area in the northeastern part of the Peloponnesus.

410   *married power*   After his exile from Thebes, Polyneikes' marriage to the daughter of Adrastos, king of Argos, gave him access to the Argive warrior class, which he persuaded to lay siege to Thebes. Antigone calls her brother's marriage "deadly" (*Antigone,* 954–55) because it led to the attack that doomed both him and her.

422   *I have new oracles*   It appears from the plural that Ismene has learned of two distinct oracles (probably sought by Eteokles and/or Kreon). One identified Oedipus, living or dead, as a magical defensive barrier that would protect Thebes from attack. Another promised that Oedipus himself would be transformed into a *heros* whose powers would extend beyond his physical death (see 424–33).

428   *When I'm nothing . . . be a man*   Oedipus does not yet know he has been tapped for heroization. In the course of his next long speech (458–98) he realizes the power he's been granted and begins to wield it.

435   *Theban frontier*   There were no exact, demarcated borders between Greek city-states like the ones that exist between modern contiguous countries. The-bans would therefore be making a judgment call when choosing the place near Thebes in which to hold Oedipus; it had to be far enough away so that Thebes wouldn't be contaminated by his parricidal guilt but close enough to the city to interfere with an Athenian attack force.

438–39   *If they don't pay . . . serious trouble*   The trouble might refer to the possibility of placing Oedipus' future Theban tomb in the wrong location or to some other form of neglect, such as failing to honor the dead king with libations of wine and honey.

448   *Your rage . . . your tomb.*   In their new oracles the gods promise that Oedipus' crucial power will be manifest in his rage. The scene envisioned in this line probably refers to Oedipus' tomb should it be located in Athens. The Thebans would deploy around it and be overwhelmed by the Athenian defenders as they fight; the dead *heros'* rage would add firepower to the attack against his former countrymen. Sophokles might allude here to the Theban raiding party that Athenian forces repulsed at Kolonos a few years before he wrote the play.

450   *Sacred envoys*   Lit. *theoron,* a spectator or witness of a sacred rite or event. In this line Sophokles specifically mentions that the envoys went to Delphi. In *Oed. King* he uses the same word (*theoros,* a different grammatical case) to explain Laios' journey "close to god"—but he purposely withholds the king's destination. See *Oed. King* n. 129–30.

450   *Delphic hearth*   Apollo's oracle resided at Delphi. The hearth refers to the smoky fire that enveloped the Pythoness as she delivered her versified answer to the questions posed to her by envoys. See *Oed King* n. 1104.

458–61   *Gods, don't interfere . . . dead set*   Oedipus here frames the wish that his sons both die as a request to the gods; later, at 1495–520, he will himself deliver the same malevolence as both curse and prophecy.

464–65   *When I was driven . . . no move to stop it or help me.*   At the end of *Oed King* Oedipus had asked Kreon to exile him, but Kreon refused. As implied in the *Kolonos,* Oedipus had become reconciled to Thebes and wished to remain there. Here he refers to his sons' failure to honor that wish, as well as to their dereliction of a duty fundamental in Greek law: to care for, support, and protect an aged parent.

470   *The far-off day when my fury seethed*   Oedipus refers to the day he became aware of the incest and parricide he had unwittingly committed—the day on which he blinded himself and asked Kreon to banish him from Thebes. See *Oed King* 1629–30.

489   *I recalled some prophecies*   Without explaining the specifics, Oedipus makes clear that he now sees the connection between the two new prophecies brought by Ismene—that he will be transformed at death and that his dead body will have military potency—and the much earlier prophecy at Delphi, which said he would find a final home in the Eumenides' grove.

503   *Whatever my host wants done*   Oedipus addresses the Leader in his specific role as advisor to strangers on the local laws and customs. As Oedipus grows more and more alienated from (and obstinate in) his relationships with his sons, the Old Men, and Kreon, he becomes increasingly acquiescent in his position as a suppliant—and he gains in divine authority.

504–31   *Ask atonement . . . If you don't . . . I'm afraid for you.*   This lengthy passage, in which the Leader specifies the procedure that Oedipus, as suppliant, must follow in his ritual offering to the Eumenides, serves a dramatic purpose: Ismene, by volunteering to perform the rituals, is sent offstage long enough to be kidnapped by Kreon. But the passage also marks the beginning of Oedipus' religious involvement mentioned in n. 503.

519   *Just pure water*   The Eumenides differed from other gods because they did not receive offerings of wine. See n. 107–8.

529   *without looking back, leave.*   It was customary when making offerings to most gods, and especially these "dread-eyed goddesses," to avert one's eyes from the actual shrine while pouring the offerings, to pray quietly, and then to leave the shrine "without looking back."

549–603   *Unpleasant it may be . . . ignorance*   This colloquy in which the Old Men press Oedipus to confess to his incest and parricide, and during which Oedipus both admits to the facts but defends the innocence of his motives, is a choral ode and was set in the ancient productions to music and sung.

562–66   *I suffered anguish . . . I chose to do none.*   In this coolly rational defense of his moral innocence, Oedipus focuses on the huge imbalance between the misery he's suffered and his lack of culpability for actions he committed in ignorance.

In successive restatements he will add passion to his logic, especially when replying to Kreon's accusations.

568–69   *Thebes married me . . . woman who would destroy me.*   The Thebans, who were grateful that Oedipus had saved them from the Sphinx, rewarded him with the throne—and Laios' widow, Jokasta, who became his wife. See introduction to *Oed King*, p. 22.

575   *scourges*   Lit. *ata,* or "curses." Oedipus does not mean that his two much-loved daughters are literally curses but rather that they are constant reminders of the defilement and pain his acts have caused. Speaking metaphorically, no matter how deeply they care for him, his daughters are constant scourges who pursue him in order to punish his incest and parricide.

One of Theseus' Men   I infer this stage direction to make sense of the Leader's next lines, in which he seems certain that Theseus intends to help Oedipus.

619   *I was also raised in exile.*   Theseus, raised by his mother Aethra, a princess of Troezen in the Peloponnesus, grew up without knowing that his father was King Aigeus of Athens. As a young man Theseus learned the truth and traveled to his father's home, performing many heroic feats along the way. Similarly, Oedipus, who was raised in Korinth by Polybos without knowing that his natural father was Laios, king of Thebes, suffered great hardship after the discovery of his true identity—and is still suffering at this point in the play.

656   *Then what superhuman pain* do *you suffer?*   Sophokles might allude here to Oedipus' imminent transformation to a *heros.*

661   *God's voice*   The oracle. Its words, from the Pythoness of Apollo, made clear to the Thebans that not bringing Oedipus home put their city at risk.

666–67   *All powerful Time ravages the rest.*   Oedipus reminds Theseus of a lesson he first learned in *Oed King:* the only thing man can be certain of is the unstable nature of all human relationships—including political alliances between cities. Oedipus elaborates his first reference to Time, or *Kronos,* as a teacher of acquiescence (7–8); he now sees time as a continuum that destroys and revives relationships. The idea is analogous to his own transformation by the gods from great king to blind beggar to honored *heros.*

679–80   *Then my dead body . . . will drink their hot blood.*   Oedipus extrapolates from the oracle he heard from Ismene: that the Thebans will be defeated in battle while they are mustered near his tomb.

690   *kindness*   The Greek word *eumeneia,* translated as "kindness," often refers to the good will of the gods. Here it echoes the name of the Eumenides, or Kindly Ones, and also alludes to a bond between Oedipus and the goddesses.

692   *our wartime ally*   Some scholars, including Blundell, think this refers to a preexisting military alliance, while others, including Knox, say that it means nothing so specific or formal, but rather a traditional courtesy extended between royal houses.

697–98   *I'll settle him . . . rights of a citizen.*   A much-disputed line that depends upon whether one reads a Greek word at 637 in the ancient mss. as *empalin* or *em-*

polin. The line could mean respectively "*on the contrary I'll settle him* in our land" or, as I believe, and as Jebb translates, "*but will establish him as a citizen in the land.*" The issue is important because the granting of the highly prized Athenian citizenship rights to a foreigner like Oedipus would be a more striking demonstration of Theseus' *charis,* or grace, toward him than would his simply offering Oedipus a place to live.

728–87   *You've come, stranger . . . Nereid's skittering feet*   This ode of welcome to Oedipus as an Athenian citizen touches on many visual features of the splendid Kolonian landscape. Its intent, however, is to celebrate the mythical and practical advantages for Athens inherent in these visual images. For an excellent discussion of the ode as both a hymn of praise to the pinnacle of Athens' greatness and as a requiem for the city's dying power see Knox 1964, 154–56.

728   *shining Kolonos*   The epithet "shining" may derive from the light, chalky color of Kolonos' soil, which has persisted to this day.

741–43   *Dionysos . . . maenads*   Dionysos, the god associated with wine and revelry, was the son of Zeus and Semele, the daughter of Kadmos, king of Thebes. In the version of the myth adapted by Euripides in *The Bakkhai,* Semele tried to test the godliness of Zeus by challenging him to appear to her in his true shape. He did—and she was struck by lightning and thunderbolts, the symbols of his divine power. Zeus then snatched the unborn Dionysos from her body, hid him in his thigh, and took him to be brought up by nymphs, or maenads, on Mount Nysa in India. There Dionysos was schooled in the joys of wine by Silenus and the satyrs; he also cultivated a following of maenads (bacchants) who eventually traveled with him through Asia and into Greece.

749–50   *Persephone and Demeter . . . golden crocus*   Demeter, the corn goddess, traveled into the underworld to find her daughter Persephone, who had been carried there (where she was forced to spend half the year) by Hades. Both goddesses are associated with death and the mysteries, which promise their initiates rebirth through the purification of death. The crocus and the nightingale also symbolize death and are fitting reminders that Oedipus will die in this grove.

751   *Bountiful . . . Kephisos*   While other rivers in Attica ran dry in the summer heat, the Kephisos flowed abundantly all year.

758–59   *Goddess of Love with golden reins in her hands*   Aphrodite, the goddess of erotic desire, was often portrayed driving a chariot drawn by sparrows, swans, or doves.

761   *Asia*   The Greeks used "Asia" to refer to what is now called the Middle East.

761–73   *A tree not found . . . guard it with tireless glare.*   Although olive trees did grow in "Asia" and the peninsula known as Peloponnesus, the first olive tree was said to have sprung up at Athena's command from the Acropolis. This sacred tree, burned during the Persian wars, was also said to have miraculously come back to life ("a tree born from itself") and, because it was protected by Athena, to have deflected later invaders ("a terror to enemy spears"). "Zeus of the Olive Groves" translates Zeus Morios, his title as "co-protector" of the sacred olives. Sophokles might be using the olive tree to symbolize more than Athens' military resilience and the divine protection it receives. The Athenians believed their race was autochthonic, i.e., they were born directly from the land. Their political system, democracy, was similarly homegrown. The olive tree, which Sophokles enjoins Athenian men (both young and old), not to shatter and destroy, might symbolize the democratic institutions at the heart of Athens' past glory.

787   *fifty Nereids*   The daughters of the sea god Nereus are sometimes portrayed escorting ships through the high seas. Sophokles' image suggests that the Nereids' presence is visible in the rhythmic circular ripples made by the oars as they dip into the water.

809   *fellow Kadmeans*   Thebans were called Kadmeans after Kadmos, the mythical son of Agenor and founder of Thebes. Kadmos seeded the earth with dragon's teeth from which the Thebans grew (see *Oed King* n. 96).

819   *first vulgar lout who comes along*   Kreon himself will soon live up to this description when he orders his troops to abduct Antigone and attempt to take her back to Thebes. But a darker irony in this passage harks back to *Antigone,* which Sophokles wrote some decades earlier, in which she is betrothed to Kreon's son Haimon.

834   *That would cause me unendurable pain.*   Oedipus knows that if he went back to Thebes, Kreon would refuse to bury his corpse; because he has committed patricide and incest, burial rites are forbidden him.

838   *you refused me*   When Oedipus first pleaded to be exiled (see *Oed King,* 1629–30) Kreon refused, saying he needed first to consult the gods. Here Oedipus suggests that Kreon acted arbitrarily without such a consultation.

909   *She's mine.*   Oedipus asked Kreon to assume guardianship of Antigone and Ismene in *Oed King,* but Antigone has hardly been under his protection, since for many years she's been wandering with Oedipus, more or less acting as his guardian.

921 22   *My city, our city is attacked!*   The issue here is not a physical attack by the Theban raiding party but the violation and abduction of Antigone, who, like Oedipus, is a suppliant under Attic protection.

927   *daughters for crutches*   The word translated as crutches, *skeptroin,* lit. means scepters. Blundell (1990, 55) writes "since scepter is in origin a staff or walking stick, the same word in Greek is used for both. Sophokles exploits this ambiguity to create a pathetic contrast between Oedipus' helplessness (here and at [Greek] l. 1109) and his sons' bid for the royal scepter of Thebes ([Greek] 425, 449, 1354). There is also a nice dramatic irony in Creon's words, since as it turns out, Oedipus will not need the support of these 'scepters' any longer." At 462, 484 and 1416 I translate *skeptroin* in its singular form as "scepter"; "power and a kingdom"; and "your throne and your power," respectively.

930   *though I'm still their king*   The kingship of Thebes remains unclear throughout the play. We're told earlier that Eteokles has reneged on his agreement with Polyneikes to relinquish the throne. But does Eteokles still rule? Kreon seems to assert here that he's in power, as we assumed he would be at the end of *Oed King.* See n. 398.

933–35   *turned your back . . . self-destructive fury*   In *Oed King* Sophokles portrays Oedipus as full of rage and fury, a man who quickly turns in anger on his friends (especially at 760–90, where Kreon, Jokasta, and the Leader attempt to calm him down to no avail). Undoubtedly Oedipus' two most self-destructive acts are the killing of Laios and his own self-blinding. In the *Kolonos,* Oedipus' anger loses its self-destructive power as it's transformed into a power that helps his new friends the Athenians and harms his enemies, a category that now includes both his sons.

943   *You might—unless our king stops you.*   Some scholars and translators attribute this line to Kreon, changing "our" to "your," as justifiably sarcastic under the circumstances.

945–51   *Goddesses . . . the curse . . . as miserable as my own*   When Oedipus invokes the Eumenides in their role as guarantors of curses he avoids calling them Kindly Ones (see 1109 and 1521). Ancient Greeks commonly cursed their enemies with the same "evils" that had been inflicted on them. The Greek word *ata* means both prayer and curse; a curse was simply a malicious or retaliatory prayer. At the end of Antigone's life she asks that her oppressors suffer a punishment equivalent to hers (*Antigone,* 1021–22).

949   *Let the Sun, who sees all there is*   Helios, the Sun God, sometimes associated with Apollo, rode a golden chariot across the sky, a perfect vantage point to take in everything that happens on earth.

978   *the two I have left*   At this point, having disowned his sons, he's effectively given them up as dead. Antigone will similarly treat Ismene as nonexistent after she refuses to help bury Polyneikes (*Antigone,* 95ff.).

1017   *permanent residence*   Theseus makes Kreon an offer he can't refuse: bring the girls back unless he wants to be taken prisoner.

1029   *morally toxic father-killer*   The Greek word translated "morally toxic" is *anagnon,* which in Jebb's words "refers to the taint of murder aggravated by union with the wife of the slain." Kreon implies that Oedipus' crimes are present in his physical person and contagious. Oedipus himself agrees; at 1241 he will shrink back from his own instinctual gesture to shake Theseus' hand.

1031   *Council of Mount Ares*   The ancient Athenian Council of Areopagos, which met on a hill near the Acropolis, had jurisdiction over murder and matters of impiety; it imposed penalties including fines, exile with loss of property, and death, and its judgments were final.

1048–50   *none of which I chose . . . whole life*   Oedipus continues with increasing conviction to plead his case: because he was ignorant of the identity of his father and mother when he committed parricide and incest he believes that he is not responsible for or guilty of the crimes.

1050   *ancestors*   The House of Labdakos. See n. 242–44.

1145–1205   *Oh let us . . . help this land and our people*   In this rousing ode the Old Men imagine the action and outcome of the skirmish that ensues when Theseus and his troops set out to free Antigone and Ismene from the Thebans.

1148   *Pythian shore*   The Old Men name two possible points, both on the Bay of
        Eleusis, where Theseus' horsemen could overtake Kreon's men, who had fled
        with the kidnapped daughters. The first, the "Pythian shore," would be reached
        via Daphni, a town in a mountain pass about six miles from Kolonos. Daphni
        was the site of a temple to Apollo, who is sometimes called Pythian.

1149–54 *torch-lit beaches . . . rites for the dead.*   The second interception point would
        be at the sacred town of Eleusis, where an annual torch-lit procession was
        held in honor of Demeter and Persephone—the "two great queens" of the
        underworld (see n. 749–50). Eleusis was about five miles south of the
        Pythian shore. The Eleusinian rites, known as the Mysteries, were tightly
        guarded secrets kept from all but initiates. The priests who carried out the ini-
        tiations and enforced the pledge of secrecy were always members of the family
        of Eumolpidae.

1162–63 *snowy rock in the town of Oea*   The Old Men now propose a third escape route
        for Kreon's men. Jebb (1886, n. 1059) cites an ancient scholiast who identifies
        the "snowy rock" as an outcrop of Mt. Aigaleos near the Athenian rural dis-
        trict or deme of Oea, several miles northwest of Kolonos.

1172   *Athena*   Athena, also a goddess of horses, shared an altar at Kolonos with Po-
        seidon, presumably the altar where Theseus has been making sacrifices.

1175   *goddess Rhea*   Poseidon was the son of Kronos and Rhea.

1198–99 *Apollo, bring Artemis*   Apollo, the god whose weapon of choice was the bow
        and arrow, was the brother of Artemis, the goddess of hunting.

1294–316 *Father, please hear me . . . repay it.*   Antigone's substantial speech is noteworthy
        in several respects. It demonstrates her intense sisterly concern for Polyneikes.
        In asking her father to show compassion she invokes the damage the family
        curse has inflicted by having parents punish their children. Antigone fears that
        Oedipus' cruelty will affect others besides Polyneikes. She's right; Oedipus re-
        jection of Polyneikes will have a role in Antigone's own death.

1326–69 *Anyone who craves . . . northern mountains*   In this starkly unsentimental
        and keenly detailed picture of aging, the Old Men remind the audience of an
        implied alternative to accepting one's painful final years. Death and the ulti-
        mate home of the dead, Hades, become a wished-for release. The outlook re-
        sembles that of Hamlet's "To be or not to be" soliloquy.

1344–50 *By any measure . . . place he came from*   The sentiments in this famously pes-
        simistic Greek proverb—the story goes back at least to the archaic period—
        belong to Silenus, the leader of the satyrs in Dionysos' band of revelers. When
        asked (while drunk) "What's best?" he answered, "Never to be born at all." Sec-
        ond best, if one was unlucky enough to be born, was to go back wherever one
        came from as quickly as possible. Easterling (52–53) writes, "Death never
        ceased to be a defining feature of tragedy in Greek tradition; it is perhaps not
        an accident that the presiding deity of the festivals which included tragedy
        [i.e., Dionysos] should have such strong connexions with the world of the
        dead." See introduction to this volume passim for examples of the Dionysiac
        influence on Athens' great theatre festival.

1389   *Respect*   Lit. *aidos.* Many scholars and translators use "Mercy" here, but I follow Blundell in interpreting Respect as the goddess that Polyneikes personifies as an attendant of Zeus. The tenor of Polyneikes' speech suggests that he is appealing precisely for respect rather than begging for mercy. Oedipus counters and rejects Polyneikes' invocation by personifying Justice as Zeus' attendant at 1508.

1395   *Will you deny me with silent contempt?*   As a suppliant Polyneikes is due the honor of an answer to a request, but as both Theseus and Antigone explain at 1291–93 and 1294–316, Oedipus is not bound to grant the request. Oedipus might be silent for the moment but he unleashes his wrath at 1480ff.

1415–16   *elder son . . . to inherit your throne*   Since primogeniture was not customary in ancient Greece, Polyneikes' argument loses some of its force.

1420   *persuaded Thebes to back him*   Polyneikes implies that Eteokles manipulated the Thebans into backing him—a tactic, writes Blundell (1990, n. 139), that democrats in Sophokles' time would have approved. The word literally translated as persuade, *peisas,* often euphemistically connotes bribery, writes Knox (1982, n. 1467).

1421–22   *the Fury who stalks you strengthened his case*   Polyneikes, with characteristic tactlessness, blames the ancient curse on Oedipus for the quarrel between the brothers.

1428–29   *seven companies of spearmen to fight Thebes*   Polyneikes has convinced six Argive warlords to join his attack on the seven gates of Thebes and put him back in power. They will not succeed. Here Polyneikes presents his strategy for the assault, presumably hoping for his father's approval. The most colorful of the seven participants are noted below. Also see *Antigone* n. 20.

1435   *Amphiaraos*   Amphiaraos, a prophet who foresaw the deaths of all the Theban leaders, refused to take part in the siege until his wife "persuaded" him to join the battle. (Polyneikes had bribed her with a magic necklace.)

1441   *Kapaneus*   Kapaneus, who boasted that nothing could stop him from scaling the walls of Thebes to set its houses on fire, was struck down for his arrogance by a thunderbolt from Zeus. See *Antigone,* 148.

1444   *Atalanta*   Atalanta, the late-life mother of Parthenopaios, was disowned by her father and raised in the woods by a she-bear in Arcadia. She swore never to marry unless the successful suitor outran her in a foot race. In some versions of the myth, Milanion, who fathered her son, met Atalanta's conditions by dropping three golden apples along the route of a race, each of which she stopped to pick up. He thereby overtook her.

1457   *fountains of home*   Springs, the source of fresh water essential for life, were considered symbolic of the land and often protected by nymphs.

1459–60   *I'm a beggar . . . but so are you.*   Polyneikes overlooks a crucial difference between Oedipus' status as beggar and exile and his own: Oedipus brings with him a helpful "gift" for his benefactor; Polyneikes only pleads for help.

1498–99   *The blood you shed will defile you . . . as he dies*   Oedipus means that the brothers will defile each other by committing simultaneous fratricide.

1500–1522 *I cursed you both . . . Ares the Destroyer.*   Oedipus imagines his curses (lit. *arai*) almost as having physical force. He speaks of them as allies, as fellow fighters in his campaign to teach his sons to respect their parents. Jebb (1886, n. 1375) writes, "the *arai*, when they have once passed the father's lips, are henceforth personal agencies of vengeance." Tartaros is the part of the underworld where evildoers are punished for their crimes. The native spirits Oedipus summons are the Eumenides in their punitive mode.

1508 *Justice*   Oedipus responds to Polyneikes' personification of Respect at 1389 by invoking Justice, a goddess who can be expected to carry out Zeus' will without mitigation.

1538–39 *don't dishonor me . . . Perform the rituals.*   In *Antigone* she will honor her brother by performing the burial rites he requests, but by doing so she risks her own life.

1580–628 *We've just seen . . . Zeus!*   In this choral ode the gods begin their final and benign intervention in Oedipus' life. The heightened musical energy from song and wind instruments accompanies Oedipus' understanding and acceptance that he is being called to his death.

1594 *That was thunder! O Zeus!*   In Apollo's original oracle thunder and lightning were two of the three signs that would announce Oedipus' death and transformation.

1652 *My life is weighted to sink down.*   This ancient image is of a balance scale in which Zeus decides the outcome of life-or-death matters by weighting the scale so that it sinks the doomed person or people.

1698 *Hermes*   As the messenger of Zeus, one of Hermes' duties was to escort the souls of the dead to the underworld.

1708 *unseen goddess*   Persephone, queen of the underworld, was called the unseen goddess, perhaps because her husband's name, Hades, literally means "unseen."

1711 *Aidoneus*   Aidoneus is a longer version of Hades' name. The Old Men address him tentatively because he is notoriously resistant to prayer. See *Antigone,* 857, where Kreon makes a jibe at Antigone by snidely suggesting she pray to Hades to save her life.

1715 *house of Styx*   A reference to the River Styx that runs through the underworld.

1719 *Earth Goddesses!*   The Eumenides.

1721 *Savage guard-dog!*   Cerberus, the monstrous three-headed dog who stands guard at the entrance to the underworld, was said to be docile to those who entered but to devour all who attempted to leave.

1743 *steep brass steps*   See n. 65.

1744 *a maze of crossing paths*   This might allude to the crossroads were Oedipus killed Laios and to the maze of fated events in his life.

1746–47 *immortal pact that Theseus made with Peirithous*   Before attempting to rescue Persephone from the underworld, Theseus and his friend Peirithous pledged their everlasting friendship at a place "where a bowl had been hollowed from a rock shelf." But Hades trapped and detained them both. In most versions of the myth Herakles rescued Theseus but left Peirithous to suffer the torments of the criminal dead.

1748–50 *rock of Thoricos . . . stone tomb*   These local landmarks (and their significance) would have been familiar to Sophokles' audience. Although the exact location of the spot where Oedipus is transformed must remain a secret, the detailed geographical description adds credibility to the miraculous destination of Oedipus' final journey.

1758–59 *washed . . . white clothes customary*   Lit. "gave him the bath and the prescribed clothing." Greek burial rituals included washing the corpse and dressing it in white garments. See *Antigone* introduction, p. 163.

1762 *Zeus of the Underworld thundered*   A reference to Hades. Both Hades and the Olympian Zeus are the supreme gods of their respective realms below and above the earth. The earthquake is the third and last of the signs that Apollo told Oedipus would signal his imminent death.

1778 *enormous voice called him*   Blundell (1990, n. 190) suggests that the god who beckons Oedipus might be identified with Hermes, Persephone, or perhaps Hades himself, but the anonymity of the god's voice adds to the mystery.

1818–20 *Earth's lower world . . . welcoming kindness*   For a discussion of this passage see *Kolonos* introduction, pp. 98–100.

1924 *the Earth Powers have shown us all so much grace*   Theseus reminds the grieving Antigone and Ismene that by allowing their father to die a painless death in this sacred grove, the gods of Hades have blessed both Oedipus and Athens.

1936 *Horkos*   The son of Eris, or Strife. His role is to witness and enforce oaths, and therefore to end contention and war by bringing mortals together in binding agreements.

Antigone

Scene   Antigone's awareness of Kreon's decree and Polyneikes' unburied corpse suggests that she has left the palace to visit the city (and perhaps the battlefield) during the predawn darkness. If so, she would enter from outside the palace gates.

1–2 *born . . . womb*   The Greek word *autadelphon,* translated "born from that same womb," lit. means "self-same womb." *Koinon,* subsumed into the phrase as "like me," may also be rendered as "kindred" (Jebb) or "linked to me" (Lloyd-Jones). Antigone's first words to Ismene thus strike a chord that reverberates throughout the drama: their shared family inheritance includes horrific misfortunes that go back to their conceptions and births. The Greek word *kara* is translated "dear one." Tyrrell and Bennett (31) write that "Sophokles' avoidance of a usual word for sister may also point to Ismene as less important to Antigone in that capacity than as a 'wombmate' . . . and also suggests the excessive closeness brought about by Oedipus, their common father and brother."

5–8   *our lives . . . you and I haven't seen and shared*   Antigone speaks of her sister
and herself as united by common interests, as well as blood, until 94. After Ismene refuses to help bury Polyneikes (95–96), Antigone stops referring to herself and Ismene as a pair.

9   *new order*   Kreon, the girls' uncle, Thebes' military leader, or *strategos,* and
now its new king, presumably declared this edict only hours earlier, as soon as
the Argive army's retreat was apparent.

15   *same as our enemies*   This suggests that the bodies of all the dead Argive attackers have been left unburied. We later learn from Tiresias that this is indeed
the case. Polyneikes fits both the category of *philos,* loved one or family member, and that of *ekthros,* enemy.

20   *the double blow*   After Oedipus departed Thebes in exile to Athens, his sons
Eteokles and Polyneikes agreed to alternate as king. But Eteokles refused to
step down at the end of his year and banished his brother. Polyneikes moved
to Argos, married King Adrastos' daughter, and solicited support for a campaign to regain power in his home city. He and six other Argive captains attacked the seven gates of Thebes. During the battle, the brothers apparently
struck each other with simultaneous deadly spear thrusts, a mode of death that
fulfilled the curse against his sons delivered by Oedipus in the *Kolonos.* (Aspects of this war are the subject of Aeschylus' *Seven Against Thebes* and Euripides' *Phoenician Women* and *The Suppliants.*)

24   *past the gates*   Refers to the house gates, not the outer palace gates that lead to
the town.

32   *The dead will respect him*   According to fifth-century Greek religious belief,
failure to mound earth over a dead family member and perform the required
funeral rituals would cause those already dead in Hades to shun and scorn such
a shade when it arrived among them.

43   *stoned to death*   Since communal stoning by many citizens would have been
an appropriate method of execution for Polyneikes, a traitor to his own people,
a citizen who defied the city to bury a traitor would be fittingly sentenced to
the same method of execution.

48–49   *yanking the knot . . . pry it loose*   The image comes from weaving, strictly a
woman's occupation for the Greeks. Ismene might be sarcastically asking her
sister how her weaving skills could be of any use in burying Polyneikes and
confronting Kreon.

52   *lift his body*   To cover Polyneikes heavy body with the substantial mounding
of earth that Antigone envisions at 97–98, she will need Ismene's help. Without that help she would be forced to perform a more limited ceremony—a
dusting with earth, a poured libation, screams of grief—such as the Guard will
soon describe.

58–70   *our father's destruction . . . kin murder!*   Ismene recalls the gods' savage punishment of their parents to highlight the difference between Oedipus' and
Jokasta's "horrible deeds" and the lesser matter of a failed ritual, which she
hopes the gods and the dead (*the Spirits,* 79) will understand and forgive.

71–72   *how much worse our own deaths*   Ismene imagines the threatened stoning as a much harsher method of death than their mother's hanging, but "much worse" could also refer to the fact that there are no women left in the family to perform the sacred burial rituals mentioned in n. 52—rituals that only women could perform. See *Antigone* introduction, p. 163.

87–88   *lie down next to*   The Greek word Antigone uses here for lying down, *keiso-mai,* would be equally appropriate to describe lying in death (either before burial or in Hades) or to having sexual relations with a lover (Blundell 1989, 110). The words used to describe their kinship, *philê* with *philou,* (translated here as "I who love him" next to "him who loves me") accentuate both the emotional bond and the physical proximity of the bodies (Griffith, 135).

89   *criminal conduct*   The Greek words *hosia panourgesas* (lit. "sacred transgressions") refer primarily to the outlawed act of burying her "traitor" brother, but they also allude, given the way they are embedded in the sentence, to the incestuous love Antigone might feel for Polyneikes.

107   *those who matter*   Most likely the gods; perhaps also Polyneikes. See 487–508, an elaboration of Antigone's intention to please Hades and the gods of the underworld.

Exit Antigone   She leaves abruptly to look for Polyneikes' body on the battlefield, ignoring Ismene's warning and concern.

121–22   *Morning sunlight . . . on Thebes*   The Elders begin a song that celebrates Thebes' victory over Argos. Notably missing from the song is any reference to what preoccupies Kreon: punishing the dead body of Polyneikes. Joy and celebration, gratitude to Dionysos, Ares, and all the other gods, are paramount.

124   *Dirke*   One of two rivers flowing through Thebes. The other is the Ismenos.

127   *white shield*   The name of the region from which the attacking army comes, Argos, suggests silvery or shining whiteness.

128   *sharp piercing bit*   The Argive army is portrayed as a wild vicious horse and the defending Thebans as the horse tamer who subdues it—by using a particularly nasty bit that digs into the horse's jaw.

131   *quarrelsome*   A pun, since Polyneikes' name means literally "serial battler."

133   *white-feathered Eagle*   An emblem of Argos.

141–42   *Firegod's incendiary pinetar*   lit. "Hephestos' pine-fed flame." Balls of pine pitch were set afire and lobbed via catapult over defensive walls and onto wooden houses in besieged cities.

146   *Dragon*   The ancestral "snake" with whom Thebans identified. See *Oed King* n. 96.

148   *Zeus hates a proud tongue*   A reference to Kapaneus. See *Kolonos* n. 1441.

169–70   *trophies for Zeus*   At the end of a battle the armor of the defeated troops was collected and fastened to totem-like structures in honor of Zeus.

174   *Victory*   The wingèd and female goddess Nike.

181   *each god's temple*   With the fighting over and victory secured, every god who might have played a part in helping Thebes win must be honored in his or her own temple, hence the festive midnight rounds.

183–84   *Bakkhos, the god whose dancing rocks Thebes*   Bakkhos, an alternate name for Dionysos, is characteristically worshipped by song and a drum-accompanied dance. He often makes his presence felt by causing an earthquake. See *Oed King* n. 250.

185–91   *our new king . . . Council of Elders*   This will be Kreon's first consultation with this body of seasoned politicians since his assumption of power the previous day. It will turn out that he neither solicits nor welcomes their opinions.

204   *defiled by his own brother's blood*   Kin murder had been for centuries an intensely feared crime, since it inflicted infamy and uncleanness on the guilty; such defilement was difficult to cleanse. In this case it will be impossible because the guilty brothers are both dead.

207–12   *character, policies . . . sound advice*   By setting standards according to which a ruler should be judged, Kreon focuses attention on his coming failures and blunders as a leader.

222–23   *It's only on board . . . true friends*   Kreon's assessment of friendship, for him defined in the context of loyalty to one's city, differs startlingly from Antigone's. She believes that friends are made only at birth, an indication of her strong ties to family. The Greek word used in both of their assessments of "friendship" is *philia*. See n. 567–68.

239   *ugly . . . disgrace*   The practice of refusing burial to dead enemies was a contentious political issue in fifth-century Greece that was dramatized in two other surviving plays, *The Suppliants* of Aeschylus and *The Suppliant Women* of Euripides.

266   *talking annihilation*   I follow here Griffith's interpretation and suggested translation of *to medon exerô* (Gk 234) as expressing the Guard's fear that his story might turn him into "nothing"—i.e., get him killed.

279–80   *thirsty dust . . . rituals*   Polyneikes' body was not buried or entombed as would have been customary, but appears to have received a minimal ritual from a source unknown. See n. 310.

310   *inspired by the gods*   The mysterious circumstances of the burial described by the Guard—no tracks, no footprints—suggest to the Leader that the gods have either performed or otherwise prompted the minimal burial of Polyneikes. If so, punishing a human agent would be dangerously offensive to the gods who have intervened on Polyneikes' behalf.

340   *strung up—and you'll hang*   Kreon, with characteristic bluster, threatens to torture and kill anyone within earshot who refuses to track down and hand over the person who buried Polyneikes.

352   *since you were born*   Implies that the Guard is a household servant or slave with whom Kreon has been long acquainted.

364–65   *Wonders abound . . . astounding than man* Lit. "There are many wonders/ terrors but none as wonderful/terrible as man." The Greek word *ta deina* can mean either "wonderful" or "terrible." Most scholars and translators stress both the positive and negative capacities of men in the context of this ode (364–413). I omit the "terrifying" dimension in 364 because, on inspection, virtually all the examples of mankind's activity in the ode are welcome contributions to civilization. (The killed and domesticated animals might not agree with this assessment.) But my choice of the word "astounding" in 365 alludes to man's capacity for evil. At the end of the ode, when man's "terrifying" or destructive aspect does surface, the Elders condemn it. The city's banishment of an isolated "reckless and corrupt" over-reacher delivers the final judgment.

373   *stallion-sired mules* Lit. "the children of horses." Mules were the preferred draft animals used on Greek farms.

404–5   *follow the laws Earth teaches him* With these lines Sophokles reminds us that Kreon and Antigone not only differ about which laws and which gods to obey, but that they understand "earth" in very different terms: "for Kreon, earth is the political territory of Thebes, defined by human law; for Antigone it is the realm of the gods below, who protect the rites of the dead" (Segal 2003, 130–31).

463–64   *piercing scream . . . nest robbed* Grieving women were often compared to mother birds robbed of their nestlings. But here Sophokles' simile suggests that Antigone is, in the traditional Greek sense, a bird as omen, thus a vehicle for delivering the gods' will. Images of Polyneikes' corpse, exposed as human carrion, intensify the significance. Other readings are equally pertinent and foreboding: the empty nest recalls the children that might have been born to Antigone and Haimon; Polyneikes' empty grave, the result of battle and the marriage to King Adrastos' daughter Argeia (see n. 954–55); and the empty nest of Kreon after the suicide of his son and wife. See Tyrrell and Bennett, 66– 67. (Also cf. Sophokles' use of the metaphor in *Oed King* [62] when the Priest calls Oedipus "a bird from god.")

469   *three cool swallows* As a part of funeral ritual, ancient Greeks poured libations directly onto the grave for a dead relative to drink.

471–73   *charged her . . . now this one . . . didn't deny a thing* Sophoklean scholars have long debated whether Antigone performed only the second or both "burials" of Polyneikes, especially since the first burial, according to the Guard, seems to have been performed by a being who left no evidence behind, and might well be a divine or other airborne creature. Here Antigone accepts blame for both burials. The difficulties in believing Antigone was the first duster of the body, however, are considerable: How did she do it without leaving a trace? The gods were entirely capable of intervening to *protect* Polyneikes' body from animals until it could be given a proper honoring. (In Homer's *Iliad* gods protected both Sarpedon and Hector.) What the gods cannot do is perform full burial rites, which are the responsibility of blood kin alone. For a most interesting and persuasive discussion of this issue see Tyrrell and Bennett, 54–62.

492   *unwritten and infallible laws* Such laws were a prominent part of both legal and religious thought. Examples of unwritten laws would include the imper-

ative to bury the dead according to precise ancient customs, the prohibition against killing blood kin, and the permanent defilement of kin-slayers.

509–10   *girl's nature . . . her father's*   In both his Theban and Athenian incarnations (in *Oed King* and *Kolonos*) Sophokles' character Oedipus displays a reckless and hasty violence in thought and action that the Leader now finds in Antigone. Antigone's "savage" (or *oumós*, "raw") nature primarily attacks Kreon and the politics he represents, and Ismene for her refusal to help Antigone perform Polyneikes' burial rituals. Griffith (204) notes that *oumós* "is a very strong term to apply to anyone, esp. a young woman (elsewhere in tragedy used only of men)." Segal (1981, 34) notes that the word is reserved for the worst crimes and especially strong taboos pertaining to family. It might therefore be interpreted to include her incestuous feeling for Polyneikes implied at 87–88.

531   *screaming, hysterical, deranged*   Ismene's fit could be the result of fear for Antigone's recklessness or of distress at her own refusal to help her sister bury Polyneikes. It is surely not what Kreon assumes: a fit of guilt as she contemplates treachery.

550   *bite their tongues*   The verb Antigone uses here, *upillousin,* which I translate as "bite," refers to the way in which a cowering dog puts its tail between its legs.

563   *Hades . . . rituals*   Antigone insists Hades makes no distinctions or exceptions among the dead. He demands they all be honored and buried.

567–68   *I made no enemies . . . friends*   Traditionally this line has been translated as Jebb does: "Tis not my nature to join in hating, only in loving." Lloyd-Jones and Wilson (126), however, state that *physis,* which Jebb translates as "nature," must refer in this context to "one's birth." They argue that the Greeks believed one can make *friends* by birth, but never *enemies.* So translated in this context, the line makes clearer sense of Antigone's conduct in the drama, since the Greeks' sense of "hating," and certainly our own, is evident throughout in Antigone's temperament and her words. Lloyd-Jones and Wilson's solution spares scholars many an interpretive contortion. Those producing the play who believe Antigone is referring to her loving nature might substitute: "It's my nature to share love, not hatred."

594   *sprang to his defense*   At 56 Ismene admitted she was afraid of betraying Kreon, and at 95–96 she declared her refusal to defy the city.

602   *Some think you're right*   Those who agree with Ismene are living, principally Kreon; those who agree with Antigone, her dead family and the underworld gods, are in Hades.

603   *equally wrong*   They can't be equally wrong—at least in the gods' eyes: Hades' demand that kin be buried is confirmed in the resolution of the drama.

615   *fields to plow*   The metaphor of a woman's body as a field or furrow for plowing, common in ancient Greece, echoes Athenian marriage contracts (Blundell 1989, 120). Athenian audiences would not have normally found Kreon's use of it offensive, but his insensitivity to both Antigone and Haimon could have struck them as obscene (Tyrrell and Bennett, 78–79).

628–91   *Lucky are those . . . catastrophe*   The particular evil the Elders have in mind in this ode is peculiar to families, and it cannot be evaded or defeated by any action or virtue of a family member. The ray of hope suggested by Antigone's character and vigor as "the last rootstock" is snuffed out by her insistence on burying her brother and by Kreon's "reckless talk" and mental "Furies," but the failure of a generation to "protect its own youth" also applies to Kreon and Haimon as well. The ode offers a more general theory of human futility in its latter section: The gods punish humankind for achievement itself, and though hope sometimes is justified, it's usually delusive and deadly. Also, the foolish can't distinguish evil from noble motives; catastrophe results. If Kreon (onstage in the background) hears this ode, he seems unaware that it targets him.

644   *Labdakids*   Oedipus' ancestral family.

657   *blood-drenched dust*   The image recalls the latest act committed by a member of the doomed House of Labdakos—Antigone's sprinkling of dust over Polyneikes. But it also evokes the brothers' dead bodies on the battlefield and, perhaps, the dust storm that swirled when Antigone performed the burial rites.

658   *death gods*   Hades, Acheron, Persephone, Hermes.

660   *Furies in the mind*   The goddesses called Furies—also referred to as the Erinys—typically punish the conscience for crimes committed against the family, especially kin murder, and they are often credited with unbalancing a person's judgment. The Furies first "appear" in ancient tragedy (in Aeschylus' *Libation Bearers*) to punish Orestes for killing his mother. Although the audience realizes that the goddesses have manifested themselves in Orestes' mind, none of the other characters onstage is aware of their presence. For more on their role in *Kolonos,* where they preside in their more benevolent incarnation as the Eumenides, see n. 44–50 and n. 92 in that play.

670   *Olympos*   The mountain, visible from ancient Thebes, was the home base of the Olympian gods, from Zeus through Hephestos.

686–91   *"Evil seems noble . . . hold off catastrophe"*   These words of wisdom refer to the ancient Greeks' belief that the gods "destroy the judgment of a person bent on evil and destruction. As we might phrase it in our more psychologizing terms, the gods collaborate with the evil tendencies of the prospective criminal to lead him to his ruin" (Segal 2003, 140–41).

693   *youngest of your sons*   Haimon has an older brother, Megareus. See n. 1095.

721   *turn ice cold in your arms*   Here Kreon's words foreshadow how Haimon will wrap his arms around Antigone not long after she commits suicide, at 1237/1371. Sophokles intensifies the irony with Kreon's avowal at 631/700 that "we'll soon have an answer" as to whether Haimon will defend his bride or support Kreon's sentencing her to death—an answer that is "better than any prophet's."

730–31   *Zeus of family life*   Zeus Herkeios, lit. Zeus of the Fence *(herkos)* is a manifestation of Zeus who protects an extended family's welfare. He was worshipped within the boundaries of the house, usually at an inner courtyard shrine. Kreon implies that this "household" Zeus would disapprove of Antigone's burial of Polyneikes (and her invocation of kinship law as the motive behind it) since he would not approve a family member's rebellion against the head of its household.

756   *sapped my wits*   The Leader alludes ironically to Kreon's earlier insult at 312, where he accused the Leader of sounding old and senile.

785   *open him up*   Haimon compares his father to a clay writing tablet that opened and closed like a modern book. Kreon, says his son, has nothing inside him.

828   *You will not marry her while she's* on *this earth*   Another example of the irony in Kreon's "prophetic" powers. The "marriage" of Haimon and Antigone will indeed take place after her death. See 1240–41/1373–75.

855–56   *enough food to evade defilement*   The city would be defiled if Antigone, Kreon's blood relative, was executed at his command. By leaving enough food to sustain her for a while, Kreon might hope that she'll commit suicide in despair, as indeed she will, and thus relieve Thebes of defilement. But Kreon was wrong to think his conduct could elude the defilement that will harm all Thebes. See Tiresias' denunciation of Kreon at 1179–91.

857   *pray there to Hades*   Since Hades is Antigone's favored deity, he would logically be the one she turns to in a desperate situation. But Hades has no reputation for saving lives. By saying "Maybe he will spare her" Kreon sneers at Antigone's self-delusion.

861–80   *Love, you win . . . our lives*   The Elders sing a brief celebration of Aphrodite and her son Eros, gods of Love—the emotion that Kreon leaves out of his calculations. He may remain on stage to hear the Elders enumerate Love's power over humans and beasts, and to hear them give Love its rightful place among the ancient powers and laws, written or unwritten. The ode presents a double paradox: The allure of the bride is both irresistible and destructive, as Antigone's allure for Haimon will prove to be. And what humans consider to be disastrous, the gods of Love deem as play or even mockery. See Griffith, 260.

863   *havoc with our herds*   A literal translation. The word translated as "herds," *ktemasi,* can also refer to what the herds represent economically: wealth. The line could mean something like "love who . . . impoverishes us." I interpret it with Griffith (257) to mean that erotic power also drives animals into frenzy.

872–73   *wrench men's minds . . . off course*   The image is of a chariot overturning on a race course. Love at the intensity the Elders register here made even the ancients unsafe drivers.

Dressed in purple as a bride   Throughout her final scene Antigone conducts herself as if she were preparing for her wedding. Her spoken and sung speeches are dense with allusions, both ironic and plaintive, to a bride's expectations. Having her appear in a traditional Greek purple bridal costume would visually reinforce Sophokles' verbal imagery. Indeed, wedding and funeral rituals were deeply associative of each other in Athenian culture; they both signified a similar transition in life. Upon leaving her father's house, the bride entered the house of another man and perished as a virgin; the dead entered Hades' house, never to return (Tyrrell and Bennett, 98). Sophokles' audience would have been attuned to the visual and verbal clues that connected the rituals of marriage and death.

891   *Acheron*   The rivergod of a stream that flows through Hades.

895   *River of Pain*   A literal rendering of the meaning of Acheron.

901   *enter Hades . . . still alive*   A bit of sophistry on the Elders' part. Antigone will be imprisoned below ground, thus in proximity to Hades, and she will still be alive. But only the truly dead ever enter the real place. The Elders probably want to emphasize Antigone's exercise of free choice in committing the act that led to her death sentence.

903–5   *Phrygian stranger . . . Mt. Sipylos*   The Phyrigian stranger, or Niobe, was the daughter of King Tantalos of Lydia. She married Amphion, a king of Thebes, and bore him an equal number of sons and daughters (six of each, according to Homer; other versions of the myth say seven, nine, or ten). After Niobe boasted that she was superior to the goddess Leto, who had only one of each, Leto sent her children, who just happened to be Apollo and Artemis, to kill Niobe's. Niobe wept for nine days and nights, and the Olympian gods turned her to stone, dripping tears, on Mt. Sipylos (where her father lived). In other versions of the myth Niobe is a mortal whose boast of being superior to a divinity provoked her punishment. Sophokles' audience would have recognized his artistic license in making her a god. Tyrrell and Bennett (107) suggest that Sophokles' purpose was to accentuate Antigone's own likening of herself to a god, considered by fifth-century Greeks as "boastfulness beyond the pale." Sophokles also could have intended to soften the Leader's reproach at 914–19, where he calls her godlike fate "no small honor."

906   *living rock*   In Niobe's case, the metaphor of a body turned to stone alludes to the end of her fertility; in Antigone's case the allusion is first to her never-to-be penetrated virgin body. Seaford interprets the stone in both cases as enclosing them with their natal families. (See Tyrrell and Bennett, 143, 107.)

932   *heaped-up rock-bound prison*   Suggests that Antigone's "tomb" was not a geologically formed cave but man-made, with earth piled above a hollowed lower chamber.

933   *without a friend*   Antigone may have admirers in Thebes (as Haimon insists), but none comes forward to grieve for her, presumably out of fear. And of course Antigone no longer considers her sister Ismene to be a *philê*, or family member, and thus, not a possible mourner.

943–56   *You've touched . . . so was I*   In this lyric Antigone traces her family curse not to Laios' original disobedience of Apollo, but to her mother's incest. (The focus on her mother's responsibility echoes her opening words to Ismene, "born . . . from that same womb.") As Segal (1981, 183) notes, "kinship as a function of female procreative power [was] embedded in Greek culture." Throughout this meditation Antigone sees marriage as a maker of defilement and death, not of children and life (see n. 954–55 and the counterpart to her speech, Oedipus' howl of pain against marriages in *Oed King*, 1403–8/1591–96).

954–55   *deadly marriage*   By marrying Argeia, the daughter of the Argive king Adrastos, Polyneikes gained the military support he needed to attack Thebes; thus his marriage contributed to his death in battle.

980   *pure as far as she's concerned*   Kreon assumes his precautions—leaving her a small ration of food and enclosing her in a tomb away from the city—will be enough to the evade the defilement of kin murder.

983–84   *My tomb . . . dug from rock*   The tomb has three identities for Antigone: it is the grave Kreon sentenced her to in punishment for attempting to violate his decree; it is the nuptial bedroom in which she will wed Hades; it is the hollow in which she will dwell with her parents and dead brothers (Tyrrell and Bennett, 111).

996–1013   *I honored you . . . hollow tomb*   The authenticity of these lines has been questioned at least since Goethe (in 1827) famously expressed the hope that some classical scholar would prove them spurious. Though many editors and critics have impugned the lines, including Jebb and Winnington-Ingram, confidence in their genuineness has grown in recent years. On the one hand, Lloyd-Jones and Wilson correctly state that objections to them are invariably subjective. On the other hand, contemporary scholars, e.g., Tyrrell and Bennett, and Griffith, have argued that their content conforms to Antigone's understanding of both herself and the duties to kin as prescribed by divine law. For those producing the play and unconvinced of their authenticity, or who believe including them would divert audience attention into seemingly arid and arcane matters, these lines can be omitted en bloc without disrupting the flow and logic of the remaining lines. See *Antigone* introduction pp. 174–76.

1009   *he pulls me by the wrist*   After the wedding feast the bride was traditionally pulled by the wrist (from a table with other women) in a symbolic act of abduction, and led away by the bridegroom. Although Antigone imagines Hades as her bridegroom, she seems here to allude to Kreon as the person who prevents her from a marriage on earth. Kreon does not actually lead Antigone away himself but delegates the act to his men.

1021–22   *I want* them *to suffer the pain*   Antigone's call for vengeance might be directed at the citizens of Thebes who did not defend her and her cause, but Kreon is her primary target. Not having any *philoi* left to mourn her or to take vengeance on Kreon, she must depend on the gods, she thinks, and she appeals to them directly.

1032   *Look at me, princely citizens*   In the moments before she gives herself to Hades Antigone enacts her own version of *anakaptêria,* the bride's traditional lifting of her veil for the first time among men. The penetration of the men's eyes was symbolic of her imminent loss of virginity. The gesture of showing her face, as made by a Greek bride whose passivity was taken for granted, was a speechless invitation. But here Antigone acts aggressively, as she did in performing burial rituals for Polyneikes, and calls out to the Elders.

1036   *Danae*   Danae's father Akrisios, king of Argos, locked her in a bronze tower because an oracle prophesied that a son of hers would someday kill him. Zeus impregnated her with a shower of gold, and she gave birth to Perseus, who did in fact kill Akrisios accidentally while throwing a discus. Two other mythological characters in this ode were in some way imprisoned; see nn. 1051 and 1081–84.

1051   *Lycurgos*   According to Homer's *Iliad* (6.130 ff.) Lycurgos attacked Dionysos, forcing the god and his nurses to take refuge in the sea. Soon after Dionysos retaliated by blinding him, Lycurgos died. Sophokles likely knew other versions of the myth, and seems to draw here on the versions of Apollodorus (I. 35) and Hyginus (*Fab.* 132), in which Dionysos drives Lycurgos mad.

1066–68 *Black Rocks . . . Bosphorus channel*   The Bosphoros, a narrow strait that joined the Black Sea with the Sea of Marmara and the Mediterranean, divided Asia and Europe; the Black Rocks, over which a swift current passed, have been worn away over the past 2,400 years.

1071 *Ares*   The god of cruel bloodshed, considered to be of Thracian origin, was unpopular in the ancient world, and important only in Thebes and perhaps Athens. In mythology he is nearly always portrayed as an instigator of violence or a tempestuous lover; he never develops a moral function, as do Zeus, Apollo, and Dionysos, on his own terms, as the people's god.

1073 *savage wife of Phineus*   When Phineus, a Thracian king, cast off his wife Kleopatra—who was the daughter of Boreas, the North Wind—he married Eidothea, who blinded Phineus' two sons (for reasons unclear in the various versions of the myth).

1081–84 *a woman unhappy . . . Erektheids*   The unhappy woman, distraught because her marriage ended, is Kleopatra, the mother of Phineus' blinded sons. Her mother was Oreithyia, daughter of Erektheus, a king of Athens. Sophokles supposed Kleopatra's story to be familiar to his audience—although he doesn't mention it here, she was imprisoned by Phineas—and clearly means to connect her fate to Antigone's (Jebb 1888, n. 966).

Tiresias . . . Lad   Thebes' resident prophet, always accompanied by a young boy, also appears at critical moments in *Oed King* and Euripides' *Bakkhai*.

1095 *questioned the advice*   This may be a reference to advice Tiresias had given within the last few days concerning how best to divinely protect Thebes against the Argive onslaught (see n. 20). In one version of the myth of the Seven Against Thebes, Tiresias advises Kreon to sacrifice his eldest son, Megareus, mentioned at 1455, in order for Thebes to prevail.

1096 *straight course*   Tiresias' use of "straight," or *orthos*, echoes Kreon's repeated use of the word in various forms to characterize his statesmanlike virtues of being upright and on course. His obsession with "straightness" carries over to manipulating people as expertly as one might steer a ship.

1106–7 *They screeched . . . was drowned out*   Birds were a major medium of communication between gods and mortals. Because the birds' angry screeching has made their songs unintelligible, Tiresias interprets the screeching itself as a sign of the gods' extreme displeasure with Kreon's recent acts and decrees. See n. 463–64.

1111 *sacrificial fire*   Tiresias burns a large animal in the god's honor in order to regain his good will. Hephestos, god of fire, snuffs it out, thus blocking the gesture. At this point Tiresias' prophetic drill shifts to examining the inner organs of the animal for useful omens.

1113–17 *charred thighbones . . . fat enfolding them*   Tiresias recounts how the sacrifice failed. The offering, probably the meat of an ox, should have gone up in flames when it was ignited—the fragrant smoke ascending like a prayer to the gods above. Instead, the fire smoldered, fat oozed into the ashes, and the gall-bladder burst its stench into the air. The "vivid and repulsive description . . . [suggests] the putrescent corpse of Polyneikes" (Griffith, 299).

1117–18   *attempt at prophecy failed*   Neither the animal's organs nor the sacrifice seeking divine advice yield any readable communications from the gods. Tiresias instead gives Kreon sensible advice of his own, unsanctioned by Apollo.

1122–23   *city's altars . . . defiled*   Because neither Polyneikes nor the Argive soldiers were properly mourned and buried, their dishonored flesh, spread throughout the city by dogs and birds, defiles Thebes.

1129–30   *keen cries . . . garbled by . . . thickened blood*   Tiresias makes a direct connection between the city's defilement and the gods' displeasure at the city's leader.

1149   *silver from Sardis*   Lit. silver-gold (an alloy).

1155   *men can defile gods*   Kreon distorts Tiresias' explanation of his wrongdoing. The point is not whether men defile gods, but that Thebans and Kreon have defiled themselves.

1191   *Furies sent by Hades*   Presumably the Eumenides, who will punish Kreon for his impiety by attacking his family. See *Kolonos* n. 44–50.

1227   *Delegate this to no one*   The Leader might be alluding to the fact that Kreon, after boasting that he'd lead Antigone to her tomb himself, assigned his soldiers to the task.

1231–32   *I who locked her away will . . . free her*   At 1218–19 the Leader advised Kreon to free Antigone from her tomb and then to bury Polyneikes. Kreon makes tending to Polyneikes' body his first priority. Though going first to Antigone might not have saved her life, Kreon's mindless reversal of the logical priority further damns him.

1235–81   *God with myriad names . . . gifts*   Just before the worst calamity occurs (or is announced) in each of the three Oedipus plays, the Chorus members sing their appeal for help to Dionysos. This ode presents a vivid picture of the orgiastic worship of the god on Parnassos, a mountain northeast of Delphi that was traditionally sacred to Apollo and the muses. In the winter months, Apollo ceded his shrine at Delphi to Dionysos and his cult; a festival was held every two years and attended by a sanctioned band of maenads. (See Guthrie, 178, 202.)

1237   *Kadmos' daughter*   Semele. See *Kolonos* n. 741–43.

1240–41   *Eleusis . . . Demeter*   See *Kolonos* nn. 749–50 and 1149–54.

1254–55   *nymphs of Korykia . . . Kastalia's fountains*   Nymphs, young female spirits representing the divine powers of nature, were named specifically for their function or the locale in which they resided. Korykia, a stalactite cavern in Mt. Parnassos, was an ancient place of sacrifice. The Kastalia is a stream that flows from the fissure of a high cliff in the mountain.

1256   *Nysa's sloping hills*   The mountain where Dionysos was born in some versions of myth. See *Kolonos* n. 741–43.

1260   *Evohoi!*   A shout made by Dionysos' worshippers to signal that the god was among them.

1265–66   *mother whom the lightning killed*   Semele.

1271   *howling channel*   The windy straits between the Greek mainland and the island of Euboea.

1276   *Thyiads*   A troop of Attic women sent to join the revels of their Delphic sisters in the winter worship of Dionysos.

1279   *Iakkhos*   A secondary cult name of Bakkhos or Dionysos.

       Messenger   From his demeanor he is an educated and trusted palace servant.

1283   *Amphion and Kadmos*   Early kings of Thebes.

       Eurydike   Kreon's wife. Within days she has seen both her sons die as a result of choices made by her husband. Her name means "wide" *(eury)* "justice/ penalty/satisfaction" *(dike)* which she will fittingly exact from Kreon by leaving him without a female family member to mourn his son (or, when he dies, himself).

1321   *lived through misfortune*   This could be a reference to the (possibly) sacrificial murder of her son, Megareus, as well as to the events of Oedipus' reign. See n. 1095.

1330–31   *Goddess of Roadways . . . Pluto*   The goddess Hekate was worshipped at crossroads in the form of a statue with three heads or three bodies. Her mention brings to mind the crossroads where Oedipus killed Laios (see *Oed King,* 832). Pluto is another name for Hades.

1344   *Am I a prophet?*   Kreon has unwittingly predicted the tragic outcome of his son's relationship to Antigone. See n. 721.

1354–57   *hanging by the neck . . . bride he'd lost to Hades*   The image of Haimon embracing Antigone around the waist as she hangs from a noose of linen (perhaps made from the veil she lifted in her bridal procession) evokes another Attic wedding ritual that has been depicted in vase paintings. After the groom leads the bride by the wrist from the feast he lifts her bolt upright into the mule cart that will carry the couple to their nuptial bed. The groom demonstrates his physical strength and dominance over the bride; the bride submits in compliance and dignity by remaining rigidly in the posture (Tyrrell and Bennett, 142).

1365   *spat in his face*   Lit. *ptúsas prosopoi* This gesture reminds us of the crude advice Kreon gave his son at 653/723–24: "spit this girl out like the enemy she is," lit. *ptúsas osei te dusmene.* Sophoklean irony shows Kreon once again as a man whose arrogant behavior comes back to haunt him. The metaphorical usage of 653/723– 24 is not found elsewhere in tragedy but is common in epic and lyric; for this reason, and perhaps because genteel Victorian scholars refrained from translating literally such an ungentlemanly act as spitting, Jebb and others of his era focus on the loathing and contempt implicit in the passages. See Griffith, 236, 338.

1366   *two-edged*   Lit. *diplos,* or "double." The blade kills Haimon the son and Haimon the potential father. See Oed King n. 1415.

1371–74   *he clung to her . . . married at last*   The "marriage" is consummated with *oxeian,* lit. "spurts" of Haimon's blood, not Antigone's.

1425–26   *so much a loving mother to your son*   Lit. "the *pammêtôr* of the corpse" or, in
          the Scholiast's understanding, "the mother in all respects." *Pammêtôr* connotes
          the great Mother Earth, Gaia, the true mother of all things. Gaia repeatedly
          defends her offspring throughout the formative period of the universe against
          male aggressors who attempt to control her children or usurp her procreativ-
          ity. Sophokles' use of the term here draws on Pan-Hellenic myth in which the
          goddess unleashes her vengeance as a subordinate of Zeus. Eurydike's violent
          suicide presents Kreon with the silenced woman he wanted in Antigone, and
          it gives Antigone the vengeance she sought against Kreon—a silent funeral
          (Tyrrell and Bennett, 149–51).

1430–31   *we flood your harbor*   The dead arrive in Hades' realm by a boat that trans-
          ports them across the River Styx. Kreon imagines his own dead family as a sac-
          rifice made to Hades, but one that fails to win the gods' good will.

Works Cited and Consulted

Aeschylus. *The Complete Greek Tragedies.* Trans. Richmond Lattimore, ed. David Grene and Richmond Lattimore. Chicago: University of Chicago Press, 1959.

Aristotle. *Aristotle's Poetics.* Trans. Leon Golden. Tallahassee: Florida State University Press, 1981.

————. *The Art of Rhetoric.* Trans. John Henry Freese. Loeb Classical Library Series 193. Cambridge: Harvard University Press, 1967.

Berlin, Normand. *The Secret Cause: A Discussion of Tragedy.* Amherst: University of Massachusetts Press, 1981.

Bernardete, Seth. *Sacred Transgressions: A Reading of Sophocles'* Antigone. South Bend, Ind.: St. Augustine's Press, 1999.

Blundell, Mary Whitlock. *Helping Friends and Harming Enemies: A Study in Sophocles and Greek Ethics.* Cambridge: Cambridge University Press, 1989.

————, trans. *Antigone.* By Sophocles. Focus Classical Library. Newburyport, Mass.: Focus Information Group, 1998.

————, trans. *Oedipus at Colonus.* By Sophocles. Focus Classical Library. Newburyport, Mass.: Focus Information Group, 1990.

Carpenter, Thomas H., and Christopher A. Faraone, eds. *Masks of Dionysus.* Ithaca: Cornell University Press, 1993.

Csapo, Eric, and William J. Slater. *The Context of Ancient Drama.* Ann Arbor: University of Michigan Press, 1994.

Davidson, John N. *Courtesans and Fishcakes: The Consuming Passions of Classical Athens.* New York: St. Martin's, 1998.

Eagleton, Terry. *Sweet Violence: The Idea of the Tragic.* Malden, Mass.: Blackwell, 2003.

Easterling, P. E., ed. *The Cambridge Companion to Greek Tragedy.* Cambridge: Cambridge University Press, 1997.

Edmunds, Lowell. *Theatrical Space and Historical Place in Sophocles'* Oedipus at Colonus. Lanham, Md.: Rowman and Littlefield, 1996.

Else, Gerald F. *The Origin and Early Form of Greek Tragedy.* New York: Norton, 1965.

Euripides. *The Complete Greek Tragedies.* Vol. 4. Ed. David Grene and Richmond Lattimore. Chicago: University of Chicago Press, 1959.

Foley, Helene. *Female Acts in Greek Tragedy.* Princeton: Princeton University Press, 2001.

Garland, Robert. *The Greek Way of Death.* Ithaca: Cornell University Press, 1985.

————. *The Greek Way of Life.* Ithaca: Cornell University Press, 1990.

Goldhill, Simon. *Reading Greek Tragedy.* Cambridge: Cambridge University Press, 1986.

Gould, Thomas. *The Ancient Quarrel between Poetry and Philosophy.* Princeton: Princeton University Press, 1990.

————. trans. Oedipus the King: *A Translation with Commentary.* Englewood Cliffs, N.J.: Prentice-Hall, 1970.

Grene, David, trans. *Sophocles 1: The Complete Greek Tragedies.* 2d ed. Ed. David Grene and Richmond Lattimore. Chicago: University of Chicago Press, 1991.

Griffith, Mark, ed. *Antigone.* By Sophokles. Cambridge : Cambridge University Press, 1999.

Guthrie, W. K. C. *The Greeks and Their Gods.* Boston: Beacon Press, 1950.

Jebb, R. C., trans. *Antigone.* By Sophocles. 1888. Cambridge: Cambridge University Press, 1928.

————, trans. *Oedipus at Colonus.* By Sophocles. 1886. Cambridge: Cambridge University Press, 1928.

————, trans. *Oedipus Tyrannus.* By Sophocles. 1883. Cambridge: Cambridge University Press, 1928.

Kagan, Donald. *Pericles of Athens and the Birth of Democracy.* New York: Touchstone–Simon & Schuster, 1991.

Kirkwood, G. M. *A Study of Sophoclean Drama.* Cornell Studies in Classical Drama 31. Ithaca: Cornell University Press, 1994.

Knox, Bernard M. W. *Essays: Ancient and Modern.* Baltimore: John Hopkins University Press, 1989.

————. *The Heroic Temper: Studies in Sophoclean Tragedy.* Berkeley: University of California Press, 1964.

————. *Oedipus at Thebes.* New York: Norton, 1957.

————. Introduction and Notes. *Sophocles: The Theban Plays.* By Sophocles. Trans. Robert Fagles. New York: Viking, 1982.

Lefkowitz, Mary R. *The Lives of Greek Poets.* Baltimore: Johns Hopkins University Press, 1981.

Lloyd-Jones, Hugh, trans. *Antigone.* By Sophocles. Loeb Classical Library Series 20. Cambridge: Harvard University Press, 1994.

————, trans. *Oedipus at Colonus.* By Sophocles. Loeb Classical Library Series 20. Cambridge: Harvard University Press, 1994.

————, trans. *Oedipus Tyrannus.* By Sophocles. Loeb Classical Library Series 20. Cambridge: Harvard University Press, 1994.

Lloyd-Jones, H., and N. G. Wilson. *Sophoclea: Studies on the Text of Sophocles.* Oxford: Clarendon Press, 1990.

Moore, J. A., trans. *Selections from the Greek Elegiac, Iambic, and Lyric Poets.* Cambridge: Harvard University Press, 1947.

Pickard-Cambridge, Arthur. *The Dramatic Festivals of Athens.* Rev. John Gould and D. M. Lewis. 2d ed. Oxford: Clarendon Press, 1968.

Plutarch. *The Rise and Fall of Athens: Nine Greek Lives.* Trans. Ian Scott-Kilvert. London: Penguin, 1960.

Radice, Betty. *Who's Who in the Ancient World.* London: Penguin Books, 1971.

Rehm, Rush. *The Play of Space: Spatial Transformation in Greek Tragedy.* Princeton: Princeton University Press, 2002.

Reinhardt, Karl. *Sophocles.* New York: Barnes & Noble–Harper & Row, 1979.

Seaford, Richard. *Reciprocity and Ritual: Homer and Tragedy in the Developing City-State.* Oxford: Clarendon Press, 1994.

Segal, Charles. Notes. *Antigone.* By Sophocles. Trans. Reginald Gibbons and Charles Segal. New York: Oxford University Press, 2003.

———. Oedipus Tyrannus: *Tragic Heroism and the Limits of Knowledge.* 2d ed. New York: Oxford University Press, 2001.

———. *Sophocles' Tragic World: Divinity, Nature, Society.* Cambridge: Harvard University Press, 1995.

———. *Tragedy and Civilization: An Interpretation of Sophocles.* Cambridge: Harvard University Press, 1981.

Steiner, George. *Antigones.* New Haven: Yale University Press, 1996.

Taplin, Oliver. *Greek Tragedy in Action.* Berkeley: University of California Press, 1978.

Thucydides. *The Landmark Thucydides: A Comprehensive Guide to the Peloponnesian War.* Ed. Robert B. Strassler. New York: Touchstone–Simon & Schuster, 1996.

Tyrrell, Wm. Blake, and Larry J. Bennett. *Recapturing Sophocles'* Antigone. Lanham, Md.: Rowman & Littlefield, 1998.

Vernant, Jean-Pierre, ed. *The Greeks.* Trans. Charles Lambert and Teresa Lavender Fagan. Chicago: University of Chicago Press, 1995.

Vernant, Jean-Pierre, and Pierre Vidal-Naquet. *Myth and Tragedy in Ancient Greece.* Trans. Janet Lloyd. New York: Zone Books, 1990.

Whitman, C. E. *Sophocles.* Cambridge: Harvard University Press, 1951.

Wiles, David. *Greek Theatre Performances: An Introduction.* Cambridge: Cambridge University Press, 2000.

———. *Tragedy in Athens: Performance Space and Theatrical Meaning.* Cambridge: Cambridge University Press, 1997.

Winkler John J., and Froma I. Zeitlin, eds. *Nothing to Do with Dionysos? Athenian Drama in Its Social Context.* Princeton: Princeton University Press, 1990.

Winnington-Ingram, R. P. *Sophocles: An Interpretation.* Cambridge: Cambridge University Press, 1980.

Zimmern, Alfred. *The Greek Commonwealth: Politics and Economics in Fifth-Century Greece.* 5th ed. New York: Modern Library, 1931.